Systems Application Architecture
The IBM® SAA Strategy

Systems Application Architecture
The IBM® SAA Strategy

L. Robert Libutti

TAB Professional and Reference Books

Division of TAB BOOKS
Blue Ridge Summit, PA

FIRST EDITION
SECOND PRINTING

Library of Congress Cataloging-in-Publication Data

Libutti, L. Robert.
    Systems application architecture : the IBM SAA strategy / by L.
Robert Libutti.
        p.   cm.
    Includes bibliographical references.
    ISBN 0-8306-3516-5
    1. Computer architecture.   2. IBM computers.   I. Title.
QA76.9.A73L53   1990
004.2'525—dc20   89-20567
                                                      CIP

TAB BOOKS offers software for sale. For information and a catalog, please contact TAB Software Department, Blue Ridge Summit, PA 17294-0850.

Questions regarding the content of this book should be addressed to:

Reader Inquiry Branch
TAB BOOKS
Blue Ridge Summit, PA 17294-0850

Acquisitions Editor: Gerald T. Papke
Technical Editor: Pat Mulholland-McCarty
Production: Katherine G. Brown
Book Design: Jaclyn J. Boone

Trademarks

Systems Application Architecture™, **Operating System/2**™, **OS/2**™, **Personal System/2**™, **PS/2**™, **Systems Application Architecture**™, **Presentation Manager**™, **Micro Channel**™, **System/370**™, **Operating System/400**™, **OS/400**™, **Application System/400**™, **MVS/ESA**™, **MVS/XA**™, **PROFS**™, **DB2**™, **SQL/DS**™ and **IBM**®	International Business Machines Corp.
TieLine™	American Management Systems, Inc.
AMSOFT™	American Software, Inc.
MAC-PAC™ and **DCS/Logistics**™	Arthur Anderson & Co.
Commander™, **Redi-Mail**™, **Reminder**™, **Exec-View**™, and **Briefing Book**™	Comshare, Inc.
PM/FOCUS™	Information Builders, Inc.
HR Vision™ and **HR; Minder**™	Integral Systems, Inc.
Easel®	Interactive Images, Inc.
BrightView™	Management Science America, Inc.
Millennium™	McCormack & Dodge Corp.
Capsule™	Metaphor Computer Systems
SAS™	SAS Institute, Inc.
Presentation/Answer™ and **Micro/Answer**™	Sterling Software, Inc.
HRMS Intuition™	Tesseract Corp.
Ethernet™	Xerox Corp.
UNIX™	Bell Laboratories

Contents

Figures

Acknowledgments _____

I wish to thank all of the dedicated men and women in IBM's programming and marketing organizations around the world who have made SAA an evolving reality. I especially wish to thank Earl Wheeler, Bill Stuek and Dave Cartenuto for their reviews and support in the preparation of this book. A special thanks goes to Mrs. Terry Doscas for her assistance in the preparation of the manuscript. I also wish to recognize the many IBM customer people who are taking their time and energy to work closely with IBM in the creation of SAA.

Foreword

In the three years since Systems Application Architecture (SAA) began, it has received a great deal of publicity. However, until now no one directly involved in SAA's development has written about it. So I am very glad that Bob Libutti, who has played an important role in the development of SAA, has written this book explaining the strategy behind Systems Application Architecture, the technology that it requires, and the solutions that it is providing.

Bob clearly and concisely explains the market-driven nature of SAA. In the latter part of the 1980s, although generally pleased with the quality of most IBM products and services, many of our customers were not completely satisfied. They were concerned with how to connect their systems (both IBM and non-IBM), how to share data, how to improve programmers' skills, and how to maximize the availability of applications.

This book explains how Systems Applications Architecture developed as our response to those customer needs. Simply stated, SAA is IBM's commitment to make common what our customers have told us should be common across four of our major operating systems.

Bob has a unique perspective on SAA. He joined IBM in 1961 and held a number of systems engineering and marketing management positions. He has been working on SAA since before its announcement in 1987, when he was the executive in charge of introducing SAA to the European market. Now, as Director of SAA Marketing Strategy, he is responsible for ensuring that SAA remains market-driven and truly responsive to our customers' needs.

He also has been active in forging the business partnerships that are essential to bringing SAA solutions to as wide a range of customers as possible. Bob was instrumental in our September, 1989 AD/Cycle announcement of a comprehensive application development solution from IBM and those partners that will help attack the application backlog. In large part because of his efforts, more than 35 companies have endorsed AD/Cycle.

Bob's technical training and marketing skills blend well to make this a readable, substantive account of why and how SAA was developed, and where it is going. It is a book that will be useful to customers, consultants, and anyone else interested in Systems Application Architecture.

Earl Wheeler

Preface

Some claim that Thomas Watson, Jr. gambled the future of the IBM Corporation when he moved the company from accounting machines to the initial line of IBM Computers in the early 1950s.

The introduction of the IBM System 360 in 1964 was reviewed as a "bet your company" strategy as Thomas Wise describes the direction and decisions in his Fortune magazine article "IBM's $5,000,000,000 Gamble."

The "third gamble" may very well be on the success of IBM's Systems Application Architecture (SAA). This IBM direction involves the mobilization of thousands of IBM programmers across three continents, in 17 laboratories, involving three major computing systems and four operating systems environments. IBM has involved hundreds of customers and vendors in the venture.

IBM's success with SAA will provide its customers with an unprecedented base of computing functionality and consistency to fuel the development of their enterprise information systems.

To the extent that IBM achieves its objectives, IBM will remove one of the major inhibitors to their growth and their customer's productivity by keeping the information systems needs current and competitive.

This book describes IBM's direction and objectives in developing Systems Application Architecture. Several of its components will receive special focus due to their significance. This will include a view of the growing importance to IBM of turning to its customers and vendors for requirements in what they internally call their "market driven" strategy and how this may be reflected in their programming systems operations.

The book concludes with an assessment of the potential results and success of the "third gamble."

About This Book _____

In his book *The Fractal Geometry of Nature*, Benoit Mandelbrot asks, "Why is geometry often described as 'cold' and 'dry'? One reason lies in its inability to describe the shape of a cloud; a mountain, a coastline, or a tree," he says.

The same question has been asked about SAA. In a sense SAA is intended to provide customers and end users the tools and services that can describe the information and system's "clouds" and "trees" encountered in developing modern application systems.

The general objective of SAA is to provide a technical framework in which customers who are developing applications can leverage their current investment in database, network, and applications and take advantage of emerging new technologies. The scope of SAA is such that the resulting solutions span the enterprise and automate the business processes. This should result in providing companies more timely access to more accurate information supporting the customer business objectives. SAA is the framework for the tools and services operating on IBM hardware and software systems evolving in increasingly complex computing configurations.

There are a number of attributes that are inherent in the course adopted by IBM in the creation of SAA and its implementation across multiple computer hardware and software systems. The first of these is a fundamental orientation toward exploiting the power of the programmable workstation, explicitly the PS/2 with its OS/2 operating system. The second attribute, incorporated in part to support the first, is to make systems easier to use. The third focus area is connectivity of hardware, systems software, and applications across global and local networks in such a way that the interconnection is transparent to the business application. The final area is that the resulting system or application operates in an integrated fashion throughout the enterprise and that the systems resources and services are managed in a coherent manner.

This work is an attempt to describe SAA in a step-by-step fashion. Many illustrations are used to enable you to form mental pictures of the structure of SAA and move rapidly through the written descriptions.

CHAPTER 1 provides a background of the evolution of computing systems in IBM leading to the need for Systems Application Architecture.

CHAPTER 2 provides a brief introduction of the basic IBM software structures upon which SAA will evolve.

CHAPTER 3 describes the three major architectural components of SAA—the Common User Access (CUA), the Common Communication Support (CCS) and the Common Programming Interface (CPI). In addition, a number of the significant SAA product implementations are identified.

CHAPTER 4 outlines the general IBM vision and commitment to SAA as a basic corporate software strategy.

CHAPTER 5 presents cooperative processing concepts as one of the technical structures supported by SAA.

CHAPTER 6 presents the distributed nature of the underlying system assumed by SAA.

CHAPTER 7 defines the Application Development Environment required to support large complex computer installations and the IBM contribution AD/Cycle.

CHAPTER 8 gives insight into the management system being employed by IBM to manage its internal development of SAA products and systems.

CHAPTER 9 explores IBM's direction interrelating SAA and its version of Unix called the AIX operating system.

CHAPTER 10 is a further view of what to look for as SAA continues to develop during the 1990s.

CHAPTER 11 is the author's assessment of the potential impact of SAA.

Appendices are included that are intended to guide the reader to more detailed technical information and background material relevant to SAA.

This work attempts to describe the principles and central directions of Systems Application Architecture. At the same time that it avoids the technical difficulties and challenges in accomplishing all the goals, it does express the confidence the author has in all the thousands of IBM people who are developing parts of SAA and their commitment to their IBM customer needs.

1
Background

The managing directors of information processing in most companies are faced with an increasing challenge in meeting their companies' data processing requirements. The backlog of computer applications to be developed continues to increase. It is not uncommon to hear management information systems (MIS) directors speak in terms of a two-year or more backlog of work to be done on new applications and modernization of old applications.

This demand for sophisticated applications has been caused by many factors in the economy. Dominant among these is the increase of white collar workers as a percentage of the work force. The change has been dramatic since 1950 when this population represented slightly more than 20% of the work force. In 1980 that figure rose to 50% and by 1990 will exceed the 60% level.[1] These people are the professionals, the clerical, the administrative and management information users in the growing service industry sectors of our society. As John Naisbitt, the author of *Megatrends*, noted: "The Information Economy is Real."[2] This new economy has created the need for the new computer applications and new quantity and forms of information.

From the MIS director's point of view two inhibitors dominate his ability to satisfy the demand. 1) The first is the availability of skilled data processing professionals. The number of new college graduates in the fields of computer science, mathematics and physical sciences that are the core of the computer profession has not kept pace with demand. In 1990 it is projected that tens of thousands of positions will be unfilled around the world due to the lack of graduate qualified applicants. 2) A second inhibitor is a result of the richness of choice brought on by the technology explosion in the information systems industry. Nothing exemplifies this more than the growth of the IBM Corporation whose revenues in 1961 were $2.2 billion to its 1987 revenues of over $54 billion. During this period of growth came enormous technological innovation and the entry of thousands of hardware and systems providers into the marketplace.

MIS directors around the world installed equipment at dizzying rates. Larger applications demanded larger CPUs, larger disk files, and more powerful printers. These systems were being attached to each other by cable and across telephone lines creating ever-increasing complex networks of systems. Millions of computer keyboard display terminals were being attached to the systems at the same time. These terminals, with the new applications, gave the white collar worker, the end user, access to the new forms of information.

This trend continues today. The technology projections are consistent. We can expect a 25% compounded growth rate (CGR) change across the hardware components that make up computer systems for the next decade and beyond. There is not yet, anything in the science that suggests this trend will slow down.

The MIS director is faced with another new fast emerging trend to manage: the personal computer as an intelligent workstation. This device is placing computing power directly in the hands of the end user and represents a technology example of the whole decentralization trend—the decentralization of the users and computing power.[3]

The MIS director has attempted to manage the demands of his business, expand the computing capability, disperse the function across his enterprise, hire skilled people and educate his executive management. 3) Meanwhile, the third inhibitor—inconsistency—reached a level that demanded more understanding and acceptance by vendors. The solutions require fundamental short and long range change in how information systems are to be supplied and supported by information systems suppliers.

This was not a new challenge to the IBM Corporation. In the early 1960s, IBM's customers were beginning to express increasing concern about the lack of consistency among the IBM systems populating their installations. It was not uncommon at that time to find a large customer with such systems as IBM 7090s, IBM 1400s, IBM 7070s, IBM 1620s, and even some IBM 650s. Each of these systems were designed and optimized for a different environment such as commercial applications or scientific applications. Individually, they had excellent technical and economic design points for their time, but the differences in the hardware designs, the software operating systems and the application enabling software made them difficult to use together. They also required the customers to create programming and support staffs that were specialized in only one of the computing systems and its software systems.

On April 7, 1964, IBM announced the IBM 360 family of computers to replace its 1400 and 7000 series product lines.[3] As Robert Sobel relates in his book *I.B.M. Colossus in Transition* "Almost immediately competitors claimed that this was a deception, a play aimed at taking placements from under false pretenses."[4] Not only was the IBM 360 a huge success, but it was created on an architecture of systems design that has lasted to this day and will continue to be developed upon well into the 1990s. It is a tribute to the IBM design engineers of that time. In the fastest growing industrial segment, driven by the fastest developing technological revolution, they were able to lay a design foundation that has lasted over 30 years.

During the early 1970s, the integration of telecommunications with computing took on increased importance as the growth of use of display terminals and the interconnection of computing systems via telephone lines took place. This trend was accompanied by the increased use of interactive computing software that gave the users the "real time" benefits of computing and was the beginning of the move away from the exclusive "batch" processing of applications.

Once again the IBM customer was faced with a challenge of attempting to attach sets of diverse architectures. The MIS director wanted a means to interconnect systems using a wide variety of electrical interfaces, data stream formats, communication protocols, support services, programming interfaces, and communications network control facilities.

The introduction of IBM Systems Network Architecture (SNA) in 1972 provided the beginning of a base allowing systems to interconnect and interoperate in a productive way. And again, SNA is an architecture that has continued to evolve over time and will continue to be the base of IBM interconnectivity into the 1990s and beyond.

Jeremy Bernstein in his book *The Analytical Engine* in 1963 wrote:

> "If there is one word that characterizes the history of computers since 1950, the word is probably "proliferation"—proliferation in the number of computers, in the number of people using computers and the range of applications of the machines."[5]

Certainly many fundamental steps have been taken to deal with this issue. Yet again, this time in the early 1980s, IBM customers were experiencing the reoccurring lack of consistency among the IBM product line. Not only had incompatible hardware systems begun to coexist but the "proliferation" of software systems was creating major productivity losses in the customer's information systems organizations.

The IBM hardware systems families—IBM 370–3090 series, IBM Systems 34 and 36, IBM Systems 38—and the increasingly ubiquitous IBM Personal Computer, had spawned new operating systems environments such as MVS and VM operating systems for the IBM 370–3090. The IBM System 36 and System 38, although a related family, had different operating systems environments and different language levels. The IBM Personal Computer success had created a whole new industry involving thousands of companies providing operating systems, application packages and hardware devices.

In addition to the array of already mentioned product functions, there were different versions of the computer languages of COBOL, Fortran, PL/1, and RPG on the variety of operating systems, and not all systems supported some of the new important languages, such as the C language and PASCAL.

When a MIS director structured a plan for his company to establish a total system for his enterprise he found it difficult to interconnect the systems. Although IBM had standardized on

SNA, different IBM systems were at different versions and could not operate together.

In response to this need, IBM conducted numerous studies of the requirement. They formed customer advisory councils, worked with the IBM User Groups, met with software vendors and consultants, and repeatedly found the following to be the major requirements upon which a plan needed to be developed:

- *Usability* The application had to be simple to build, easier to learn and easier to use.

- *Connectivity* There must be the capability to connect systems and their peripheral hardware in a consistent and simple manner and to provide tools to manage the connected environment in an efficient manner.

- *Productivity* The capability to develop applications that operate in a variety of systems environments in a consistent way and to remove the need to rewrite applications as the move from one environment to another so that customers' skilled resources and investments in applications are better leveraged.

In March 1987, IBM introduced its Systems Application Architecture (SAA). This introduction is analogous to the System/360 announcement in 1964 that introduced a family of hardware systems. SAA defines an architecture design framework that has as its objective to provide the base for building consistent applications across IBM's major computing systems—the IBM 370, the AS/400 Follow-on system to the System/36 and System/38 mentioned earlier, and IBM's current version of personal computer, the Personal System/2.

The analogy to the System/360 announcement was further confirmed when press reports had competitors claiming that SAA was "a deception, a play at taking placements under false pretenses." SAA was dubbed "futureware" and "vaporware!" An accusation that the facts of the past two years have dispelled.

2

Introducing Systems Application Architecture (SAA)

Customer MIS directors told IBM that their systems and application expansion is significantly inhibited by the inconsistent software systems and systems architecture provided by IBM. They also said that IBM was not doing enough to address the problem. Systems Application Architecture (SAA) is a software approach intended to address this problem and to present the breadth of IBM's product line to its customers and end users as a consistent family of operating systems.

SAA also represents an opportunity for IBM to focus its investment in three or four operating systems rather than eight or nine. Compliance with SAA is directed at providing the means to develop consistent and portable applications in three IBM computing systems environments:

(1) System/370, a range of high end systems

(2) AS/400, a series of midrange systems that replaced the popular System/36 and System/38

(3) Personal System/2, the IBM personal computing system

Technology has advanced to a point that each of the above computing systems have software operating systems that are roughly equivalent in scope of function. Obviously, the large systems can store more data and perform more tasks concurrently than the smaller systems, which do not have that depth of function.

The IBM product line, ranging from the IBM PC to the System/37 – 3090 represents a power range of approximately one to one thousand. It has become evident that to support that range of computing power you will need different hardware architectures and operating systems. When a system is designed to optimize its performance and information handling capability at very high ranges for example, they tend to operate less efficiently at lower ranges. Similarly, a design such as the Personal System/2 and its operating system is designed to be optimized as an intelligent workstation for an end user. Extrapolating that design to a high-performance version on the scale of the System 370's results in an inefficient and non-competitive system.

One of the challenges of SAA is to provide the framework to operate over different systems architectures, each evolving over time and optimized for its performance range. To achieve its objective of consistency, SAA must define consistent programming interfaces across the systems implementations described above.

The SAA interfaces, as shown in Fig. 2-1, are organized into three major components:

(1) Common User Access (CUA)

(2) Common Communications Support (CCS)

(3) Common Programming Interface (CPI)

The three architectures are built around the IBM operating systems structures for the System/370, AS/400, and PS/2 as shown in Fig. 2-1. Implementation of SAA provides the consistent interface to end users, programmers and other IBM SAA systems in a communications network. These architectures have been published and noted in references 8 and 9 in the back of this book. The communications architectures that comprise CCS are extensively documented and referenced in the IBM manual *System Application Architecture: An Overview*.[10]

In the late 1970s, a general software model, shown in Fig. 2-2, was developed in IBM and used for the high-end operating systems. The model represents sets and categories of functions and provides a base for understanding the relationships of functions and

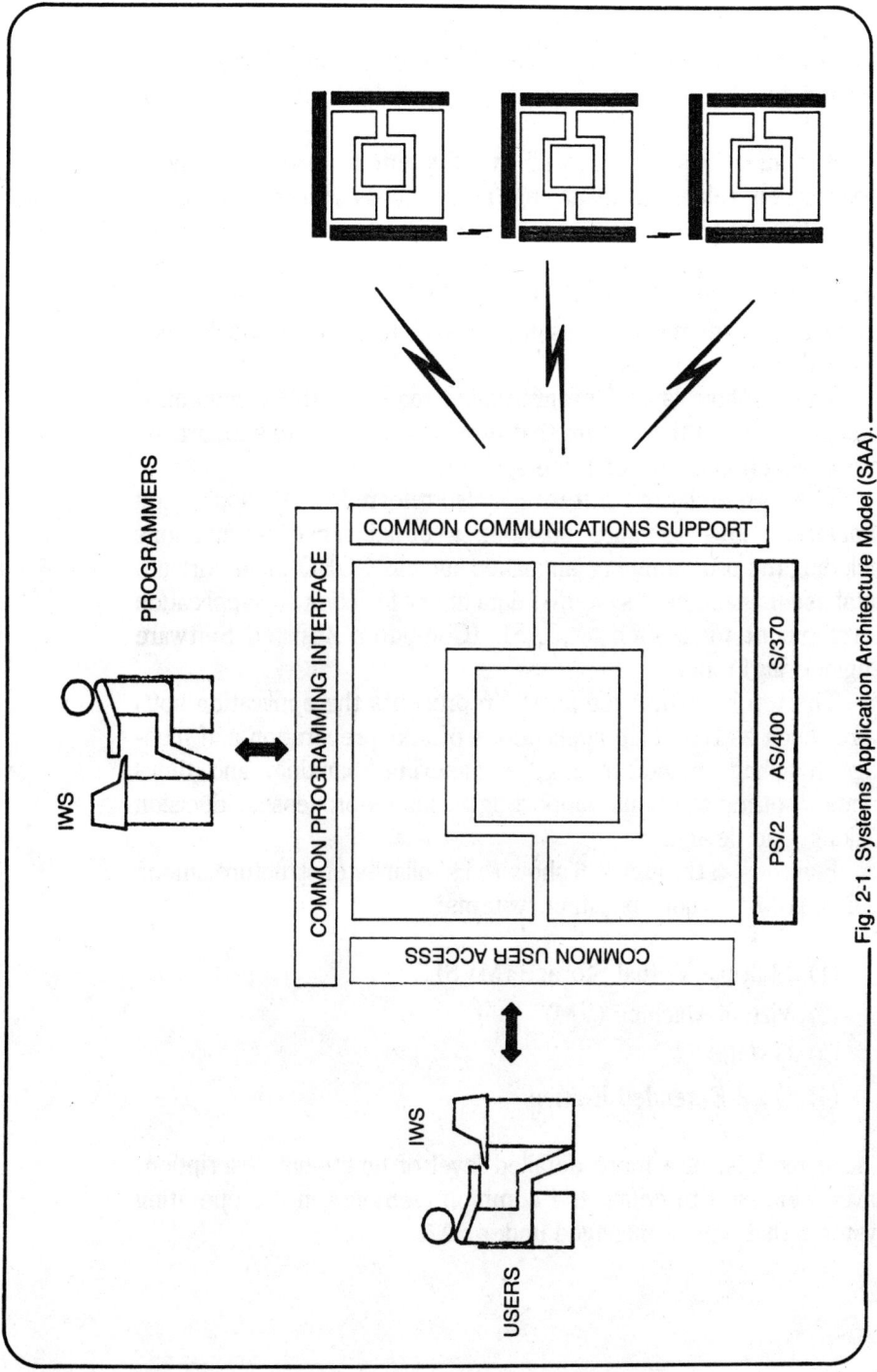

Fig. 2-1. Systems Application Architecture Model (SAA).

a convenient means of communicating directions. This model became the basis of the operating system's structure used for SAA.

The functions represented in "System Control" are those most closely related to managing the physical aspects of the computer. The program code that manages physical memory, the input-output devices such as printers and disk drives, and the various system interrupt schemes is referred to as "blue layer" code. (Each layer in the model is assigned a color to help individuals refer to the design.)

The "yellow layer" programming manages the communications functions of the system that provides the logic to support the interconnection of two or more systems.

The "green layer" software is also referred to as "application enablers." This software provides a broad range of functions including the programming languages such as COBOL and Fortran, database management systems, data query facilities and application development tools such as CASE (Computer Assisted Software Engineering) tools.

The top layer or "red layer" represents the application software, such as the office applications of text preparation and message handling, manufacturing, engineering, banking, and thousands of other solutions supporting business processes, decision making, and design.

Figures 2-3 through 2-6 show the similarity of structure among four of IBM's major operating systems:

(1) Multiple Virtual Storage (MVS)

(2) Virtual Machine (VM)

(3) OS/400

(4) OS/2 Extended Edition

These models, at a more detailed level of functional description, have been used to define the common elements in the operating systems that will be managed under SAA.

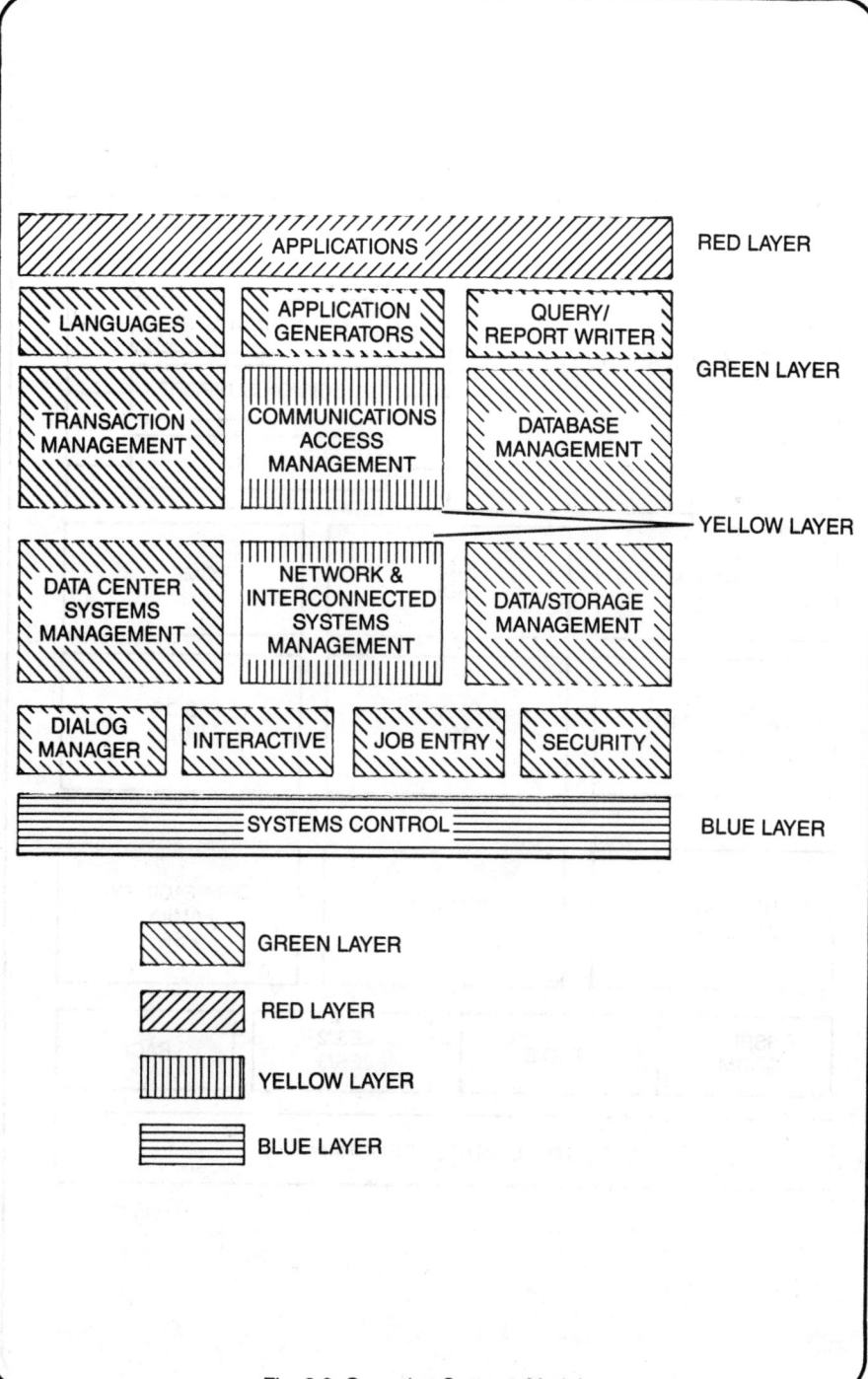

Fig. 2-2. Operating Systems Model.

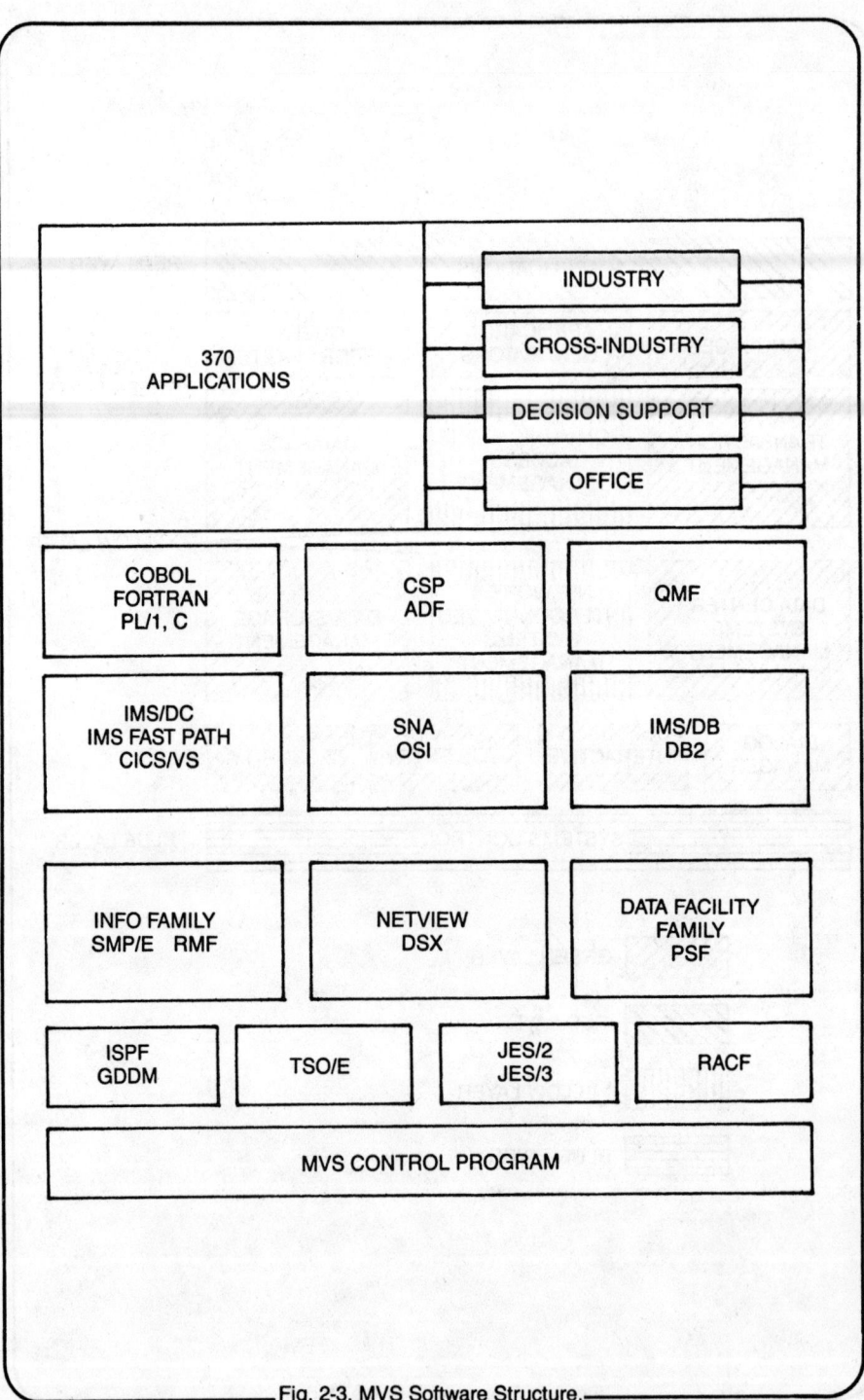

Fig. 2-3. MVS Software Structure.

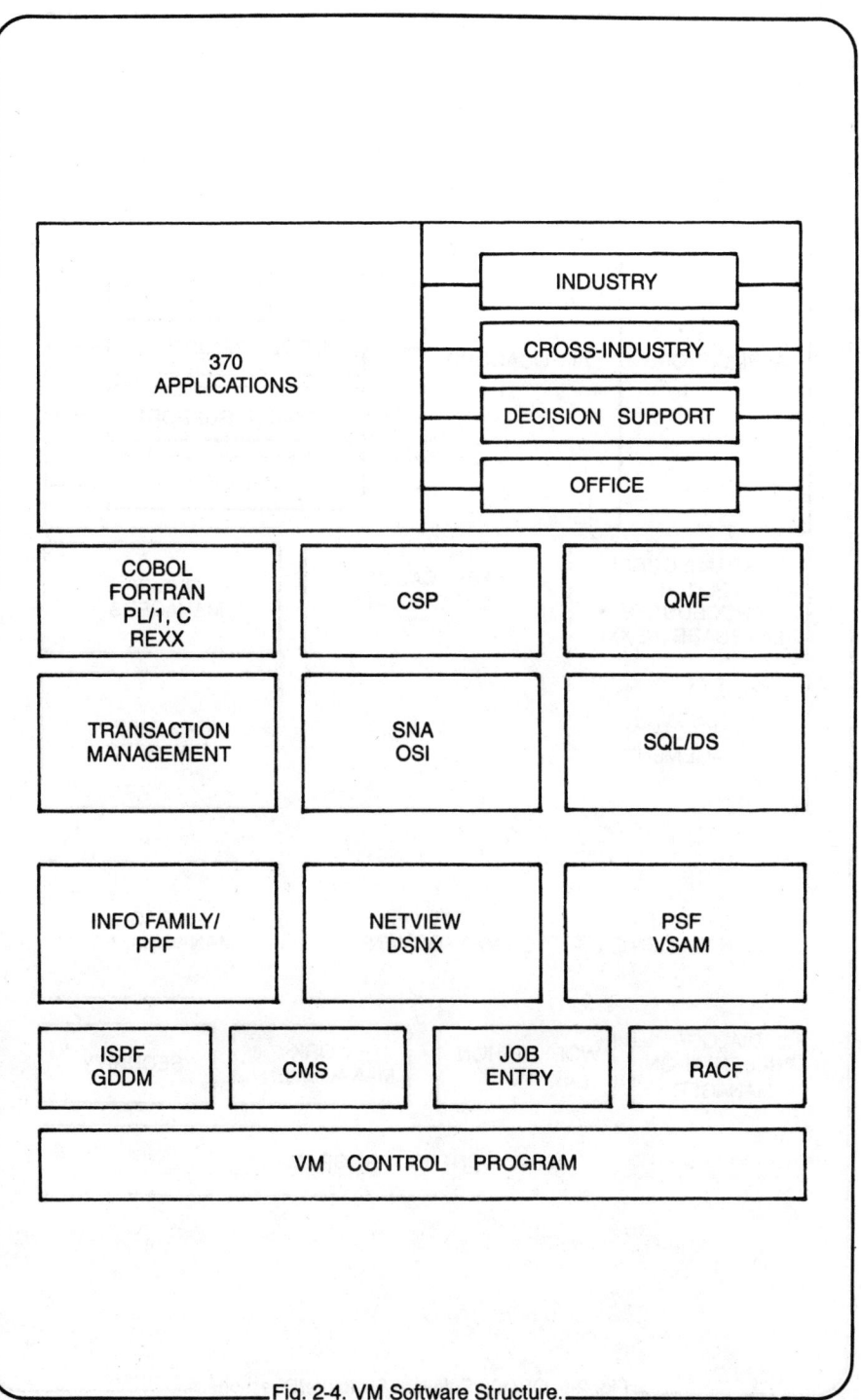

Fig. 2-4. VM Software Structure.

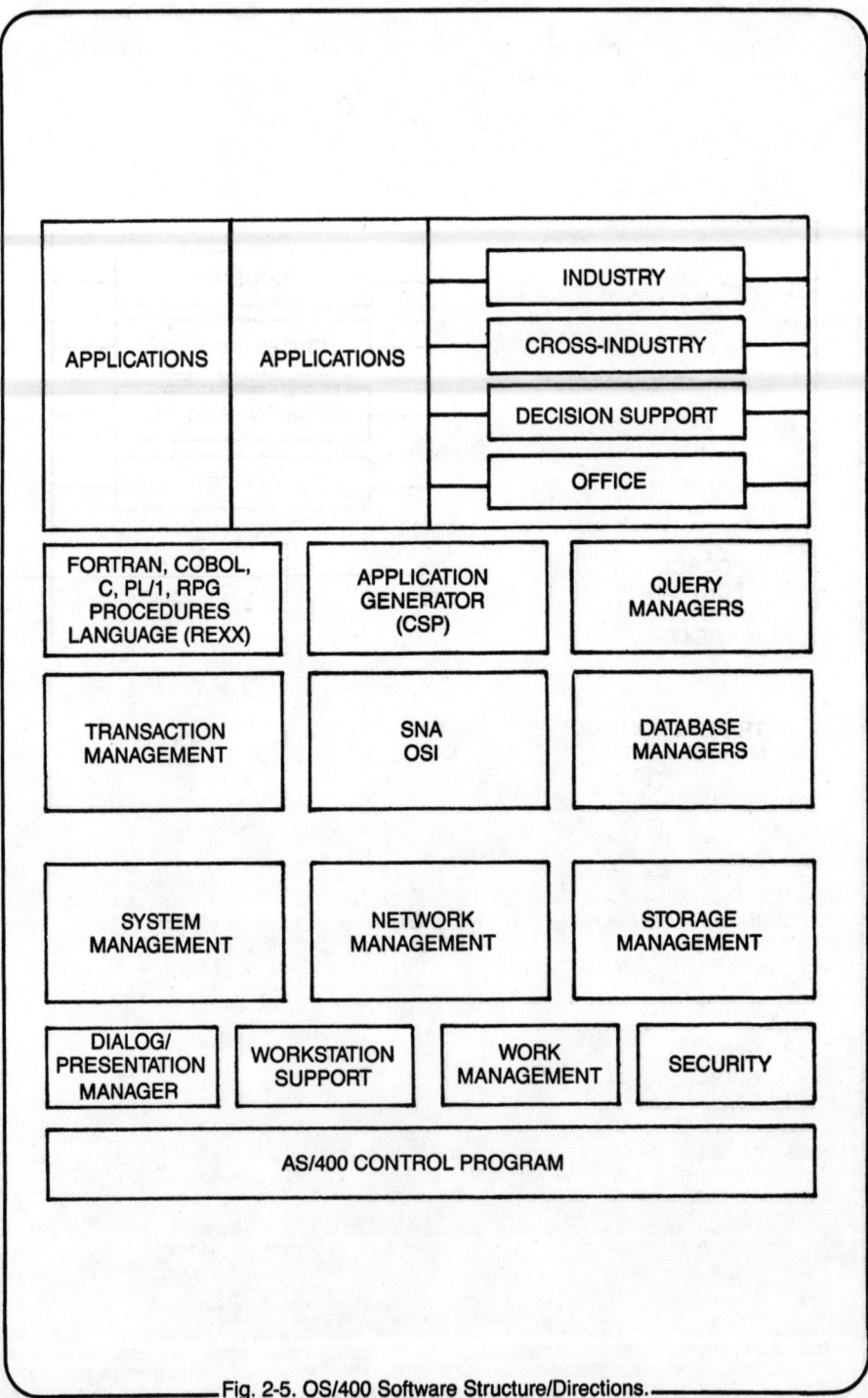

Fig. 2-5. OS/400 Software Structure/Directions.

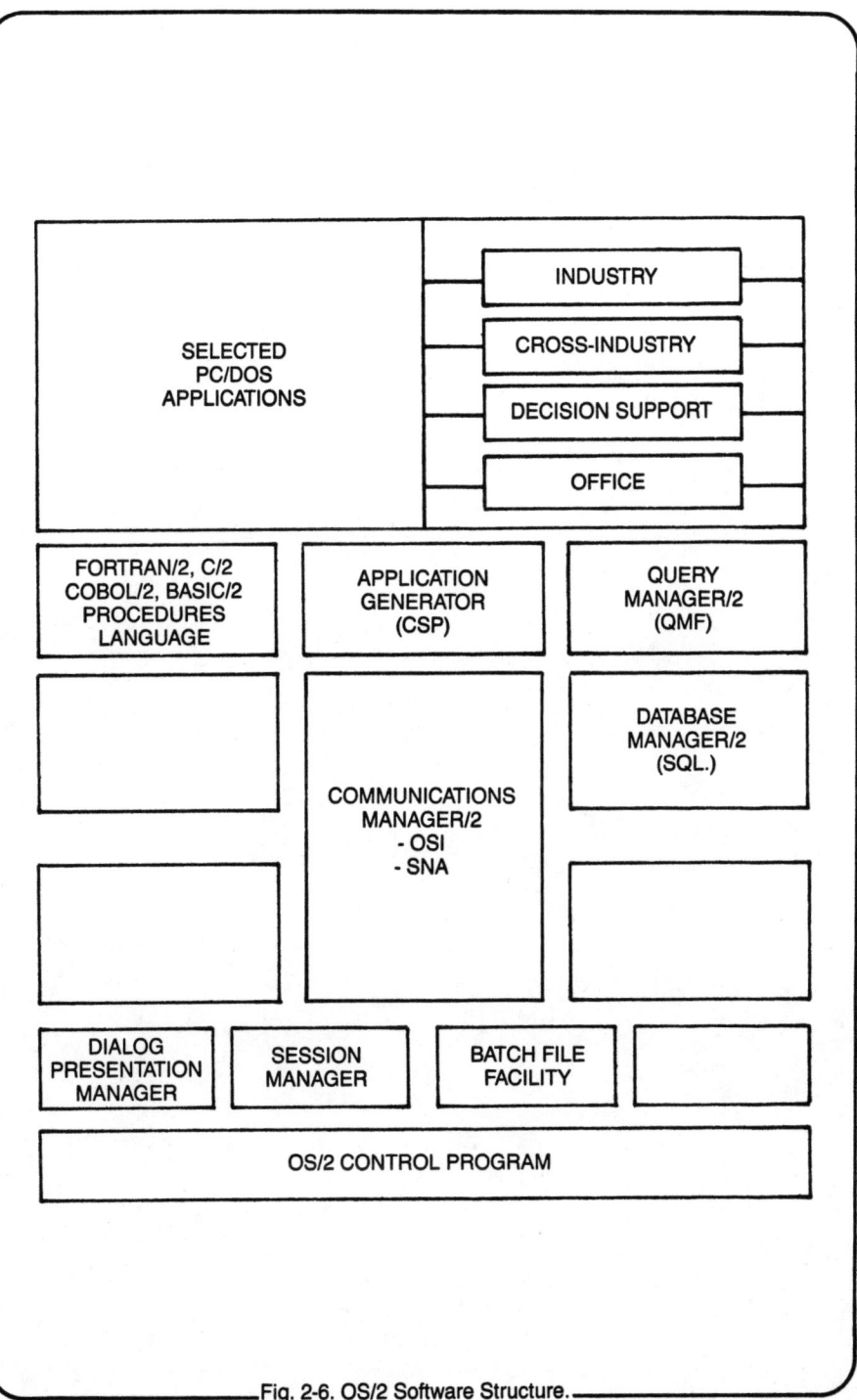

Fig. 2-6. OS/2 Software Structure.

3
SAA Components

The development of CUA, CSS,and the CPI in IBM is based on six principal objectives summarized in Fig. 3-1 and described here.

The architectures must be durable   Each of the interfaces will be subjected to an enormous variety of use by thousands of customers executing millions of lines of code. The logic and processes evoked must be implemented and executed in the defined manner. To answer that, each element of the architecture has gone through vigorous review and testing. In addition to internal testing, IBM has had the architectures reviewed by vendors and customers including the early installation of programming code executing selective functions on one of the systems. Obviously, this has resulted in excellent feedback on modification that better suit the customer requirements.

The architecture must be able to support evolutionary growth   Over the next twenty years, hardware and software systems will undergo dramatic change and evolution. Indeed, SAA will be a part of, and cause of some of that change. Its components, while being durable must also be expandable new functions. The expandability must be carefully managed across the system to maintain consistency. The architectures of System/360 and SNA

- DURABLE
- EVOLUTIONARY GROWTH
- LINK ENTERPRISE
- VARIED WORKLOADS
- CONSISTENCY
- LEVERAGE INVESTMENT

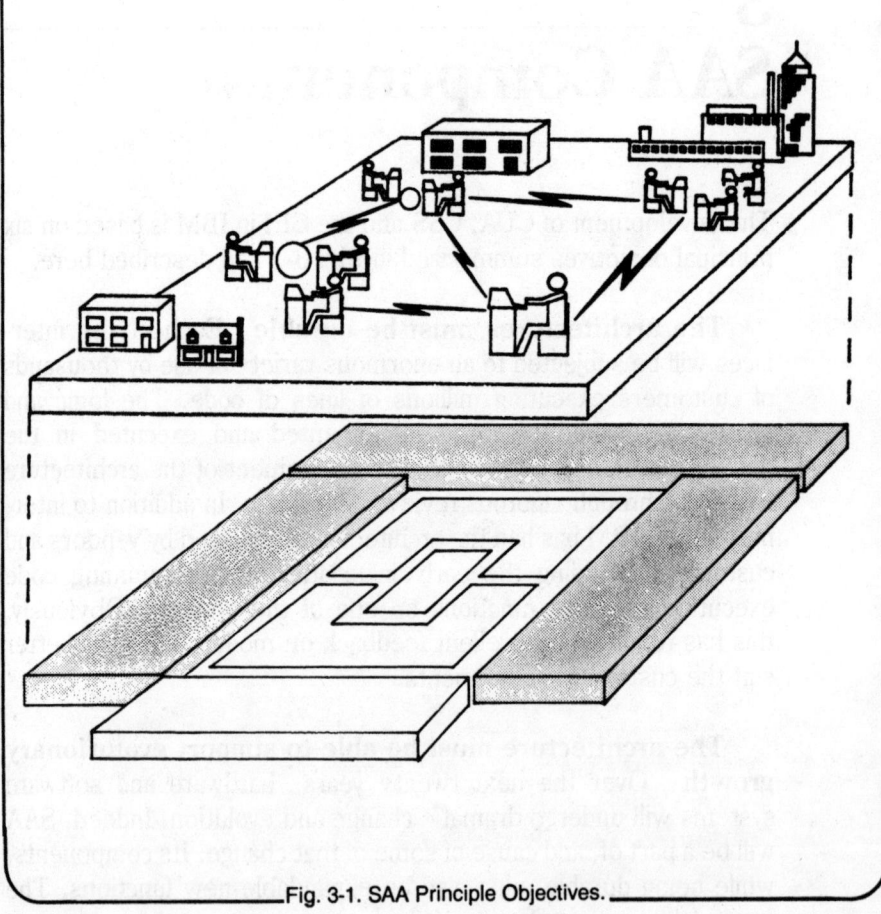

Fig. 3-1. SAA Principle Objectives.

discussed earlier, have shown the importance of the first two objectives.

Link Enterprise Ultimately, the customer's goal is to link common applications together. This way they can operate in different system environments and create a total *enterprise information system*, shown in Fig. 3-2, which is designed to meet the objective listed:

(1) Common Communications Support (CCS)

(2) Common Programming Interface (CPI)

(3) Common Applications

(4) Common User Access (CUA)

Varied Workloads, Consistency, and Leverage Investment The linked enterprise information system must handle varied workloads within the network and within individual systems. The total environment must be created and maintained through consistency of user interface, programming systems, development tools and system management tools. It is through this objective the customer will leverage his investment in application, systems, programmer productivity and service to his end user by making the system more productive and easier to use.

The specifications of CUA, CPI, and CCS that are intended to achieve these objectives are discussed in the upcoming sections.

COMMON USER ACCESS (CUA)

The user's role in SAA is largely defined by Common User Access (CUA), shown in Fig. 3-3. CUA lays down a set of rules relating to the way a user interacts with his application system. The objective is to give the user an expectation of how his computer system works and then continually reinforce that expectation both within a single application system or across many application systems. This reduces training requirements, reduces errors and increases the user's confidence in the system.

- COMMON COMMUNICATIONS SUPPORT
- COMMON PROGRAMMING INTERFACE
- COMMON APPLICATIONS
- COMMON USER ACCESS

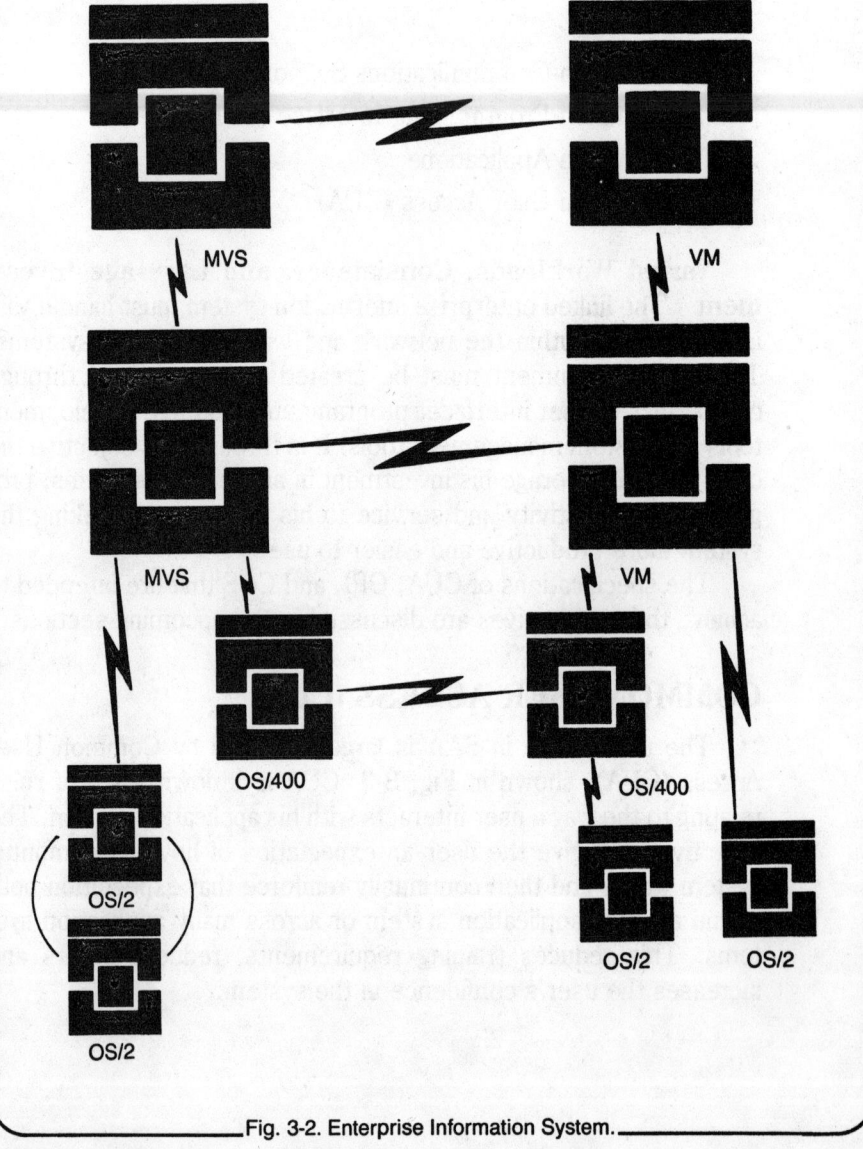

Fig. 3-2. Enterprise Information System.

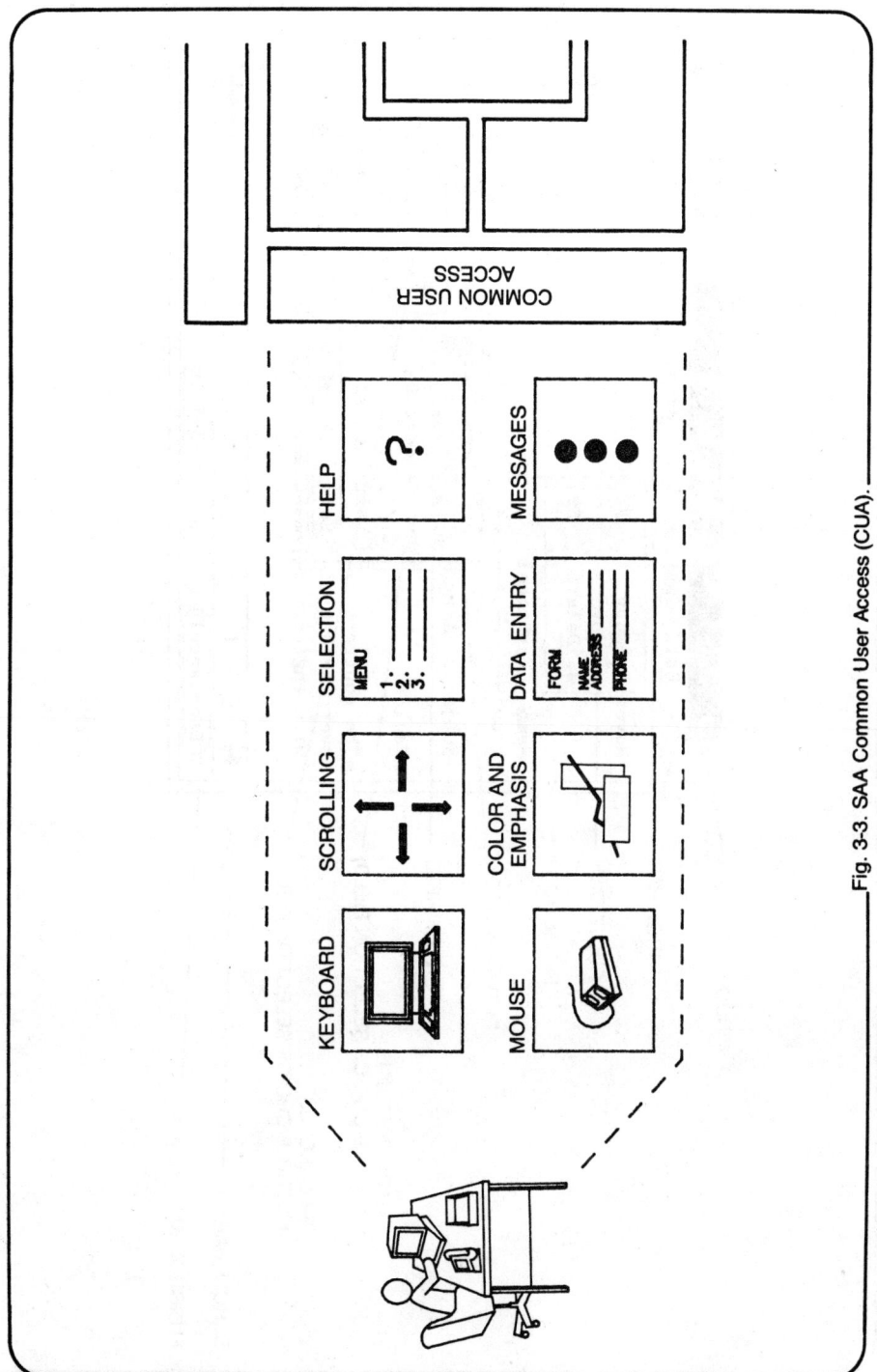

Fig. 3-3. SAA Common User Access (CUA).

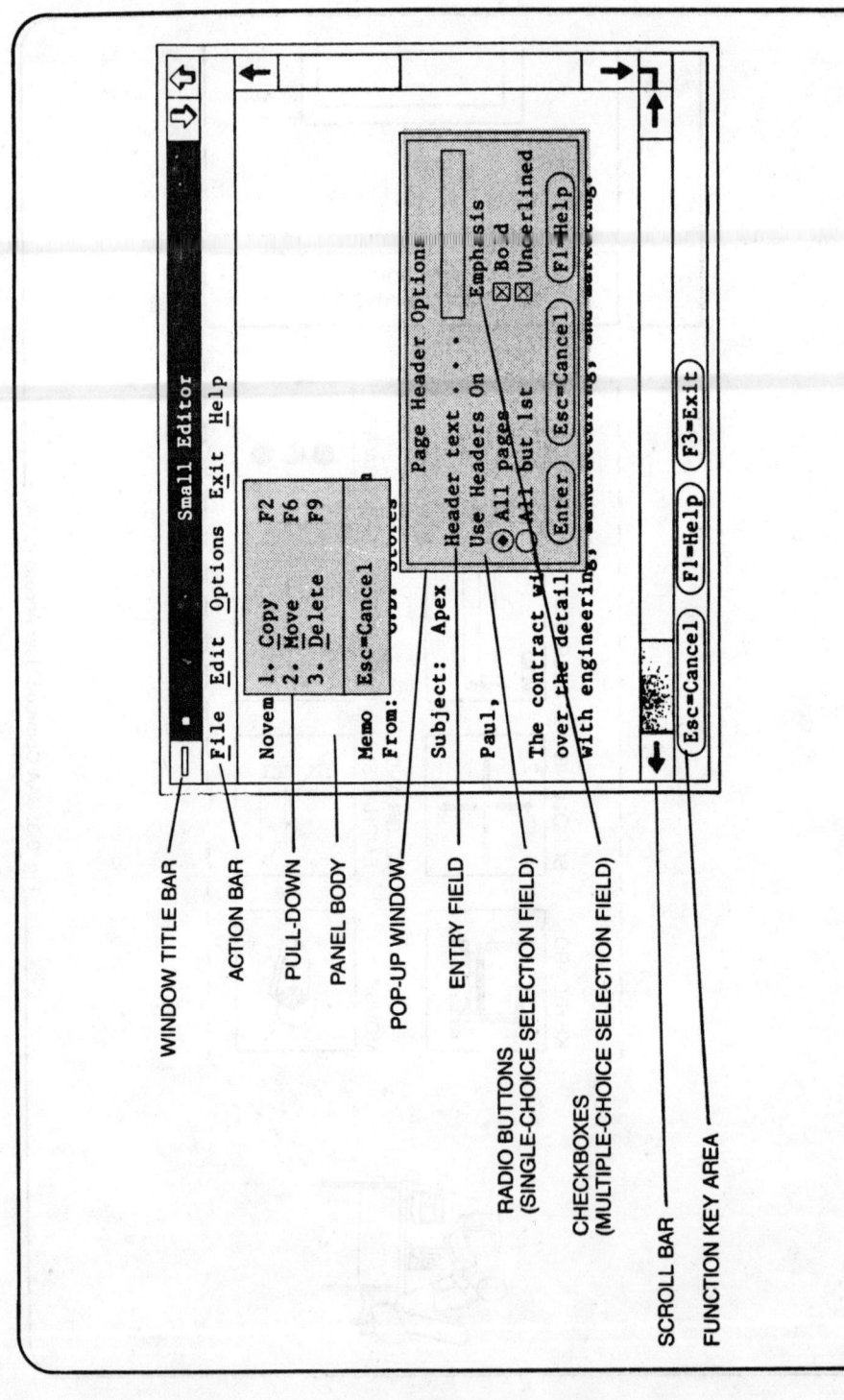

WINDOW TITLE BAR

ACTION BAR

PULL-DOWN

PANEL BODY

POP-UP WINDOW

ENTRY FIELD

RADIO BUTTONS
(SINGLE-CHOICE SELECTION FIELD)

CHECKBOXES
(MULTIPLE-CHOICE SELECTION FIELD)

SCROLL BAR

FUNCTION KEY AREA

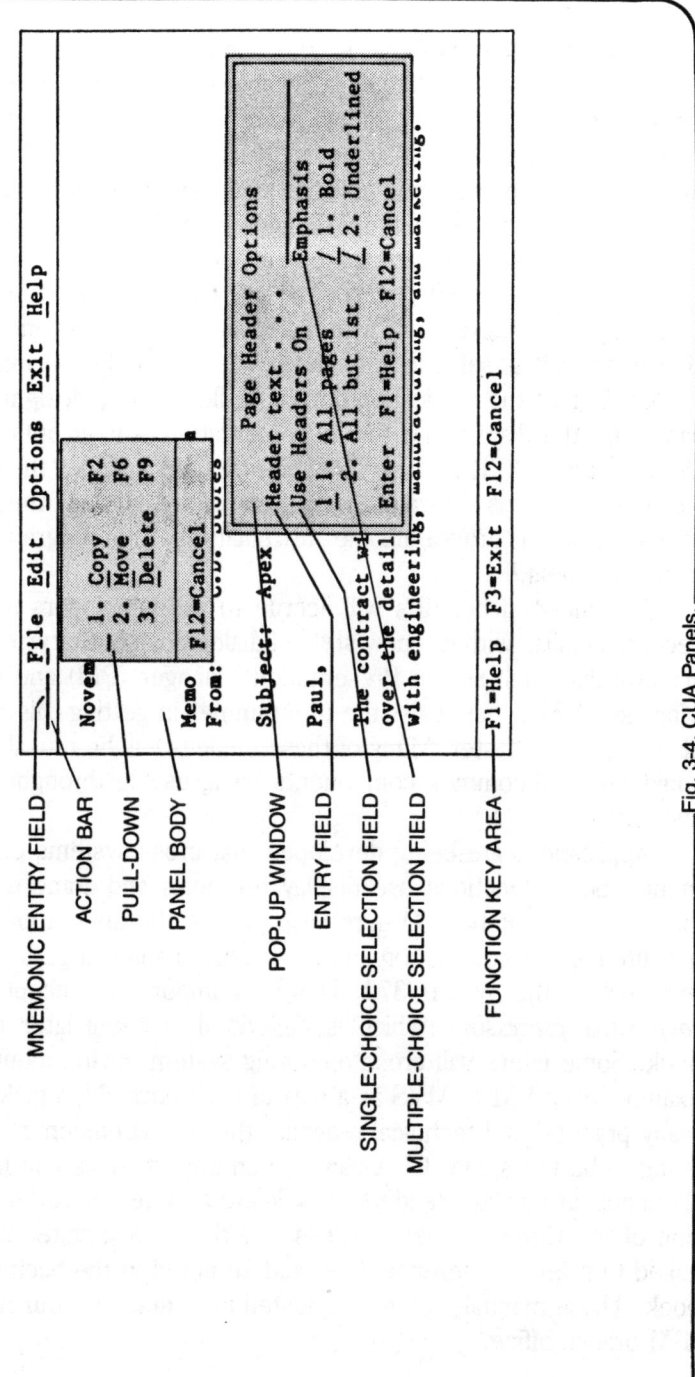

Fig. 3-4. CUA Panels.

MNEMONIC ENTRY FIELD

ACTION BAR

PULL-DOWN

PANEL BODY

POP-UP WINDOW

ENTRY FIELD

SINGLE-CHOICE SELECTION FIELD

MULTIPLE-CHOICE SELECTION FIELD

FUNCTION KEY AREA

Application consistency is the most important aspect of CUA.[11] The rules of CUA are applicable for use on an intelligent workstation such as the Personal System/2 or a display terminal, such as the IBM 3270 display family. Much of the research by IBM, Xerox, Mitre Corporation, and others in defining the right constructs for human usability have gone into the development of CUA. These results govern the use of the keyboards and mouse. On the display screen it governs the use of color and sets of user action aids for movement within applications and for indicating choice, as well as selection of specific action or help information.

CUA gives the application developer flexibility in designing the panels for the display and the implementation of user options, as shown in Fig. 3-3. R.E. Berry's article on CUA includes the examples of CUA panels shown in Fig. 3-4 and shows some of the differences between programmable terminal and nonprogrammable terminal panels.[12]

A number of benefits will accrue to the developers as they become familiar with the new style of dialog design. Software tools are available such as the Presentation Manager (PM) and Dialog Manager (DM), that assist the programmer in getting this part of his design done faster. Many of these designs will be reusable and could result in common components being usable throughout the installation.

Applications are being developed that cross systems environments. Some functions use display terminals and some use the intelligent workstation. Others have part of the application being executed in the workstation and other portions in a large host system such as the System/370. This is an important concept called *cooperative processing*, which is described in detail later in this book. Some users will cross operating system environments, for example from VM to MVS as a part of their normal job tasks. For many practical and technical reasons, these environments are not going to be the same. CUA can play an important part in making them appear similar. Readers who desire a more detailed description of the Common User Access and the SAA architecture are asked to refer to reference 8, 9, and 10 noted in the back of this book. These manuals can be requested by contacting your nearest IBM branch office.

COMMON COMMUNICATIONS SUPPORT (CCS)

Common Communications Support (CCS) is used to connect applications, systems, networks and devices within a customers' *enterprise*. The major elements come from Systems Network Architecture (SNA) and include data link control, network control and session management, application services, data streams and the object control architecture used in office applications, as shown in Fig. 3-5. CCS specifies a set of protocols for interconnection and communication among SAA systems whether they are across the room or across an ocean. In addition to SNA, selected international standards such as CCITT, IEEE, and Open System Interconnection (OSI) are included as an integral part of CCS.[13]

SAA high-level language facilities have been introduced that allow an SAA application to invoke the communications and interconnect functions and mask the complexities of CCS from the programmer and end users. The terms and concepts that describe these functions are included in the reference manual *Common Programming Interface—Communication Reference* (SC26 - 4399), which is available from the IBM Corporation.

COMMON PROGRAMMING INTERFACE (CPI)

The Common Programming Interface (CPI), shown in Fig. 3-6, defines a set of interfaces for a set of building blocks of languages and services that affects the process of developing applications.

IBM customers and software vendors want to construct a process where development of an application can be done in one environment and then executed in another environment. It follows that if the development process follows SAA rules and both environments support SAA, then this process is most likely to succeed.

In the longer term, as a consequence of easier applications operability, SAA will significantly reduce the impact of system differences and environments on application development. It will be possible to design applications as a logical whole, giving little or no attention to the specifics of the operating systems' hardware. The

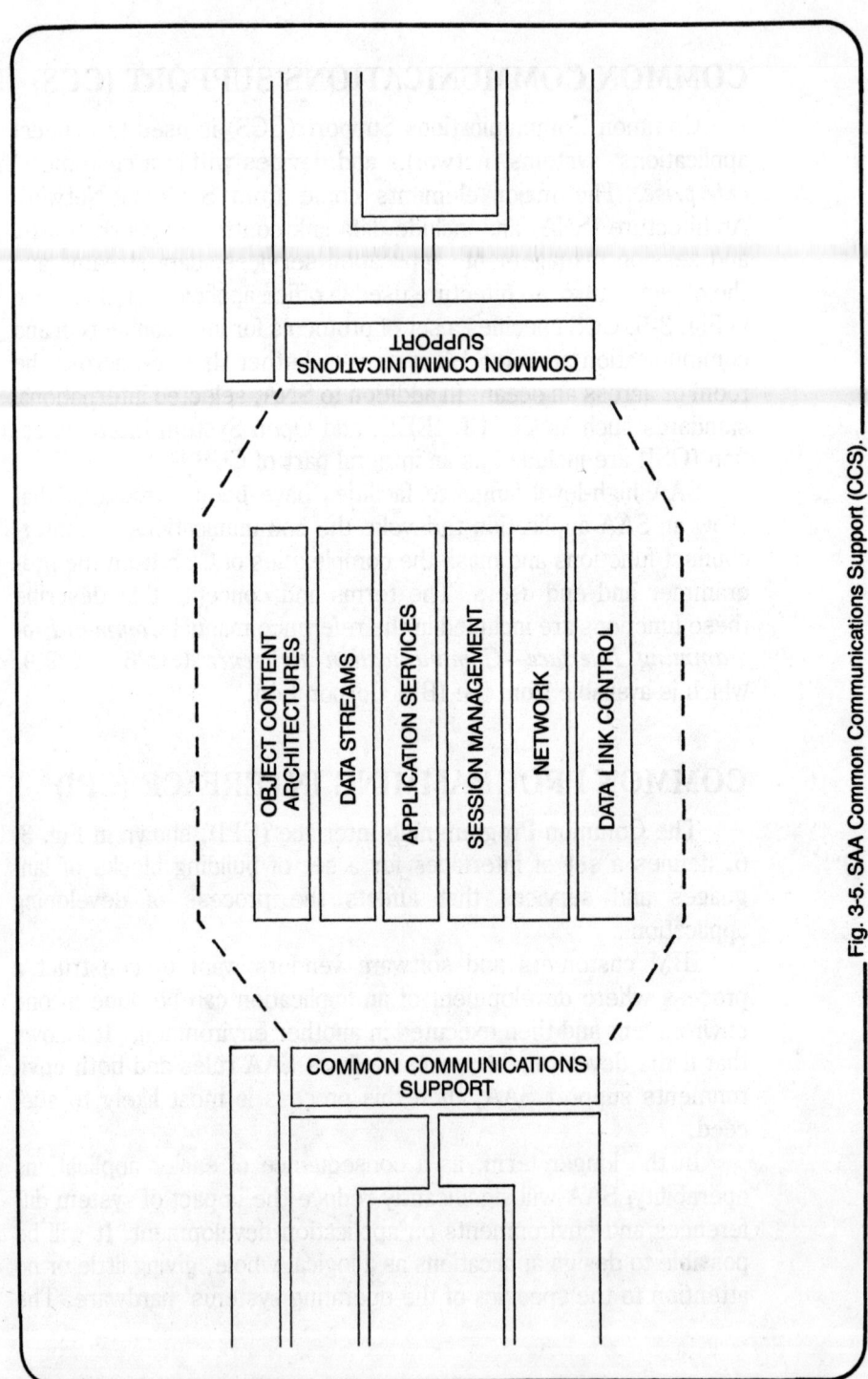

Fig. 3-5. SAA Common Communications Support (CCS).

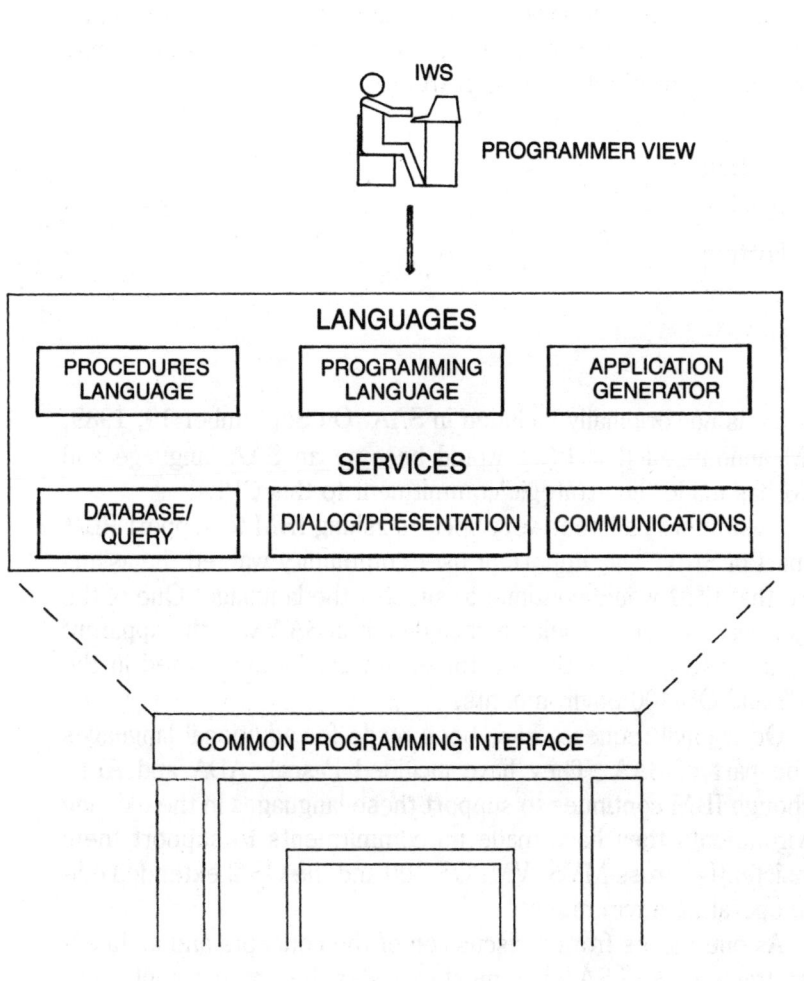

- BUILDING BLOCKS FOR APPLICATION DEVELOPMENT

- CONSISTENT INTERFACE ACROSS SYSTEMS

IWS

PROGRAMMER VIEW

LANGUAGES

| PROCEDURES LANGUAGE | PROGRAMMING LANGUAGE | APPLICATION GENERATOR |

SERVICES

| DATABASE/ QUERY | DIALOG/PRESENTATION | COMMUNICATIONS |

COMMON PROGRAMMING INTERFACE

Fig. 3-6. Common Programming Interface (CPI).

decision to execute portions of an application on a host system or the intelligent workstation could be taken at execution time by the user, the operations manager on the system itself. The CPI establishes the architectural foundation to move toward these objectives.[11]

The following section will present a short description of the major elements of the CPI as shown in Fig. 3-6.

There is an extensive set of languages that will be implemented consistently across the SAA system. The programming languages currently defined as SAA are:

COBOL

RPG

Fortran

C

PL/1

PL/1 was not originally included in SAA. On September 19, 1989, IBM announced that PL/1 would become an SAA language and IBM has made the strategic commitment to this CPI.

Customers had been very vocal in asking IBM to support PL/1 as part of SAA. This important user community wanted the assurance that IBM would continue to support the language. One of the major reasons for the delay in including it in SAA was the apparent marginal use of PL/1 that customers originally anticipated in the OS/2 and OS/400 environments.

Occasional requests have been made for additional languages to be part of SAA. They have included Pascal, ADA and APL. Although IBM continues to support these languages in the existing environments they have made no commitments to support them consistently across MVS, VM, OS/400 and the OS/2 extended edition operating environments.

As one moves from a discussion of the concepts and architectural framework of SAA you must consider the product implementations:

SAA is not a product, it is a set of architectures.

The product rules follow the definition in the preceding paragraph. Therefore, when IBM talks about a particular *function* being SAA, one should look for the software product that produces that function. It should exist in at least one of the SAA operating environments.

IBM has indicated that when it introduces an SAA product, that function will exist in all of the operating environments within a two-year time frame. This commitment has included a statement of national language support for these products to follow on a similar schedule.

Languages: The SAA procedural language is based on the REXX language. Because the command languages of the various SAA operating systems are not compatible, the developer must take precautions when writing portable applications. The REXX language provides a means of specifying an operating command interface and the procedures to be followed by the application in the current execution environment. Because the same procedural language is available in each SAA system, the skills needed to write the procedures are portable.

The SAA application generator is based on the IBM Cross System Product (CSP). An *application generator* is a generalized application development tool for the programmer sometimes referred to as a *fourth generation language*. Application generators can offer up to ten times more programmer productivity than third generation languages. The third generation languages being COBOL, Fortran, RPG and the like and the fifth generation languages belonging to an arena variously referred to as knowledge based systems, expert systems, or artificial intelligence systems.

An application generator is in one sense an application itself which produces output that is another application. This reduces the number of steps required to use conventional methods. The generator needs to use SAA interfaces to the user and to the operating systems in order to fit into the SAA structure.

The IBM direction in the whole area of supporting an application development environment is a key direction and important link to the success of SAA. Application developers want an integrated set of facilities to support and manage applications through their life cycles from the business model, requirements, design, implementation, testing and on to the maintenance phases. If customers use application development facilities that are not consistent with the SAA direction, SAA will fail to establish itself as satisfying customer requirements. Due to the critical nature of this strategy, a separate section will follow devoted to the plans that are evolving from IBM addressing this important marketplace requirement.

Services: The services portion of the CPI as shown in Fig. 3-6 currently consist of a database and query facilities, dialog and presentation management, and communications support. The embodiment of new capabilities afforded by SAA are to be exploited with these services. The object action power of end user interfaces possible under the constructs of CUA become available through the design tools of the dialog managers and presentation managers.

The concepts of distributed data can be implemented via the technologies of relational database and query facilities. I will borrow a definition of a *distributed base system* provided by Michael Killan as follows:

> "A system that effectively supports a distributed database environment is one that a) allows for access and update of data across multiple computer systems platforms b) enables a user to access and to update data on multiple systems with a single transaction and without knowing where the data exists or the type of system on which it exists and c) provides the security and performance needed for this level of computing."

One of the major objectives of SAA is to provide solutions to this requirement.

CPI-Database Access to databases in the SAA environment is provided through the Structured Query Language (SQL). It allows customers to define, build, retrieve, and manipulate information in a relational database as shown in Fig. 3-7. SQL has evolved into an industry standard adopted by a large number of data base providers as their database access method.

The implementing products for an SAA database have a variety of names depending on the execution environment. Under MVS the implementing product is called DB/2; under VM, it is SQL/DS; under OS/400, it is the OS/400 Database Manager; and on the Personal System/2 it is the Database Manager.

- RELATIONAL DATABASE
- STANDARD DATABASE LANGUAGE (SQL)
- FOUNDATION FOR INTEGRATED SYSTEMS

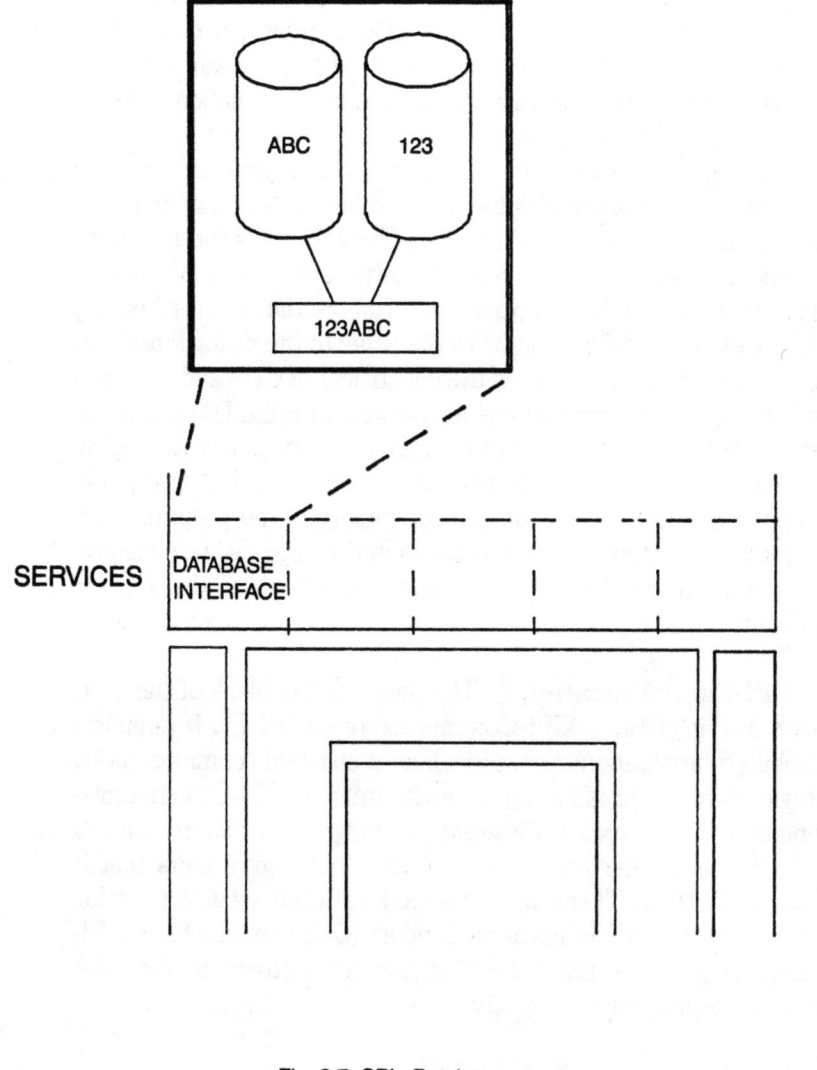

Fig. 3-7. CPI - Database.

CPI-Query Interface   The SAA Query interface as shown in Fig. 3-8, is based on an IBM product, the Query Management Facility (QMF). This facility allows an end user and a programmer to easily compose requests of a relational database, format the results, and produce a report.

CPI-Dialog/Presentation Managers   The SAA Dialog Manager (DM) and Presentation Manager (PM) as shown in Fig. 3-9, are the products that incorporate the data presentation and interaction techniques specified in the CUA architecture. The use of these products allow a customer to build display panels for his application programs that will run and display information consistently across the SAA environments.

The two interfaces of the DM and PM are provided to allow the application programmers to choose different levels of function, ease of use, consistency and control. The *PM* gives the programmer the greater degree of control down to the level of specific device type. The *DM* essentially determines the layout of panels and how the user will interact with the panel to the dialog interface. This level of interface enforces the constructs of CUA and provided the highest level of consistency. Associated with the DM is a panel language that allows the user or programmers to specify the logical elements for each panel design menus and specify printed output in his application. Depending on the complexity of the program, significant programming effort can be shifted to the dialog manager, leaving the programmer to concentrate his efforts on the application content and logic.

CPI-Communications   The final building block of the CPI, shown in Fig. 3-10, is CPI-Communications (CPI-C). It supports distributed applications by providing consistent communicating services across a broad range of environments. CPI-C is an implementation of *Advanced Program to Program Communications* (APPC), which interfaces to one of the SNA logical units that is designated LU6.2. This is documented as referenced in the section on the Common Communication Support (CCS) architecture. CPI-C support provides the foundation for connectivity in the SAA cooperative processing strategy.

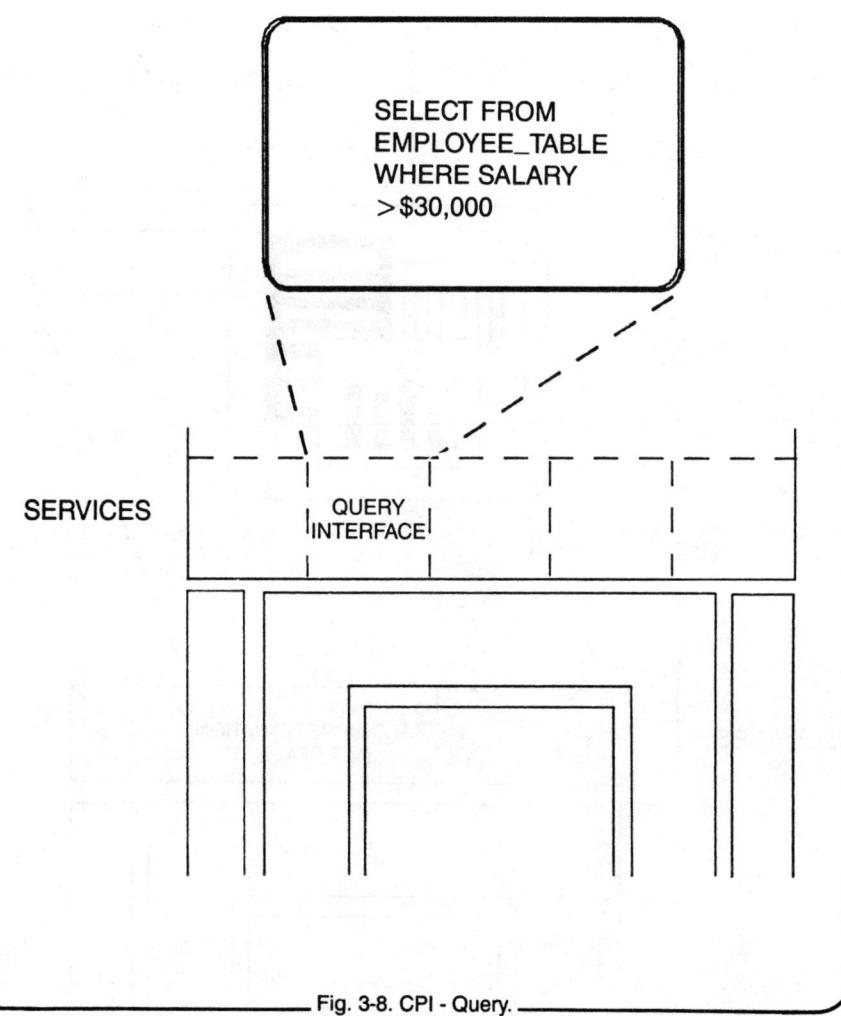

- AVAILABLE AS END USER FACILITY
  . . . AND TO OTHER PROGRAMS
- EASY TO USE LANGUAGE (QMF)
- FOUNDATION FOR ACCESS TO RELATIONAL DATA

SELECT FROM
EMPLOYEE_TABLE
WHERE SALARY
>$30,000

SERVICES

QUERY
INTERFACE

Fig. 3-8. CPI - Query.

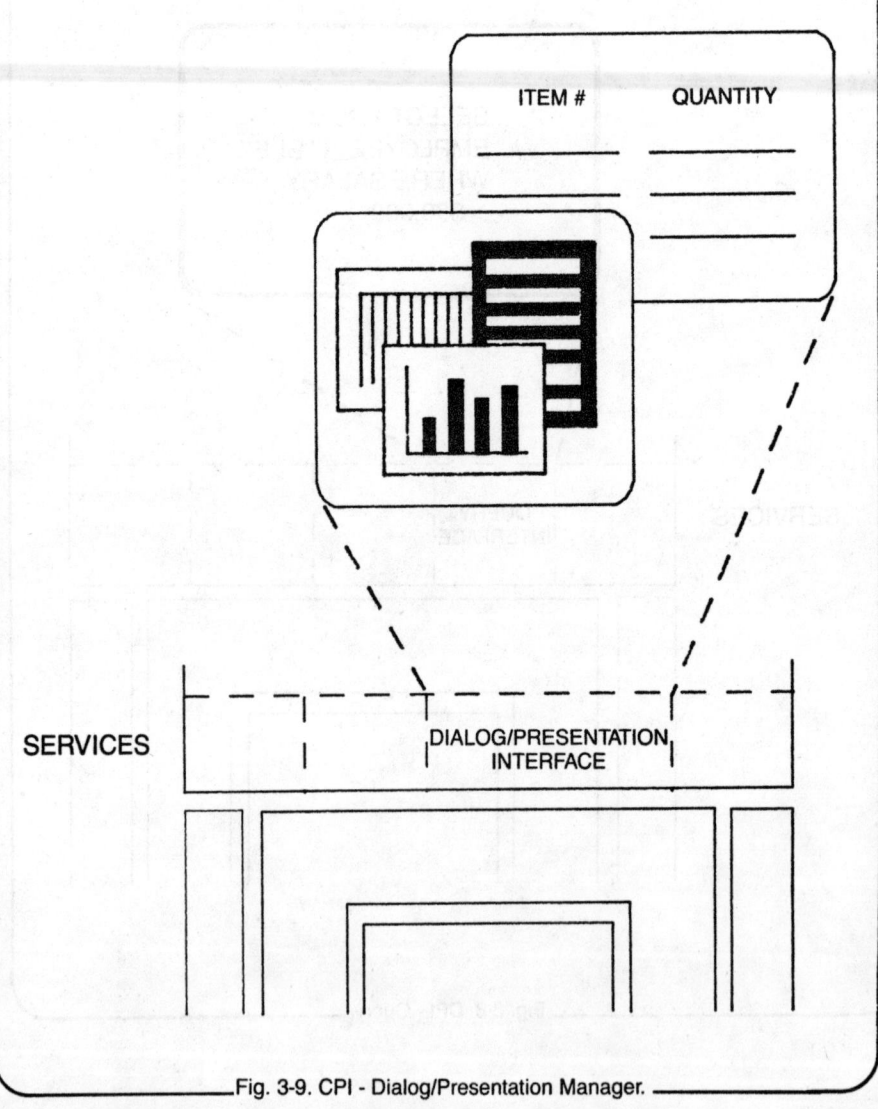

- DATA FORMAT/DISPLAY SUPPORT
- SCREENS AND PRINTERS
- FOUNDATION FOR COMMON USER ACCESS
- PANEL DEFINITION AND NAVIGATION
- MENU SELECTION AND VARIABLE FIELD INPUT

ITEM #   QUANTITY

SERVICES

DIALOG/PRESENTATION
INTERFACE

Fig. 3-9. CPI - Dialog/Presentation Manager.

- HIGH-LEVEL INTERFACE
- PROGRAM-TO-PROGRAM COMMUNICATIONS
- BASE FOR COOPERATIVE PROCESSING

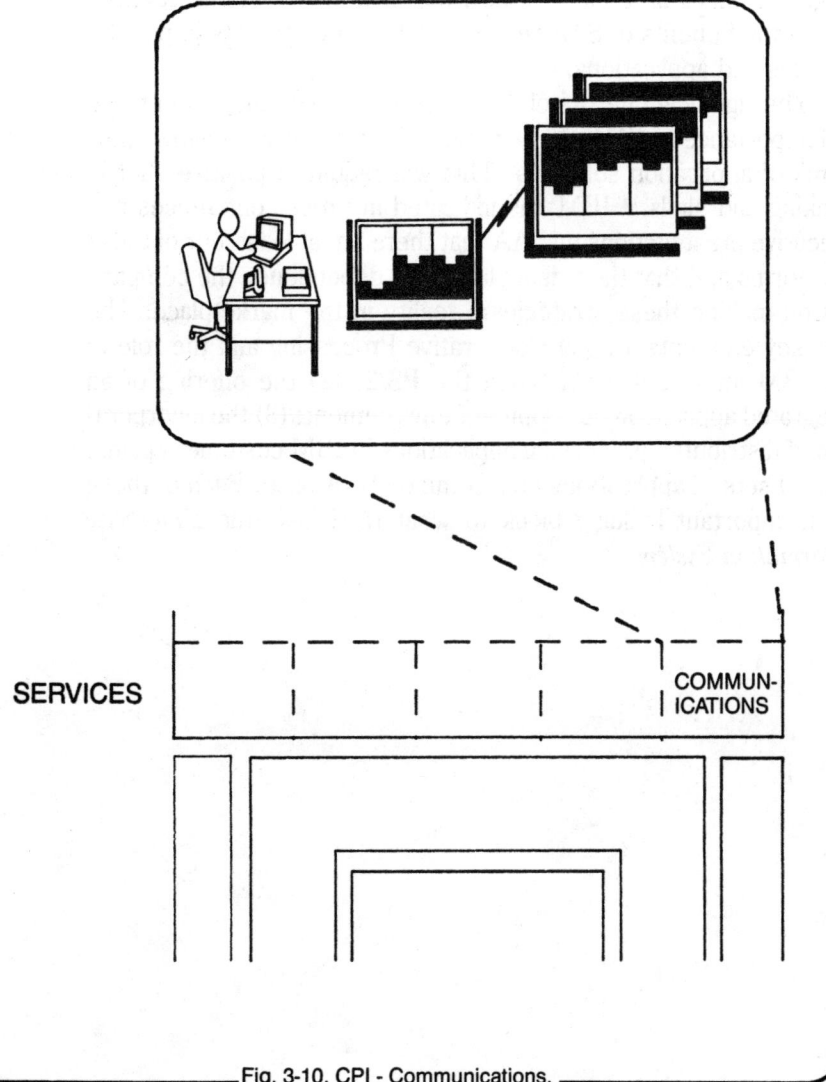

Fig. 3-10. CPI - Communications.

The SAA components describe an elegant design approach upon which IBM is basing its present and future software investments and strategy. The consistency objective of the architectures must be matched in the consistency of product implementation and ease of use. Still to be tested is the flexibility of these designs and whether they can indeed sustain the evolutionary growth that is certain to occur. The varied workloads that will be placed on their SAA systems and their accompanied networks will further challenge the initial directions. Finally, the IBM customers must experience the benefits of SAA relative to their investments in people, systems and applications.

The significant impact of SAA in terms of customer acceptance and importance to IBM will be realized by the way SAA allows new forms of application solutions. This will require a positive shift in thinking and skills.[14] IBM has indicated in press conferences and executive presentations on SAA that there are at least four of these new forms and that there is a plan and a dependency the company has on making these strategies a reality in the marketplace. The four key elements are (1) Cooperative Processing and the role of the IBM intelligent workstation the PS/2; (2) the offering of an integrated application development environment; (3) the incorporation of distributed processing applications in IBM customers plans; and (4) sets of applications on a common SAA base. Each of these is an important building block to what IBM calls the *Enterprise Information System.*

4

IBM SAA Directions

Stephen T. McClellan writes in his book, *The Coming Computer Industry Shakeout*:

> Ten years ago, fewer than one out of every five dollars that users spent on data processing went to software. Today the split is about 50-50. By 1990, the ratio will be 4-1 in favor of the programs. Now *that's a revolution*. The total market for software supplied by all U.S. companies (hardware manufacturers and independent software companies combined) was $14 billion in 1983.[15]

The above points to a shift in the software market and the impact that end user demand has and will continue to have on the evolution of computing. This impact will modify the structure of the enterprise's computing facilities and its software support. To guide its overall software development *direction*, IBM has created a vision of its customer's future computing environment. They call this vision the *Enterprise Information System*, as the conceptual model shows in Fig. 4-1. The foundation of the enterprise system is the architectural components of SAA. The enterprise builds their system utilizing "clusters" of IBM SAA products. Each major cluster is a story in this evolving enterprise system.

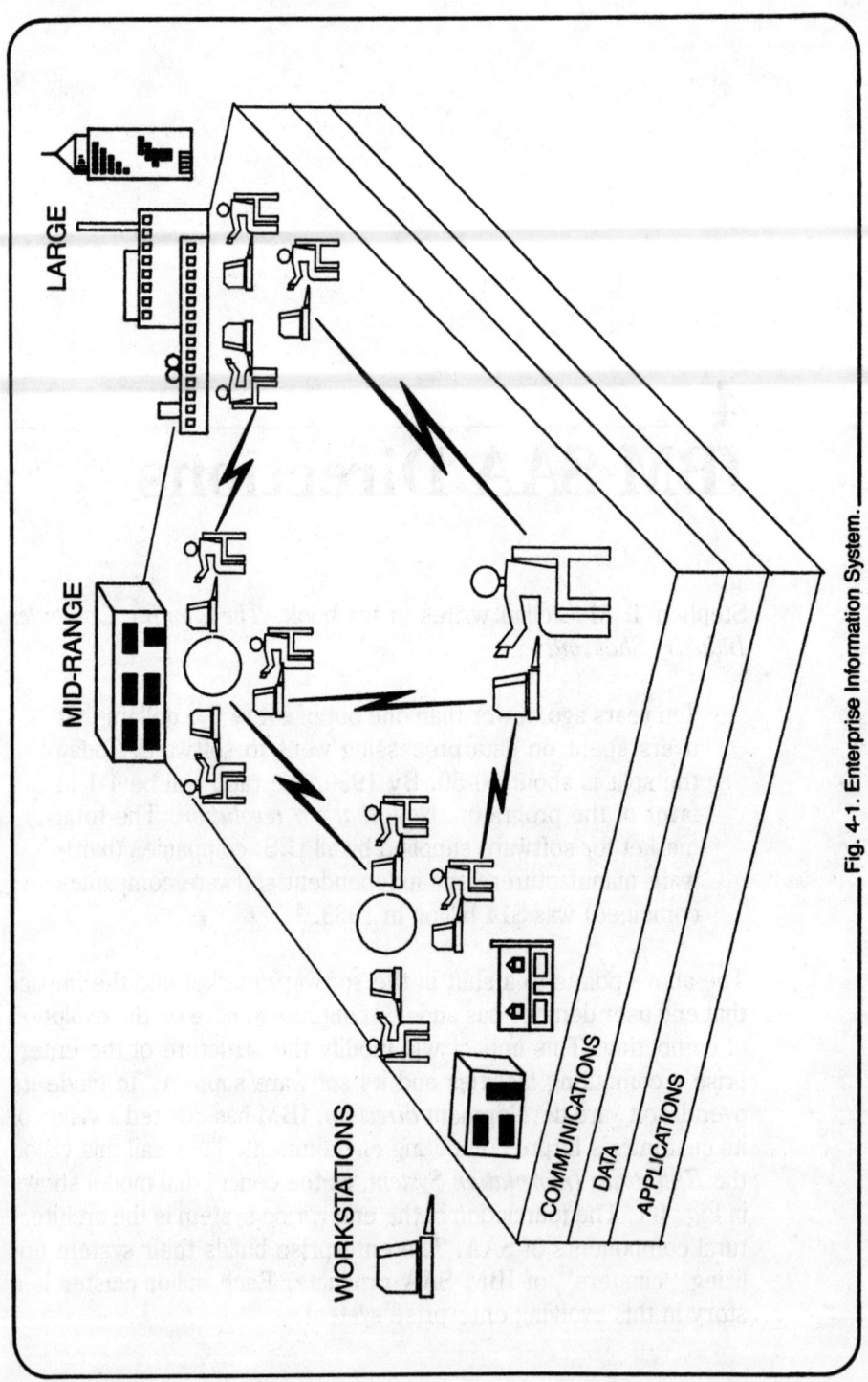

Fig. 4-1. Enterprise Information System.

At this writing, extensions to the SAA vision are being described in models that include accessing data on non-SAA and non-IBM systems and forming collections of host systems that can be described as a "data warehouse."

In the IBM SAA direction, the "window" into the enterprise is through the intelligent workstation. Through this window, end users have access to the diverse capabilities of IBM's workstation, mid-range, and large systems. This vision extends the scope of possible applications as it masks the complexity of the underlying configurations and networks by using the consistent constructs offered by SAA: its user interface, programming interface, and connectivity.

The intelligent workstation works in harmony with the enterprise system through its role in cooperative processing. The user has new powerful applications that operate on data files that can exist anywhere in the far flung geography of the enterprise with the computation performed on the system best suited for the tasks. The firm's programmers have integrated sets of tools to develop and to manage the applications. Common applications such as those supporting office systems function are provided by IBM and supplemented by software vendors.

This vision has permeated the culture of the IBM programming organization. As we shall see in a later chapter, the vision has dictated the management organization that IBM has put in place for SAA.

You have read enough now to realize that SAA is not a single IBM direction. It is a complex labyrinth of technical, business, marketing, and management plans and issues that must be coordinated on a grand scale. The desire and conviction to sustain an unprecedented investment in software development that will total in the billions of dollars can only be achieved when endorsed by the chairman of the board and given broad support across all the major lines of business of the corporation. This executive support is in place and is being reviewed through each development operating plan cycle. In addition, internal business systems are being upgraded to provide better management information of the software business and internal users are beginning to install and make wider use of SAA components.

Four major SAA strategy components—*architecture, application enabling, marketing* and the *management system*—are shown in

SAA

ARCHITECTURES

CUA

CCS

CPI

APPLICATION ENABLING	MANAGEMENT SYSTEM
Cooperative Processing	Line of Business
Distributed Processing	Executive Council
Application Processing	Technical Council
Common Application	Market Council

MARKETING

Merchandising

Product Introduction/Announcement

Market Driven Process

Fig. 4-2. Summary of Systems Application Architecture.

Fig. 4-2. The major architectural elements have been briefly described. The following chapters discuss the effects of SAA on IBM's application enabling offerings of cooperative processing, distributed processing, application development, and common applications. This will be followed by descriptions and analysis of the set of marketing directions IBM has had to structure on a worldwide basis. Finally, a major component of the SAA strategy, the management system will be described to illustrate how the implementation of this global plan is being orchestrated. The reader should gain a basic understanding of SAA and its implications in several important areas of information systems design. In addition, insight should be gained on specific IBM corporate plans in the area of marketing and organizational structure to manage the SAA strategy.

The actual report card on IBM's success with SAA will be chronicled in its business results and reported widely in the business and trade press over the next few years. It is hoped that the background provided in this book will serve to be a meaningful calibration of those results.

5
Cooperative Processing

With the advent of interactive processing in the 1960s, the keyboard display units became the "window" to the information system. All processing was done in the host computer with frames of data sent down to the terminal for display to the end user. As time passed, more function was off-loaded from the host, to be managed by intermediate controllers and more fixed function was designed into the keyboard display unit.

Technology has now advanced to a state where it is cost-effective in many applications to have a fully programmable workstation as an integral part of an application and as depicted in Fig. 5-1, they became the "window" into the enterprise. The use of the intelligent workstation provides the end user with the most advanced form of man-machine interface utilizing advanced display techniques such as windowing and high-performance graphics.

The cooperative processing model (Fig. 5-2) provides the end user the capabilities of the intelligent workstation in conjunction with host services of databases, network control, printers and computing capability not available on the workstation. In the IBM model this application approach is designed under the framework of the SAA architectures, each consistently implemented in their respective systems.

The terms *cooperative processing* and *distributed processing* are often used interchangeably. My usage of *cooperative processing*

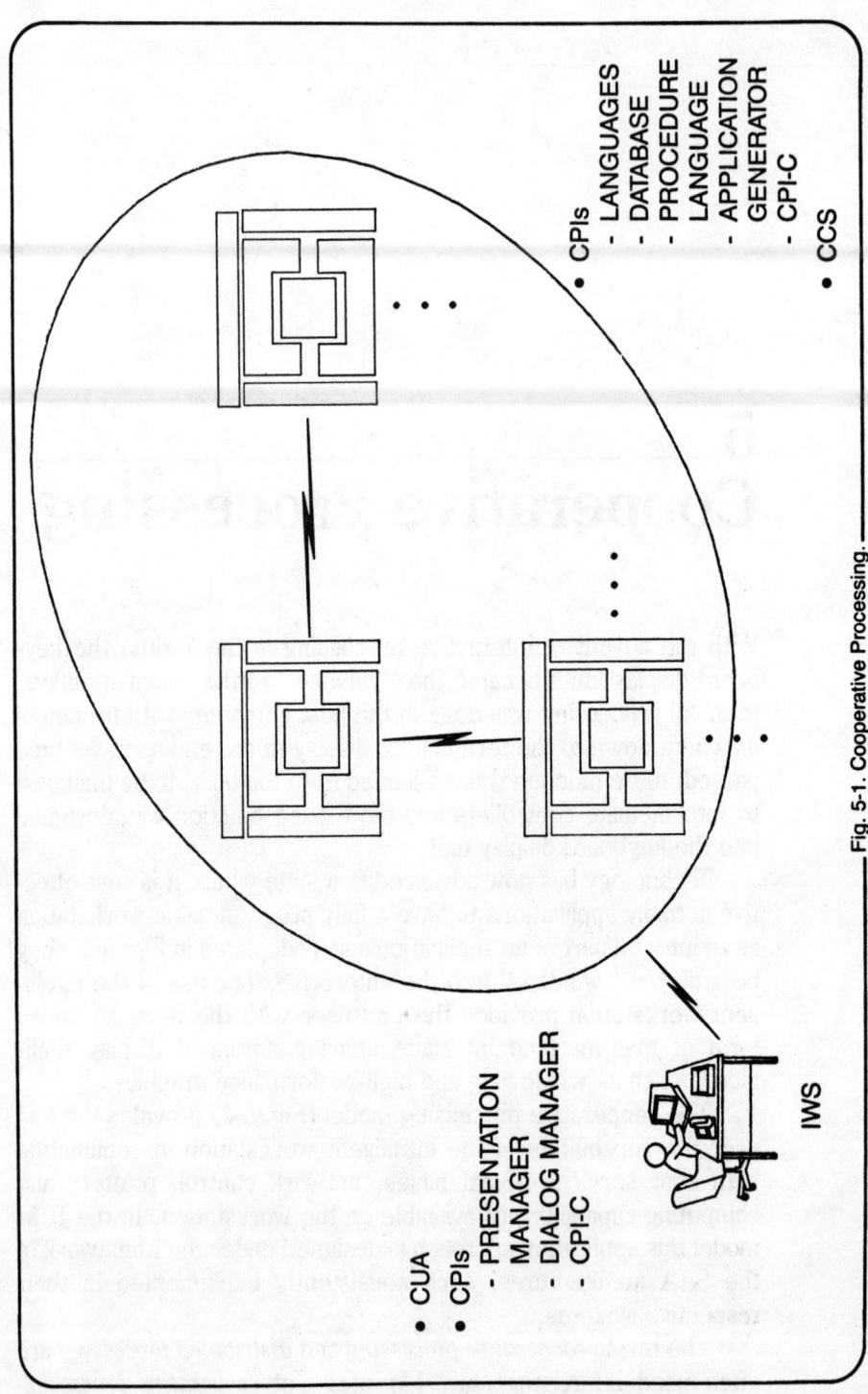

Fig. 5-1. Cooperative Processing.

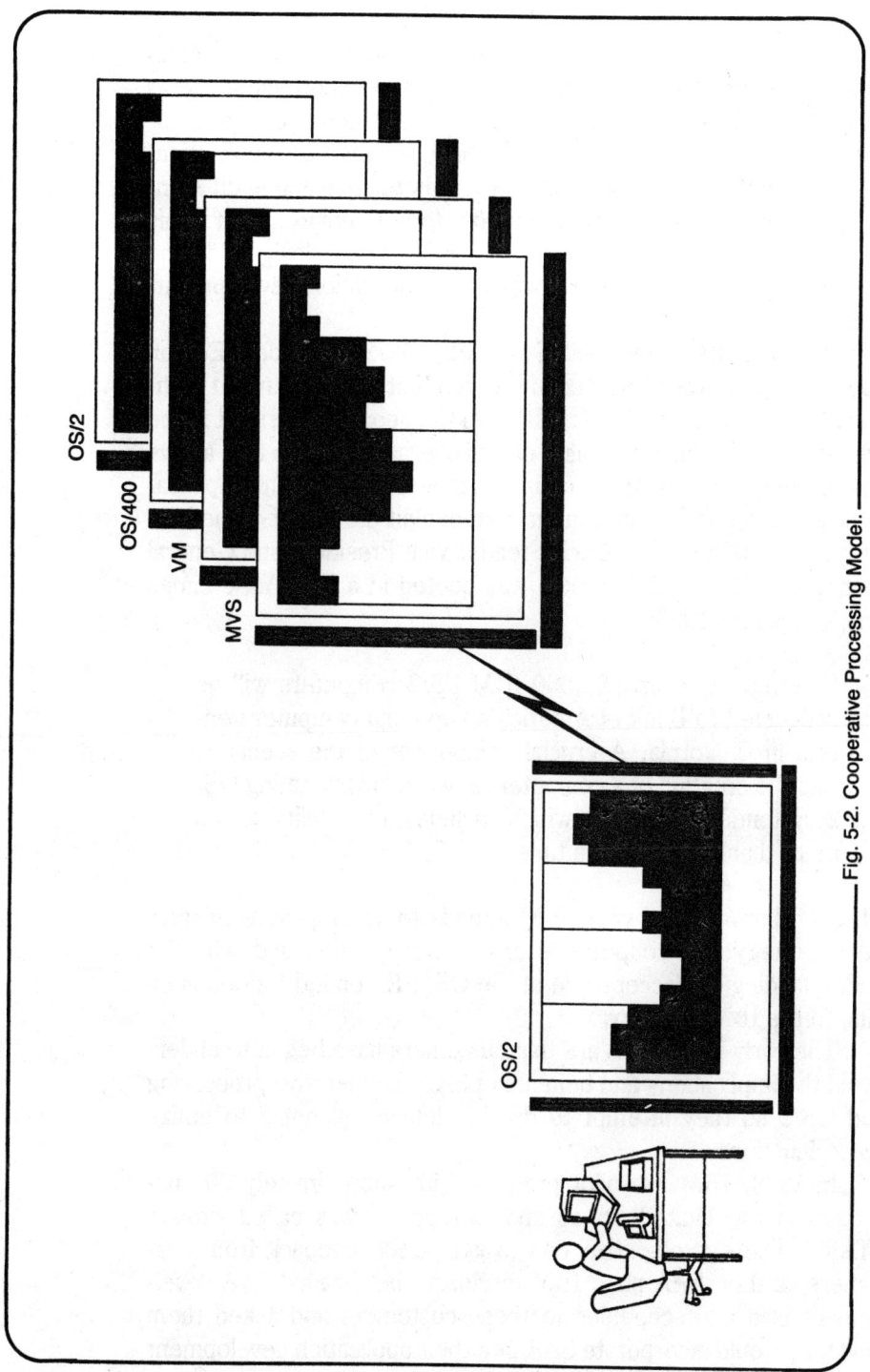

Fig. 5-2. Cooperative Processing Model.

refers specifically to the relationship of application and system function on the intelligent workstation to the application and systems function on a host system. The attachment could be direct or through a gateway on a local area network. Further, the application/ system function on the workstation in this relationship is different than the function relationship in a host-to-host environment. This implies that we need different development tools, design aids and generators, for example for workstation application development, than for the host application.

It is the IBM Personal System/2, OS/2 Extended Edition operating system represented in Fig. 5-3 that offers a current technology leadership position for IBM. In the above scenario, it is the effective multitasking capability of this operating system that allows an end user to concurrently utilize local personal computer applications and cooperative applications that exploit the power of the host systems in the network. Chris Steads, Vice President and General Manager for Bank of America, was quoted in a New York Times article, January 1989:

> "Eventually, nearly 20,000 IBM PS/2 computers will be connected to Bank of America's two main computer centers in California. A crucial component of the scenario, was the creation of a computer network incorporating OS/ 2 Extended Edition....which includes the ability to do more than one task at a time."[16]

This is a harbinger of what IBM intends to accomplish with their SAA strategy and cooperative processing function and why the understanding and acceptance of the OS/2 Extended Edition is so vital to the IBM strategy.

The early indications are that customers have begun to understand the implications and benefits of SAA, cooperative processing and OS/2 as they attempt to do the detailed planning to utilize these functions.

In 1988, IBM ran pilot projects with approximately 50 customers in the United States and Europe. It was called Project START. The key objective was to get direct feedback from customers on their SAA plan. IBM disclosed the detailed SAA development plan and schedules to these customers and asked them how they would incorporate SAA into their application development

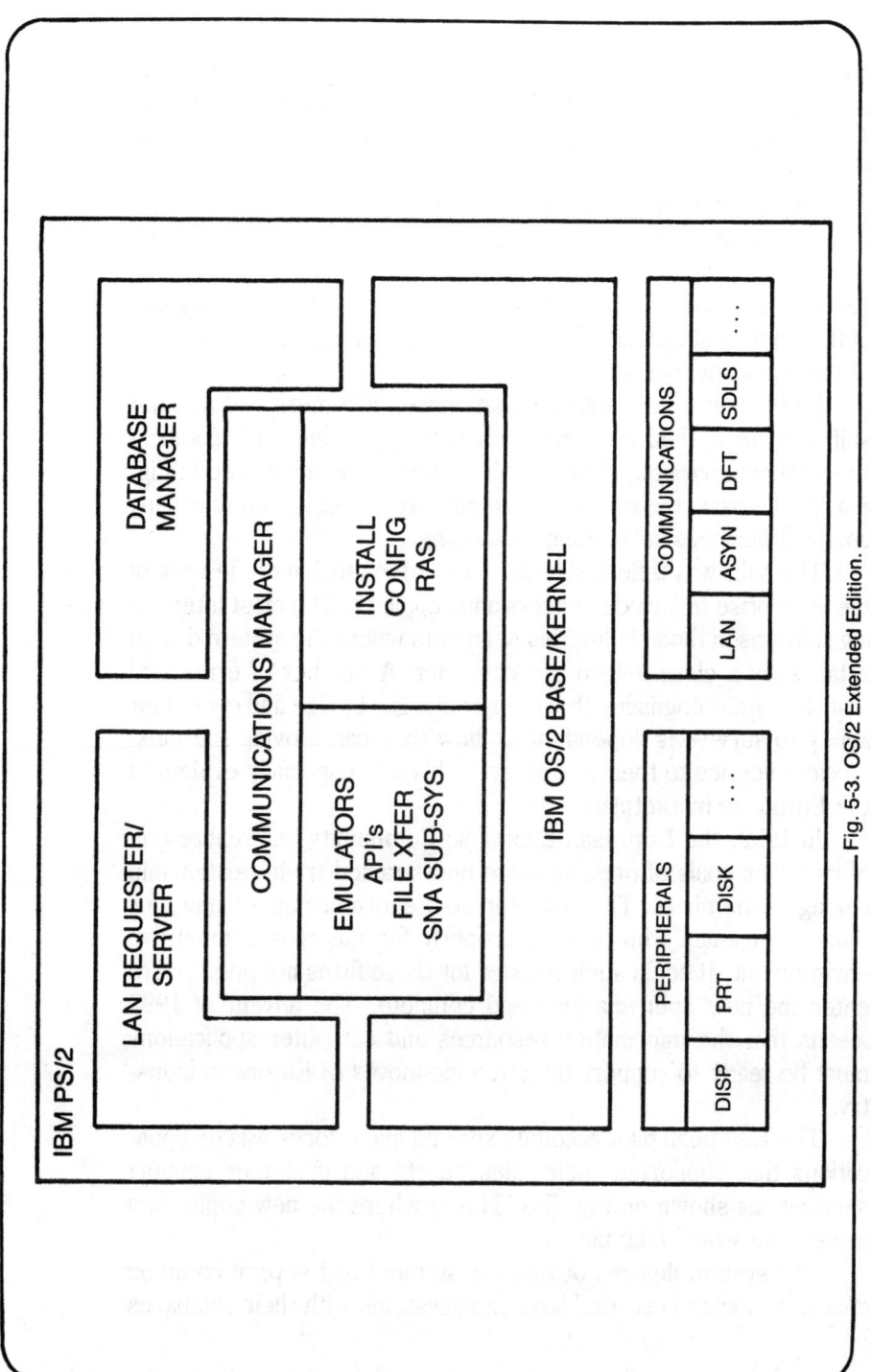

Fig. 5-3. OS/2 Extended Edition.

strategy. They were also asked to provide a critique on the benefits and the problems. The customer projects ran three to six months. At the conclusion, IBM marketing and development executives reviewed the account projects.

The customers represented a broad range of industry segments including banking, manufacturing, distribution, oil, pharmaceutical, government, hospital, airlines, and software vendors. In general, they are some of IBM's largest customers as well as some of their harshest critics. The following discussion generalizes some of the major findings and results.

First, it was very evident that these customers had a major shift in focus of their investment for new applications and modification of their current applications. This shift is demonstrated in Fig. 5-4. In the past, the major investments were focused on managing cost and business accounting processing.

The shift was reflected in the outward extension of the view of the enterprise to include vendors and suppliers. The most interesting shift was in those industries segments where the system design established a close link to the customer. A number of firms said that they are recognizing that their competitive edge and even their ability to survive is dependent on how they can provide the most efficient service to their customers. This was especially evident in the European marketplace.

In 1992, the European Economic Community will realize one of its major goals of opening more unrestrained trade relationship among its members. This will represent enormous opportunity for those companies who prepare properly for this new competitive environment. It could spell disaster for those firms not prepared to enter the new open markets and compete. The advent of 1992 means that the information resources and computer applications must be ready to support the strategic moves of European industry.

The European pilot accounts showed major focus was on applications that supported their sales efforts and customer support services, as shown on Fig. 5-5. This is where the new application investment would take place.

The system designs of these customers had several common characteristics: (1) several large host systems with their databases

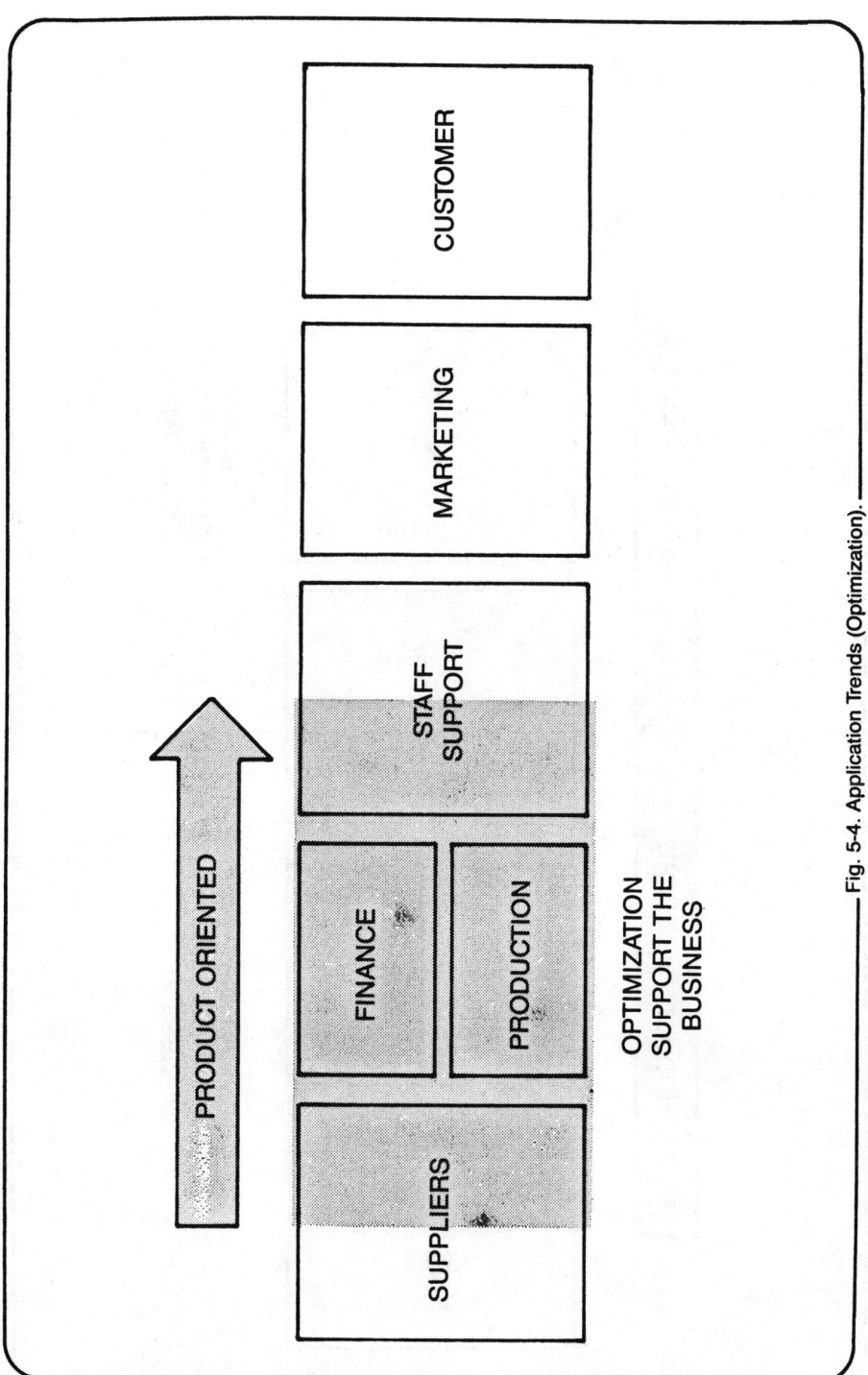

Fig. 5-4. Application Trends (Optimization).

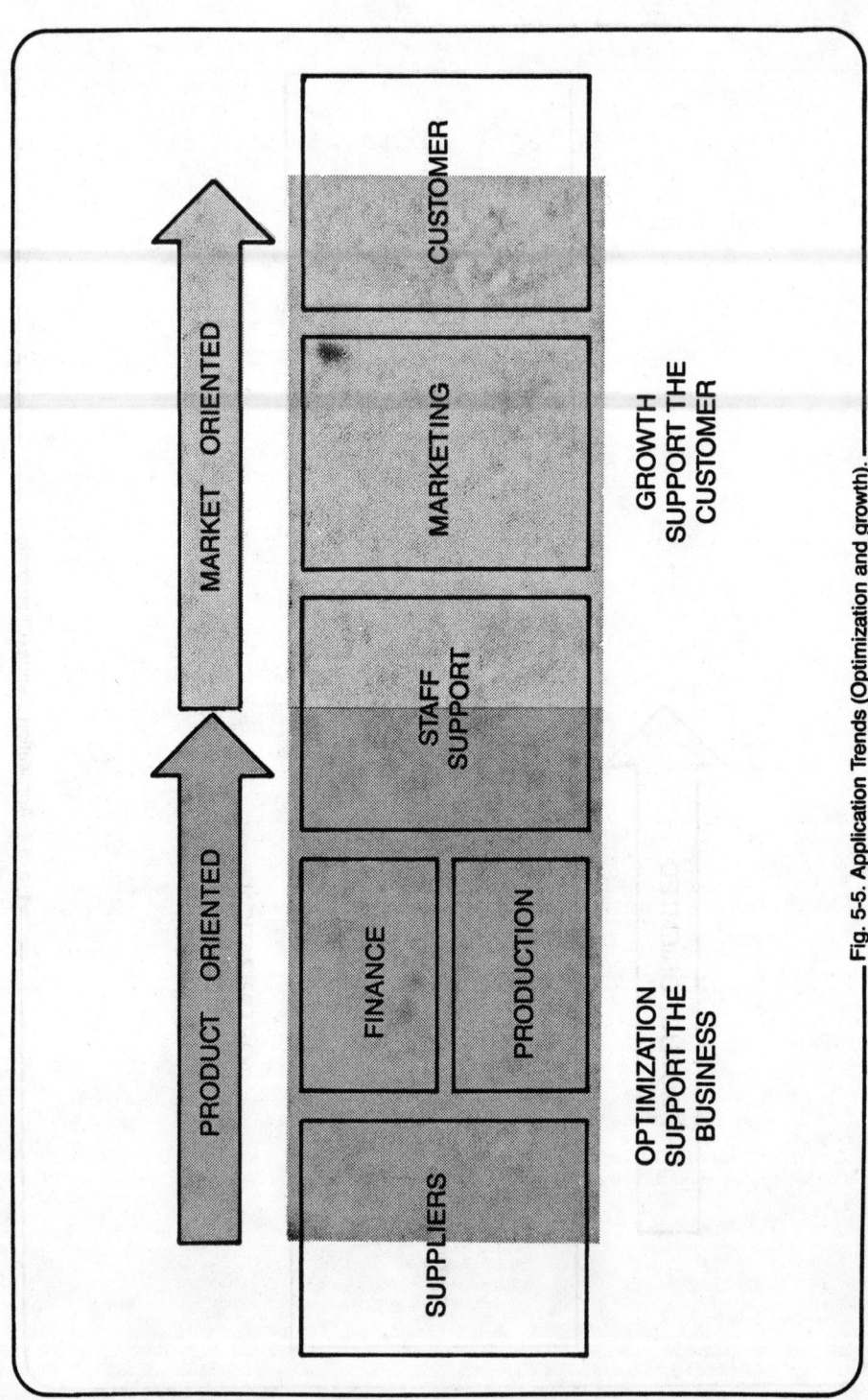

Fig. 5-5. Application Trends (Optimization and growth).

geographically dispersed; (2) a layer of distributions of smaller systems with local or specialized databases as nodes in the companies' international network; (3) attached to these nodes are intelligent terminals, PS/2 on local area networks, a ring of PS/2s and personal computers.

In the view of these customers, SAA provided a technical framework that they had confidence in to be the base of this system expansion. It would give them the ability to manage a fast buildup with a consistency of operation far exceeding today's systems. Although the SAA concept was favored by these customers there was also a long list of critiques, criticism, and recommendations generated by the detailed planning of the Project START.

The most urgent need was on availability of the products to support the SAA concepts. Schedules had to be accelerated. A few of these customers tested an early version of the PS/2 Presentation Manager. The experience was frustrating—too many "bugs." The documentation was not complete. The examples were too trivial to demonstrate how to use the function. It was too flexible. Customers wanted more specific guidance from IBM on CUA. It was too difficult for some. The Dialog Manager tool was requested earlier. Translations of the manuals into some of the European languages were not done well and so it went. The IBM executives brought lists of the complaints back to the laboratories to design action programs for the problems.

Customers also put action plans in place to exploit what they had learned about SAA, which included:

- Assigning SAA responsibility to a senior manager in the M&S organization.
- Arranging for more staff education and support.
- Implementing plans for selected projects to use SAA concepts.
- Installing some of the key SAA products such as DB/2.
- Establishing installation standards using CUA (Common User Access).
- Investigating language needs for CSP and REXX.
- Developing a detailed strategy for incorporating the IWS (Intelligent Workstation) into application plans.

Overall, IBM was told it was on the right track with the SAA direction. As one Project Start customer report concluded:

> "The team judged that SAA will become part of the infra-structure of computing in the way that SNA and SQL have. In that light, XXX should not miss any opportunity to introduce SAA conformance now, where it can be done at low cost."[17]

This early work of Project Start customers was beneficial in confirming that the SAA objective of cross systems consistency, shown in Fig. 5-6, become a customer requirement. It also became clear that the cooperative processing function within SAA is important to the customers application strategies (Fig. 5-7).

Project START continues today to be a vital source of customer requirements and feedback. The projects are now complemented with Customer Advisory Councils that meet periodically to review specific SAA implementations directions for cooperative processing application development, database, and other major elements of the SAA strategy. The insights gained in these councils will have increased importance in the formulation of SAA as we move from a focus on the individual components of CPIs to the understanding of what it means to have a SAA application and finally, to the environment of multiple SAA applications running in a distributed enterprise.

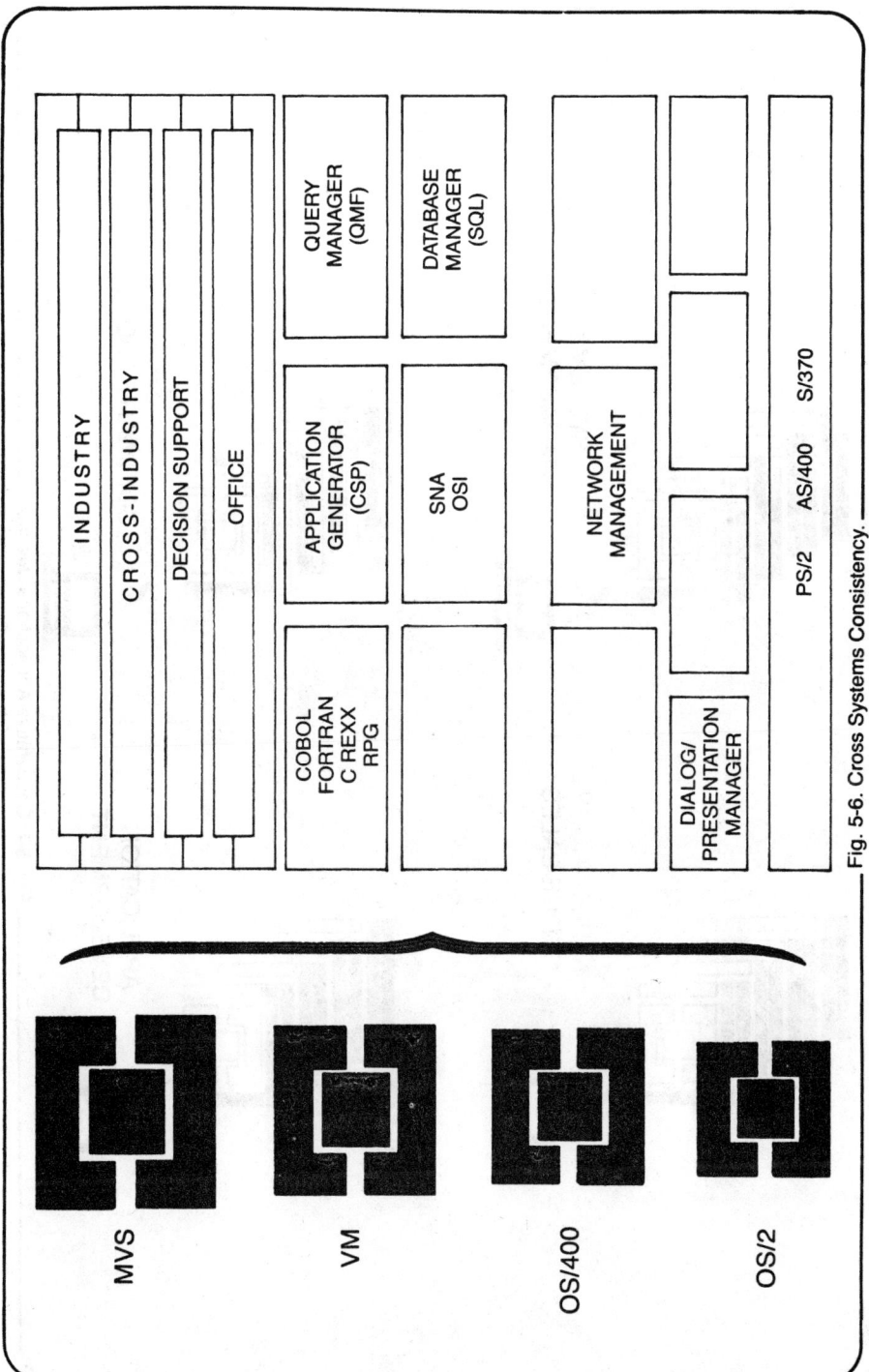

Fig. 5-6. Cross Systems Consistency.

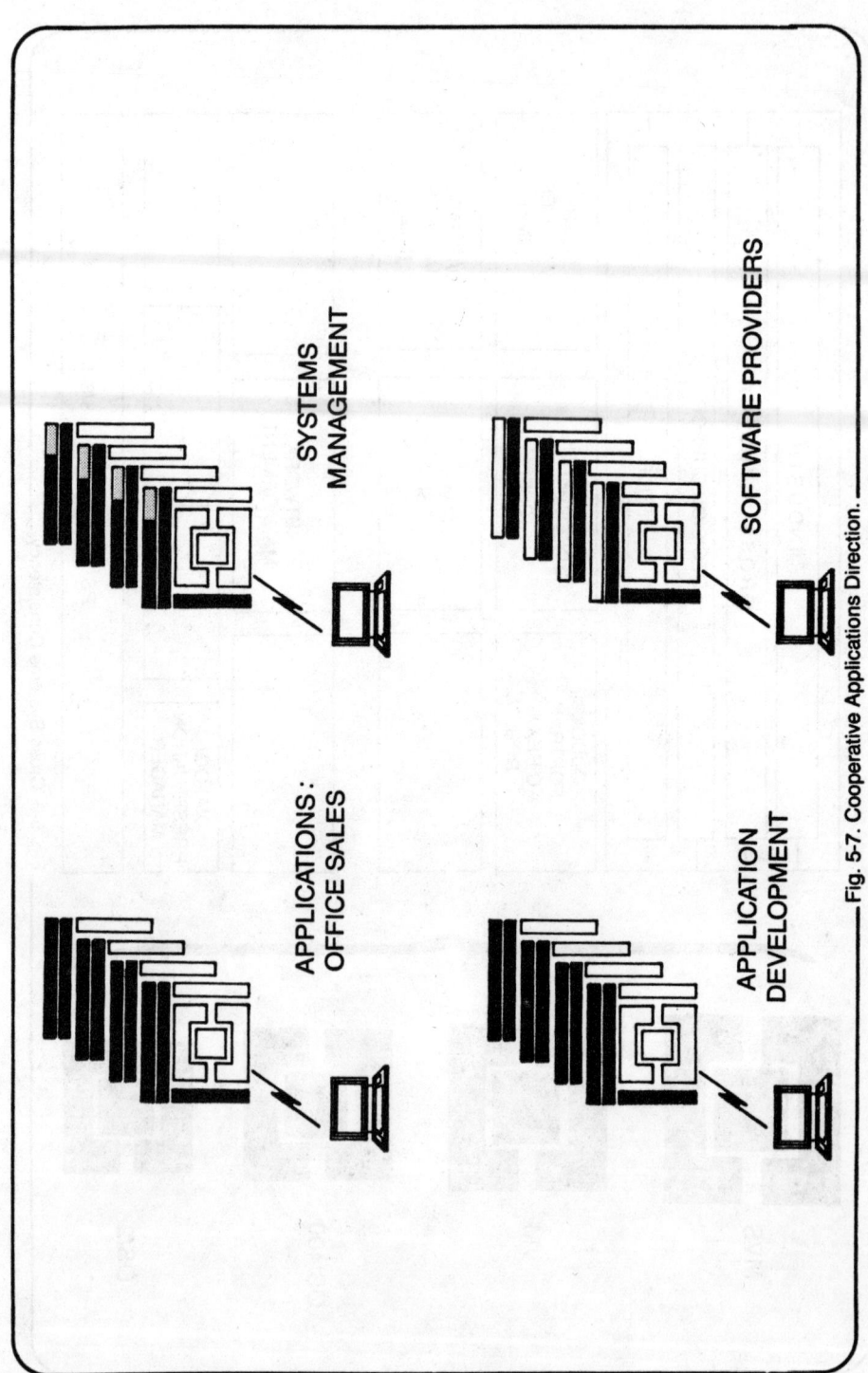

Fig. 5-7. Cooperative Applications Direction.

6
Distributed Processing

If the SAA components CUA, CPI, and CCS are the foundation of the IBM vision of the enterprise information system then the elements that construct the floors of the "building" are contained in their SAA Distributed Processing strategy as depicted in Fig. 6-1. The view is that in order for the enterprise system to be built and to operate efficiently it must be able to handle data that is distributed and supported with a wide range of services. Systems management and security functions must be available throughout the network to manage the overall operation. Finally, the distributed design of the applications should build on the concepts of cooperative processing.

Table A, from Scherr's article, shown in Table 6-1, summarizes the motivations for distributed processing. A contrast can be made with the motivations for centralized processing by examining Table B. The concept of distributed processing is as old as computing. Aspects of it can be found in Babbage's 1833 design of his Analytical Engine, the general concepts of which exist in today's most advanced computing systems.[5] Thousands of sophisticated systems are successfully operating today using all aspects of distributed processing. However, as the user population has grown in the enterprise, his demands for application support have increased and the cost of implementation, shown in Fig. 6-2, rises dramatically. The nature of the information systems installed in the enterprises

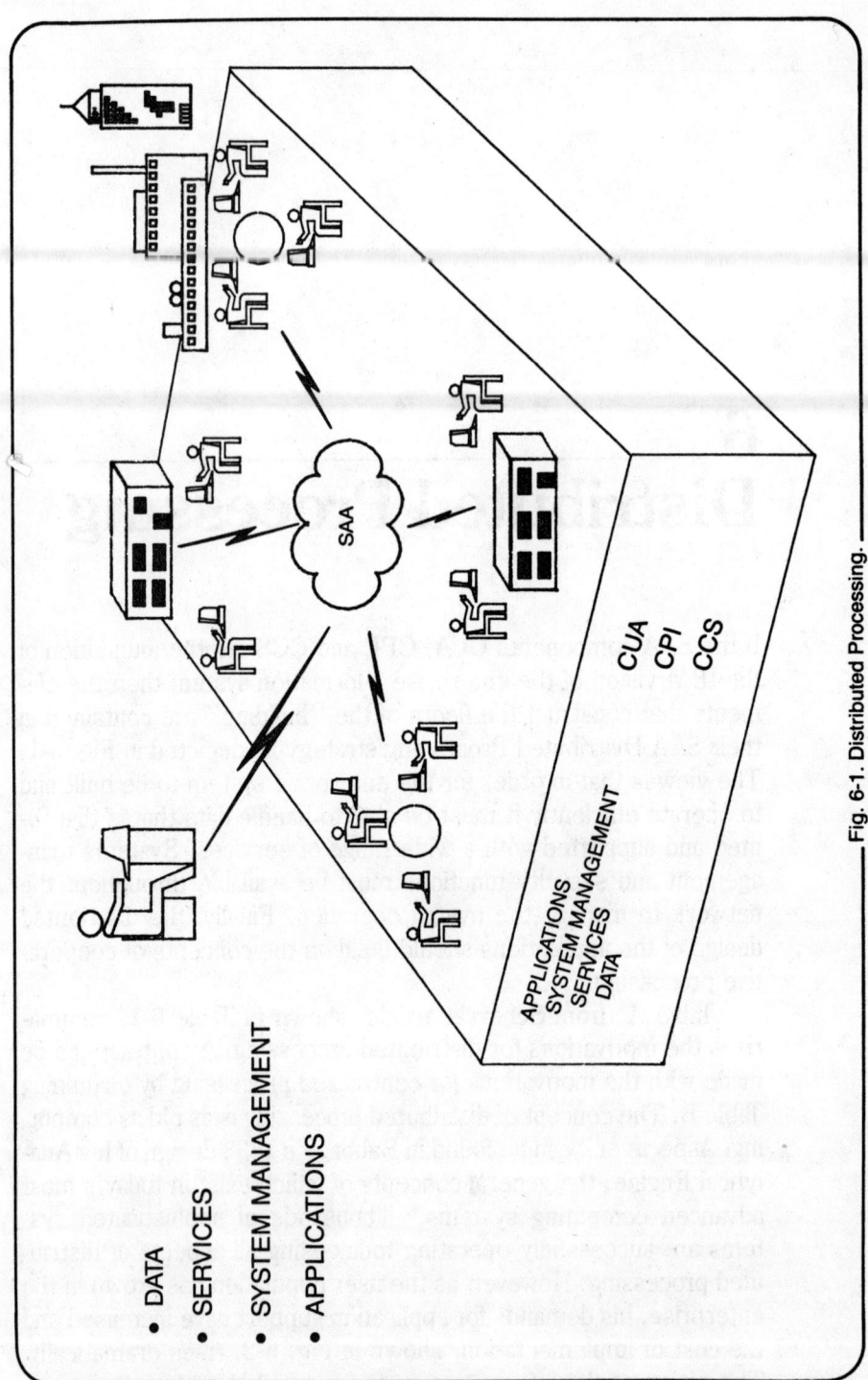

Fig. 6-1. Distributed Processing.

Table 6-1. Motivations for Distributed & Centralized Processing.

TABLE A: MOTIVATIONS FOR DISTRIBUTED PROCESSING
GEOGRAPHY
- COMPUTING VERSUS COMMUNICATIONS TRADE-OFF COSTS AND DELAYS
- RESPONSIVENESS OF THE USER INTERFACE
- BRIDGES BETWEEN EXISTING APPLICATIONS

CHARACTERISTICS OF PROCESSORS
- EXPLOITING PRICE AND PERFORMANCE DIFFERENCES
- SIMPLICITY OF SMALL MACHINES
- UNIQUE FUNCTION

HIGHER SYSTEM AVAILABILITY FOR END USERS
- SCOPE OF FAILURES LIMITED BY PARTITIONING THE WORKLOAD
- IMPACT OF FAILURES REDUCED BY REDUNDANCY IN THE FRONT END AND THE BACK END

PHYSICAL SECURITY
- PROTECTION AGAINST NATURAL DISASTERS, POWER FAILURES, SABOTAGE, ETC.
- SECURITY PROVISIONS

SINGLE-SYSTEM CAPACITY LIMITATIONS
- SINGLE COMPUTER WITH ADEQUATE CAPACITY NOT AVAILABLE
- OPERATIONAL COMPLEXITY OF LARGE CENTRALIZED SYSTEM
- COST OF MIGRATION TO LARGER SYSTEM AND/OR NEW OPERATING SYSTEMS

ORGANIZATIONAL CONSIDERATIONS
- SIZE OF CENTRALIZED DATA PROCESSING ORGANIZATION
- MANAGEMENT STYLE AND PHILOSOPHY
- HISTORICAL GROWTH
- MERGERS AND ACQUISITIONS

TABLE B: MOTIVATIONS FOR CENTRALIZED PROCESSING
ECONOMICS OF SCALE
- HARDWARE
- ORGANIZATION

SINGLE POINT OF CONTROL
- OPERATIONS
- SECURITY
- SYSTEMS AND APPLICATIONS PROGRAMMING

SIMPLICITY
- FEWER DECISIONS TO MAKE AND UNMAKE
- TUNING

SHARED-DATA APPLICATIONS
- ONLY FEASIBLE SOLUTION WHEN DATA MUST BE CURRENT AND FREQUENTLY UPDATED

ACCESSIBILITY
- SYSTEMS, DATA, AND PROGRAMS ALL EQUALLY ACCESSIBLE FROM ANYWHERE IN THE NETWORK

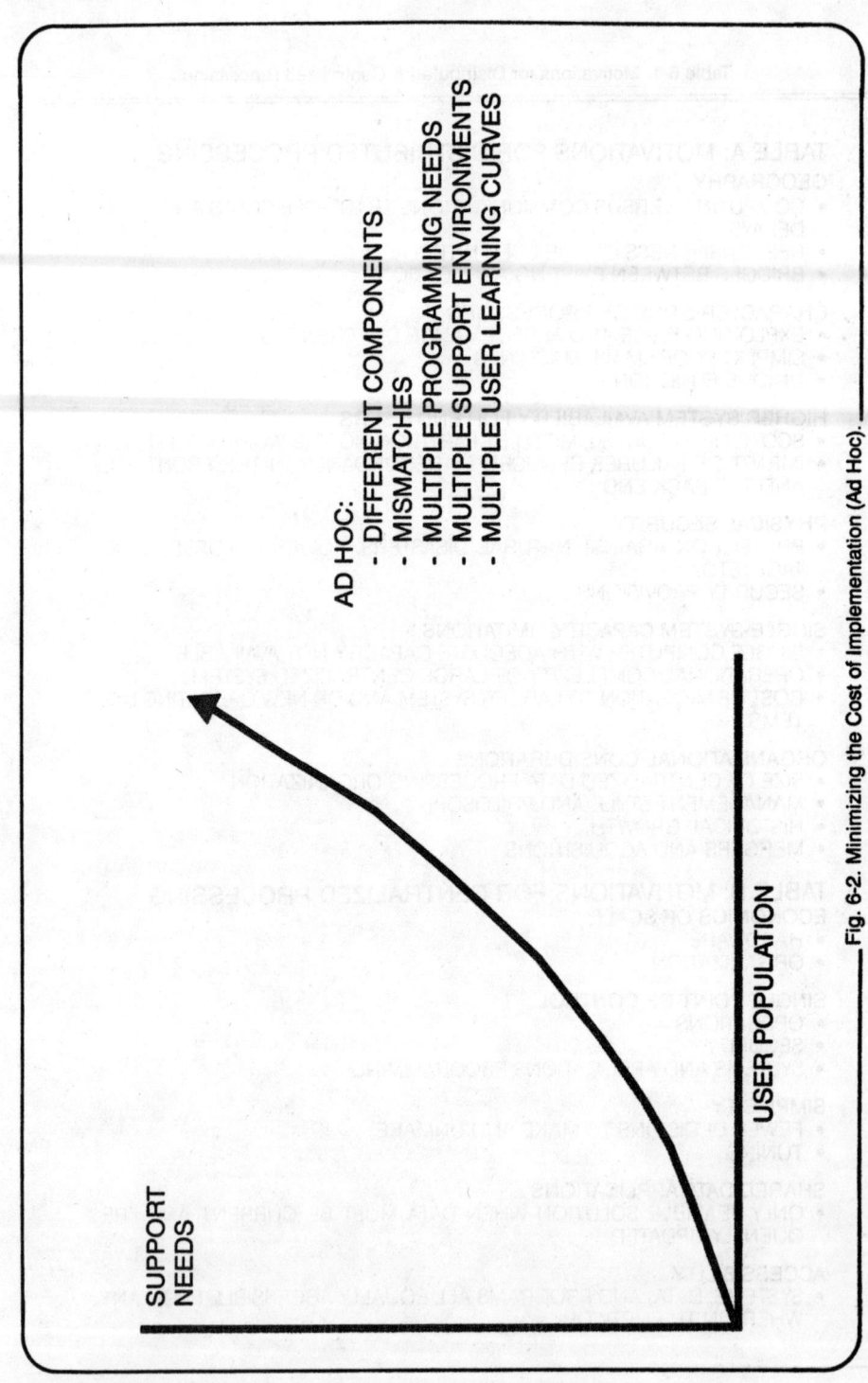

AD HOC:
- DIFFERENT COMPONENTS
- MISMATCHES
- MULTIPLE PROGRAMMING NEEDS
- MULTIPLE SUPPORT ENVIRONMENTS
- MULTIPLE USER LEARNING CURVES

SUPPORT
NEEDS

USER POPULATION

Fig. 6-2. Minimizing the Cost of Implementation (Ad Hoc).

today have brought increasing challenges to the MIS directors. The obvious are the mounting costs, increasing user demands and the risk of lowered perception of the value of the system by management. It is evident that this trend could be translated into a potential impact on IBM's growth and the growth of the industry as a whole.

On the other hand, properly addressed solutions to these challenges can represent an enormous opportunity to the information systems industry. The customers demands are not artificial. The drive for new markets, increased competition, global strategies, quality, changing consumer demand, and new technology in virtually every industry is creating the need to gather, organize and process information at an increasing rate. The information solutions positioned to address these needs in a durable, consistent and flexible manner will gain the widest acceptance.

IBM's SAA distributed processing offerings, then, can be viewed not just as a technical solution for the MIS Director but as a direct attack against the economics of the cost escalation Fig. 6-3. The opportunity for IBM is of course, to be the major provider of the matched systems and the consistency promised by SAA.

Two things became very clear at IBM. The IBM customers were facing an enormous challenge in designing and implementing the information systems they needed to run their business. It also was clear, within the IBM software development and technical community, that SAA and all of its parts could be an enormous help. The technical concepts and plans were underway to provide a distributed set of solutions for customers running under SAA.

The IBM software products that became the manifestation of SAA number into the hundreds. What was not so clear to the marketing organization was how they could evaluate and communicate the product value and associate it with the customer value judgments of software. This would be crucial on the individual SAA components as well as on the evolving rich new technology extensions promised by SAA distributed processing.

In April of 1988, the systems product marketing arm of the IBM Europe, Middle East and Africa Corporation set out to construct an evaluation tool that would be useful in mapping product attributes with customer values. The tool would be used on SAA products to validate the customer requirements and process in the

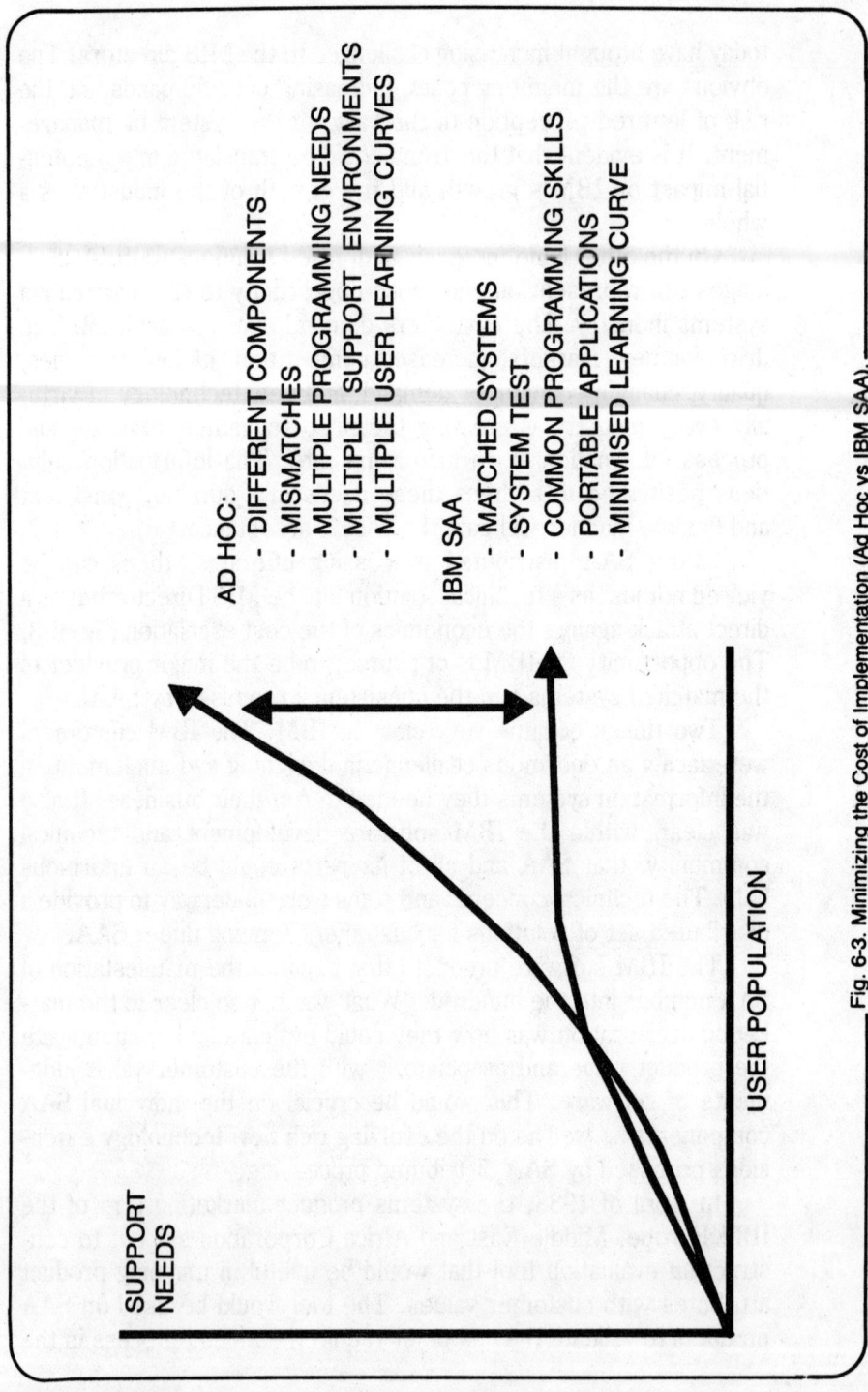

Fig. 6-3. Minimizing the Cost of Implementation (Ad Hoc vs IBM SAA).

IBM development plan. The benefit would be a value assessment on the solution orientation of the product and its value to the customer.

The customer study work was conducted with numerous customers across five industries in five countries.[17] The result was an agreed set of *value categories* for customer values and product values. The *product description matrix* shown in Fig. 6-4 is a valuable tool in preparing for the announcement and introduction of new products. It is a means of relating the individual products to specific customer value categories for the purpose of developing "themes" to categorize major announcement events as demonstrated in Fig. 6-5. Figure 6-6 shows how a particular distributed product represented by the Xs, can be assessed against a specific customer's requirement represented by the circles in the matrix. The circles and the Xs are developed jointly with the customer and is a concise summary leading to a product decision, and potentially a total distributed systems evaluation.

The definitions of the value categories are included in Appendix A. The use of this technique is currently being tested on several product areas and for incorporation into the product roll-out process.

Although the importance of the product description matrix to IBM's SAA effort has not reached its final conclusion, it demonstrates an important principle regarding SAA and IBM product development in general. That is, the desire for the IBM products to be "market driven." The tool represents one of the ways to substantiate anecdotal and intricate judgments of the customer requirement by providing an analytical base to show the marketplace assessment.

The full spectrum of distributed processing introduces new degrees of freedom for the application designer.[18] This will result in tremendous flexibility for IBM to offer new products and for new cost performance trade-offs for the customer. It is important that IBM test the value of their offering from the customer point of view as they introduce these new functions. This will give the customer and IBM the confidence to move swiftly to use the technologies of distributed processing described in the next section.

PRODUCT	CUSTOMER VALUE CATEGORIES				
	BUSINESS SOLUTIONS	PROTECTION OF INVESTMENT	END-USER PRODUCTIVITY	GROWTH ENABLING	SYSTEM MANAGEMENT
FUNCTIONALITY					
USABILITY					
PERFORMANCE					
RELIABILITY					
INSTALLABILITY					
MAINTAINABILITY					
DOCUMENTATION					
ADAPTABILITY					
EXPLOITATION					
STANDARDS & ARCHITECTURES					

CAPABILITIES

PRODUCT VALUE CATEGORIES

Fig. 6-4. Product Description Matrix.

CUSTOMER VALUE CATEGORIES

PRODUCT VALUE CATEGORIES / CAPABILITIES	BUSINESS SOLUTIONS	PROTECTION OF INVESTMENT	END-USER PRODUCTIVITY	GROWTH ENABLING	SYSTEM MANAGEMENT
FUNCTIONALITY	A		A	B,D	C
USABILITY					
PERFORMANCE	D		C	B	C
RELIABILITY			D		
INSTALLABILITY			C		C
MAINTAINABILITY					C
DOCUMENTATION	A, D		A, C, D	B,C,D	B,C
ADAPTABILITY					B, C
EXPLOITATION				B, C	
STANDARDS & ARCHITECTURES					

Fig. 6-5. Product Description Matrix for a Theme: Products A, B, C, D.

CUSTOMER VALUE CATEGORIES

PRODUCT	BUSINESS SOLUTIONS	PROTECTION OF INVESTMENT	END-USER PRODUCTIVITY	GROWTH ENABLING	SYSTEM MANAGEMENT
FUNCTIONALITY	⊗		⊗	X	⊗
USABILITY					⊗
PERFORMANCE	X		⊗	X	X
RELIABILITY			⊗		X
INSTALLABILITY			X		
MAINTAINABILITY					X
DOCUMENTATION					
ADAPTABILITY					⊗
EXPLOITATION				⊗	X
STANDARDS & ARCHITECTURES		X			

PRODUCT VALUE CATEGORIES / CAPABILITIES

Fig. 6-6. Product Description Matrix for DB/2, Version 2: Value Assessment for a Specific Customer.

DISTRIBUTED DATA

Access to data residing on another connected computer is a common requirement in distributed processing, as is the need to provide a data support services environment, shown in Fig. 6-7. As data processing and operating systems evolved increased levels of support in the forms of data storage techniques, access methods, and high-level language support also has evolved to simplify the programmers job of specifying data formats, accessing different hardware storage devices, and handling error conditions. However, different operating systems, languages, and applications address the file management needs in a different way.

The SAA CPI architecture addresses file portability by standardizing the method of interfacing to files across each of the SAA programming languages (Cobol, Fortran, RPG III PL/1, and C). The SAA programmer can access remote files through the use of the high-level languages' input-output statements shown in Fig. 6-8, which are specified in IBM's Distributed Data Management architecture, a subset of SAA.

Similarly, the SAA distributed application facilities form a base of supporting the SAA direction for data that is independent of the physical location of the data in the network. The application program invokes the industry standard, Structured Query Language (SQL), to access the relational database (Fig. 6-9). If the data is stored remotely, communication requests would be generated exploiting SAA common communications support (CCS).

IBM provides the distributed database function through its four SAA relations database managers:

DB/2,

SQL/DS,

OS/400 Database Manager with SQL400

OS/2 Database Manager

These products allow distribution of relational data across the large, mid-range and small SAA systems. Each database manager participates as a peer in distributed environments. A central data manager is not necessary. This permits the Enterprise Information System to have as much decentralization as desired, presenting all

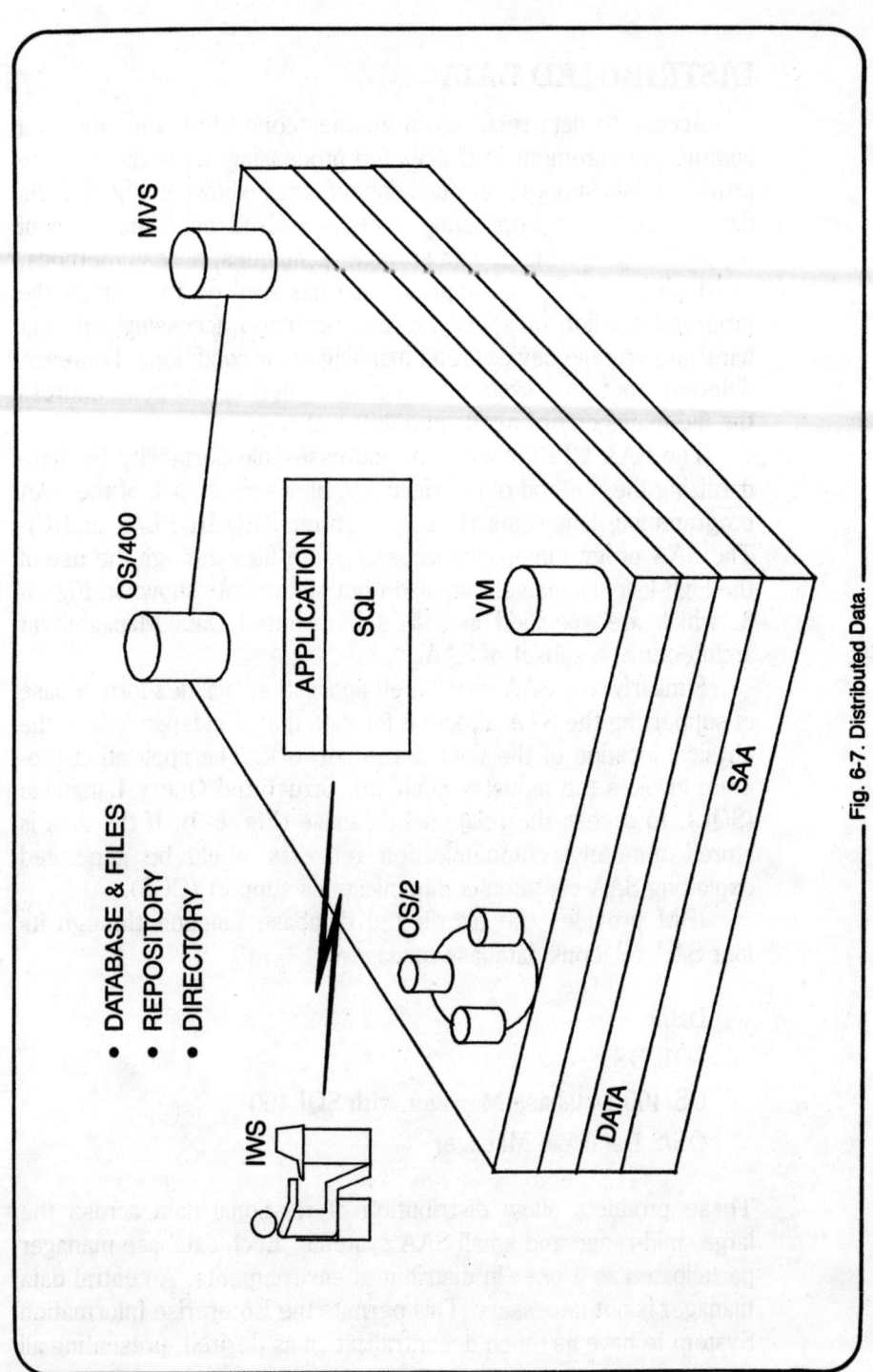

Fig. 6-7. Distributed Data.

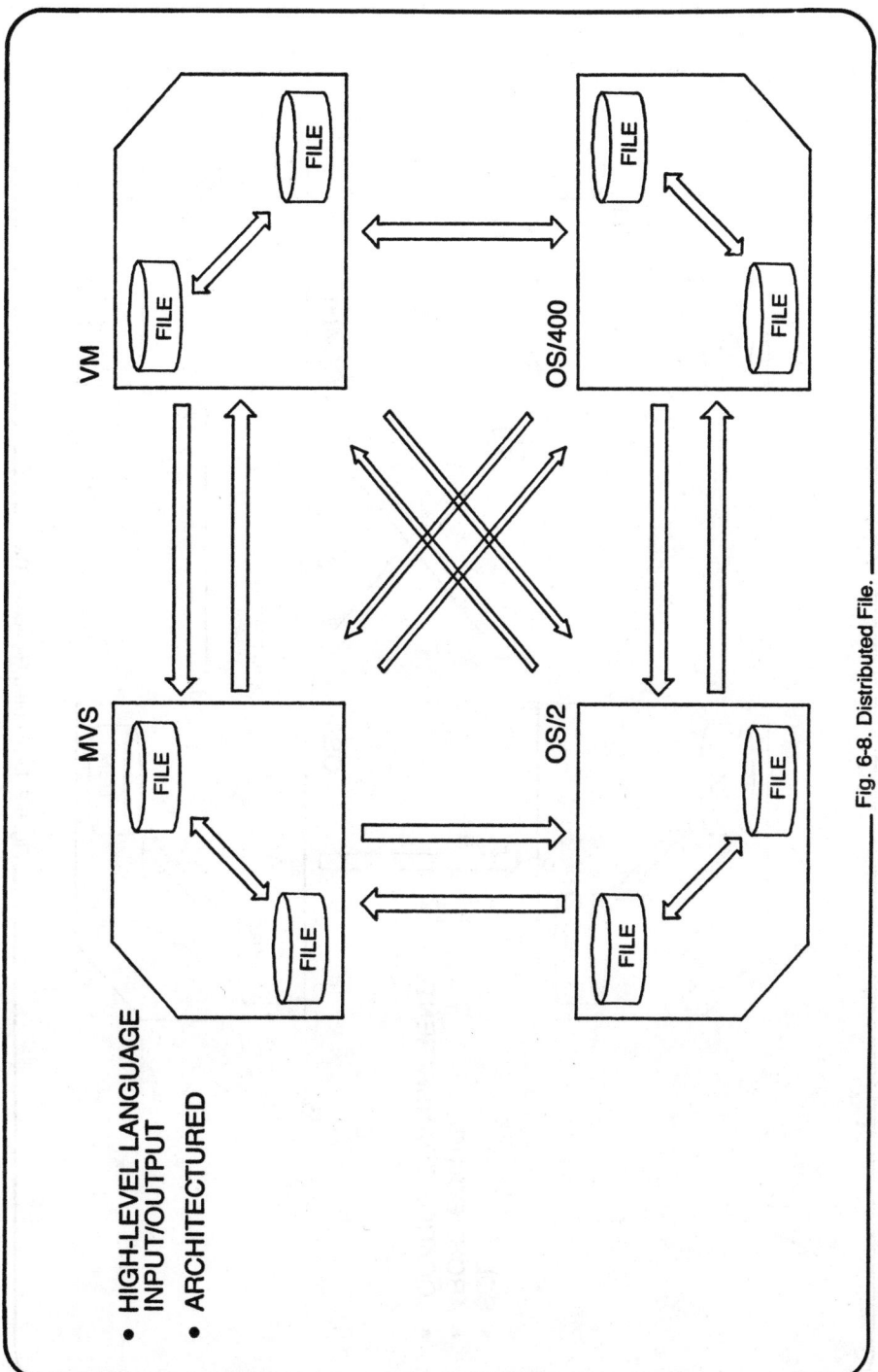

Fig. 6-8. Distributed File.

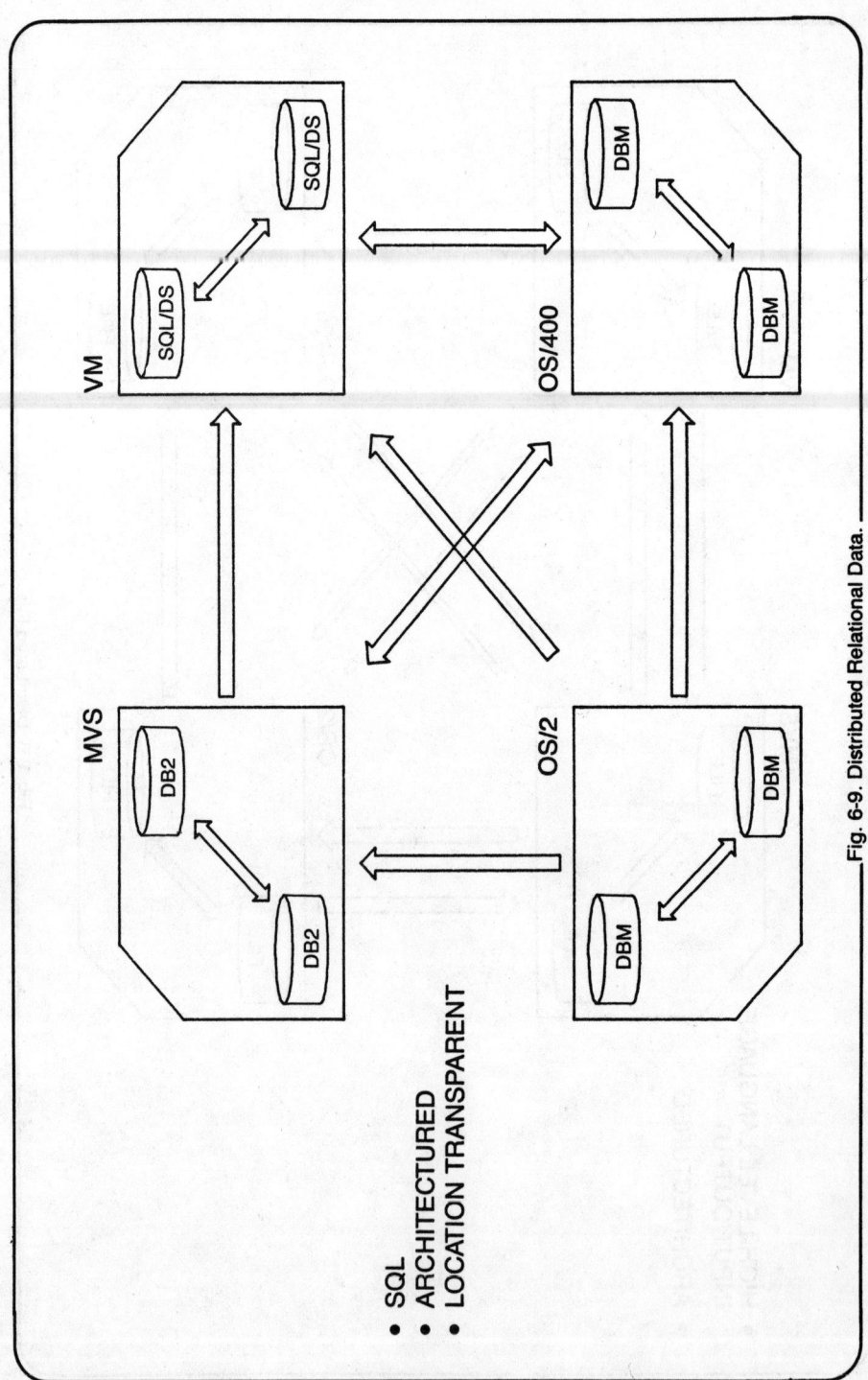

Fig. 6-9. Distributed Relational Data.

the advantages of the local database management and still partici-
pate in this distributed network.

Two important service functions are often discussed as an
integral part of a distributed data system: the data dictionary, and a
repository function.

As Aron describes the *data dictionary*:

"There is usually a strong correspondence between the
key parameters used to manage a business and the major
data items used in data processing. For this reason, the
common "business factors" are often the nucleus of the
data dictionary, which grows to include all data items relevant to the business. Each is defined as to meaning,
usage, format, source, when generated or destroyed. All
synonyms for a given piece of data are cross referenced.
The data dictionary provides the basis of a service that
would schedule and track the distribution of data files to
any or all nodes in a network and to control the collecting
of data files from the network."[19]

The introduction of the *host repository* by IBM will over time
diminish the role of the data dictionary with many of its functional
roles to be performed by the repository and its related utilities.
Transformation utilities will be provided to move and transform
data from current dictionaries into the host repository. I also sus-
pect that there will be from time to time a requirement for application specific versions of the repository, running in real time, that
update the host repository periodically.

Overall, in certain processes like application development the
programmer or analyst defines certain objects such as a business
process. The repository is the system element used to store these
object names (*entities*) and their relationship to other entities in the
process. The repository function also includes advanced services
on itself, such as "revisioning." This allows the system to keep
track of the level of a program (version).

DISTRIBUTED SERVICES

In addition to a data dictionary function and repository services, several additional services are important in designing, building, and maintaining a distributed system (Fig. 6-10). The *Dialog*

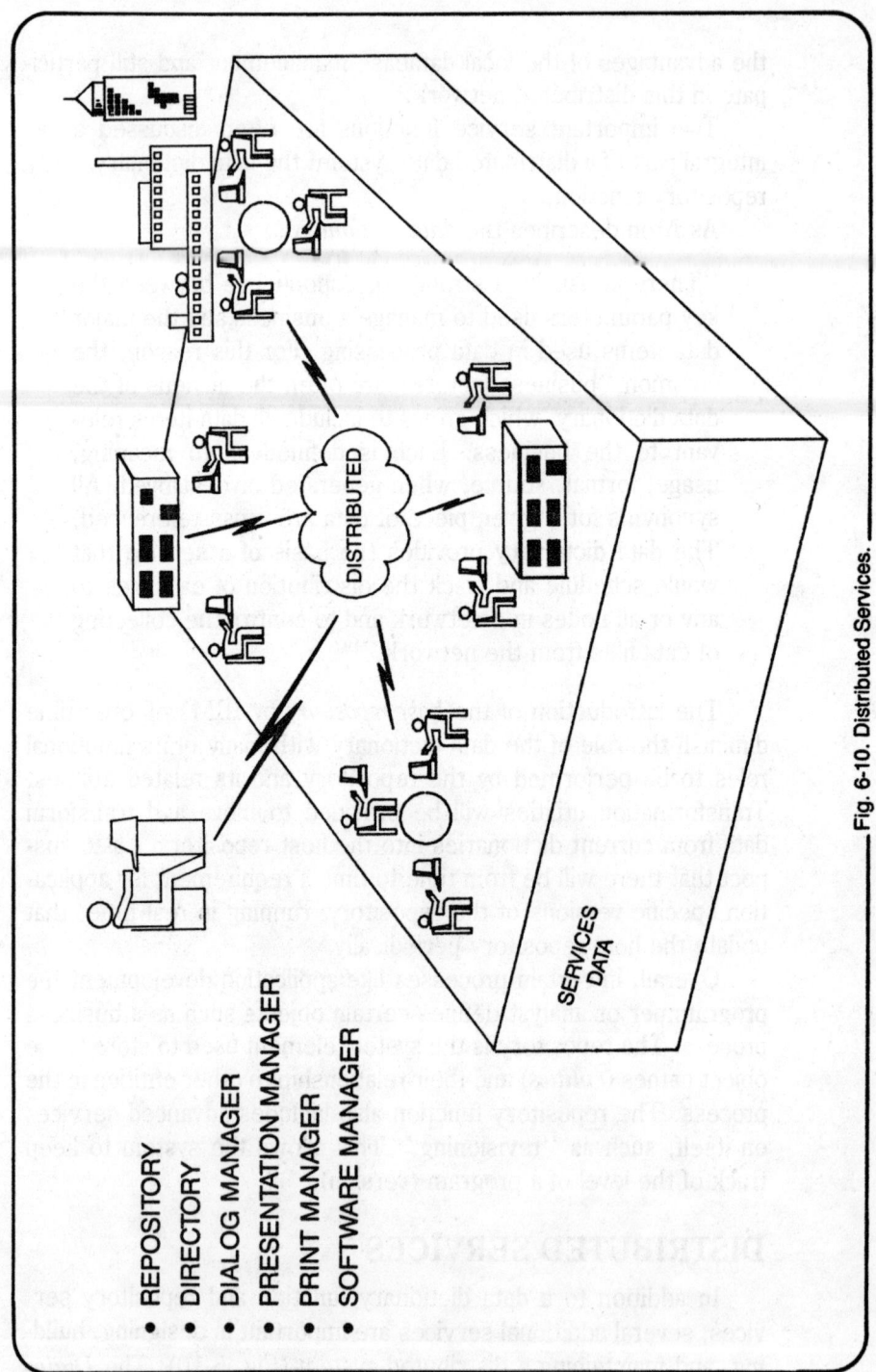

- REPOSITORY
- DIRECTORY
- DIALOG MANAGER
- PRESENTATION MANAGER
- PRINT MANAGER
- SOFTWARE MANAGER

Fig. 6-10. Distributed Services.

interface, which provides display panel management services in SAA and the *Presentation Interface*, which provides several management services are depicted in Fig. 6-11 and discussed in Chapter 3.

In a SAA distributed processing environment one must be prepared to provide accompanied services so that when an application executes on a SAA host system (MVS, VM, OS/400) the screens can be displayed elsewhere in the network. A similar set of facilities must be available for printing information remote from the host system.

Finally, an associated function is necessary, the *Software Manager*, to be able to invoke application programs on a remote system. Again, the actual communication function is handled in a transparent fashion by SAA's CCS enabling a programmer to "call" one program from another without knowing the location.

DISTRIBUTED SYSTEMS MANAGEMENT

The ability to use multiple data processing systems in an integrated fashion across the enterprise (Fig. 6-11) creates the need for a set of facilities to manage the network as a single entity. There are a number of important aspects of distributed systems management that will be addressed in a consistent implementation across the SAA environments. They can be expected to address:

- The change control and distribution of fixes and new versions of systems and application programs.
- The management of configuration charges and service of the hardware, software and communications.
- The use of tools to balance and optimize the overall performance of the network.
- Problem determination and monitoring of the network and systems devices such as the workstations and storage systems.
- Operations management facilities including administration of data, databases, and accounting.
- Security of the system and user authorization.

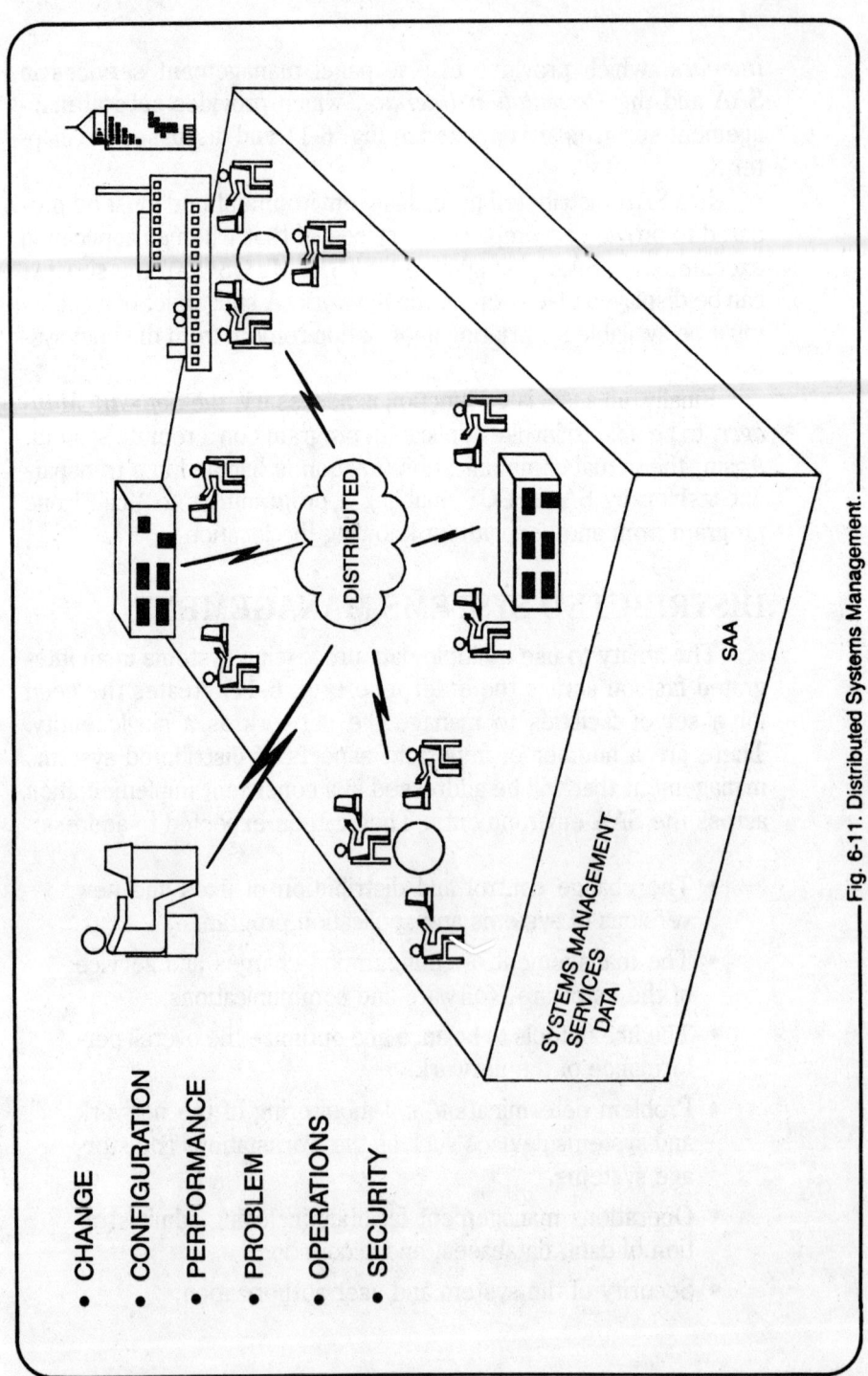

- CHANGE
- CONFIGURATION
- PERFORMANCE
- PROBLEM
- OPERATIONS
- SECURITY

Fig. 6-11. Distributed Systems Management.

In addition to a variety of tools expect to see the introduction of the IBM repository technology in such applications as configuration changes, user profiles, security schemes and addressing information that provides uniform access to data on a networkwide basis. The overall result will be consistency to the user who must manage the system and a complete array of integrated functions accessible through an SAA and CPI as suggested in Fig. 6-12.

DISTRIBUTED APPLICATIONS

All of the aforementioned SAA functions are intended to make it simpler to create and to use applications. The value of SAA is that it provides the functional framework for the integration of diverse functions and services to appear to be a "single" consistent system to the end user. (Fig. 6-13)

The power of the computer and especially the intelligent workstation is opening up the opportunity to use advanced tools of design, graphics, spreadsheets, and document creation that were in the past restricted to a few users. This can now be done in such a way that the end user no longer has to be familiar with multiple operating systems and application environments. All applications can soon be built to have a similar "feel and touch."

The SAA set of common applications will be built on the set of guidelines shown in Fig. 6-14. They will be implemented using the Presentation Services or Dialog Services Manager, which ensure compliance to the SAA Common User Access. One or several of the relational Database Managers will be at the heart of the application. The execution of the application will be selected on the appropriate system for location of data, performance, or cost reasons. Because of the SAA compliance, the application will be extendable and by definition, integrated into the system environment.

The structure will be oriented to using the power of the intelligent workstation running under the OS/2 EE operating system.

IBM's OfficeVision family of products, shown in Fig. 6-15 are a vivid demonstration of these principles.

IBM OFFICEVISION FAMILY

On May 16, 1989, IBM made a number of SAA product announcements. Most widely reported of these was IBM's OfficeVision family of products. This was a significant event in many

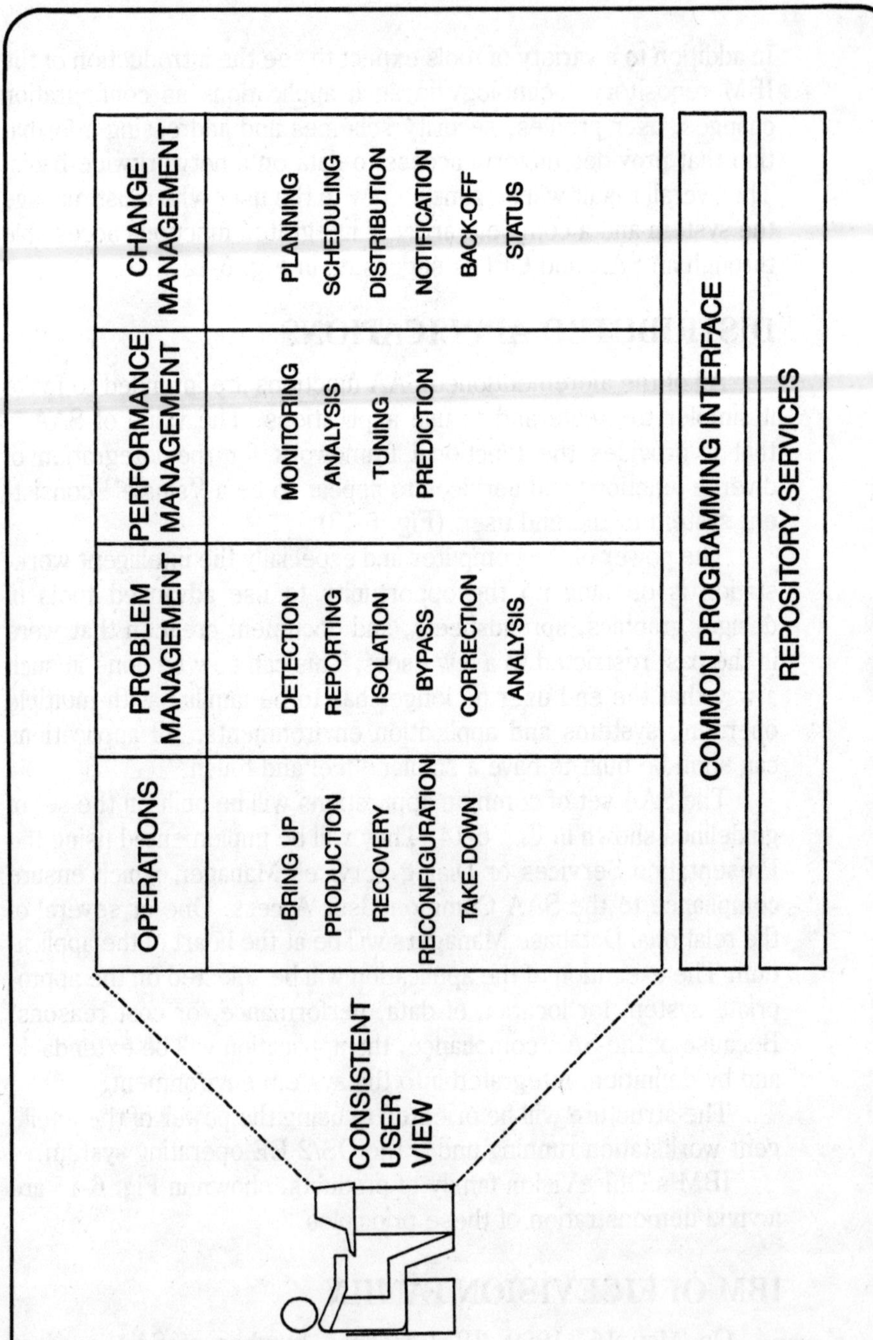

Fig. 6-12. Systems Management.

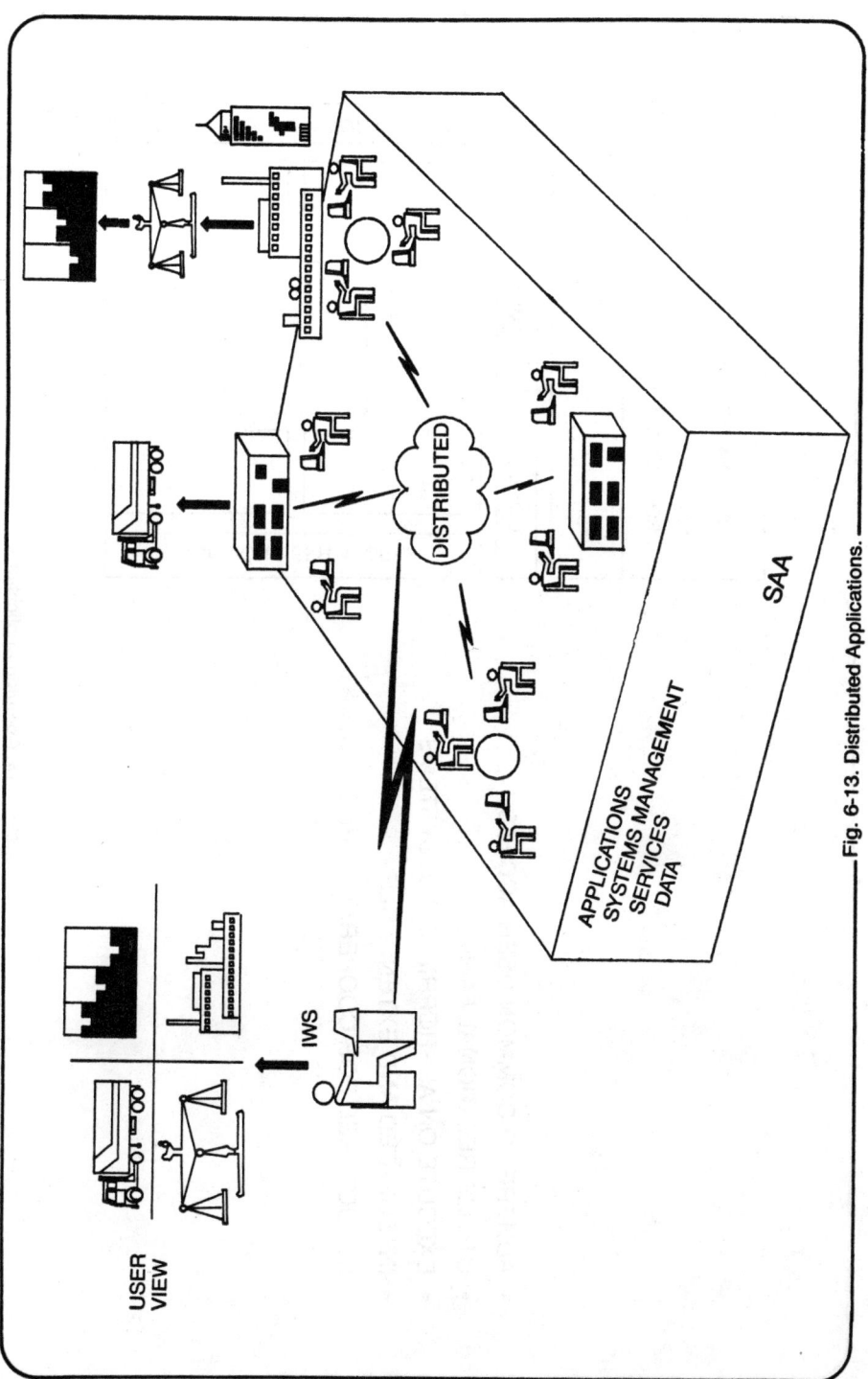

Fig. 6-13. Distributed Applications.

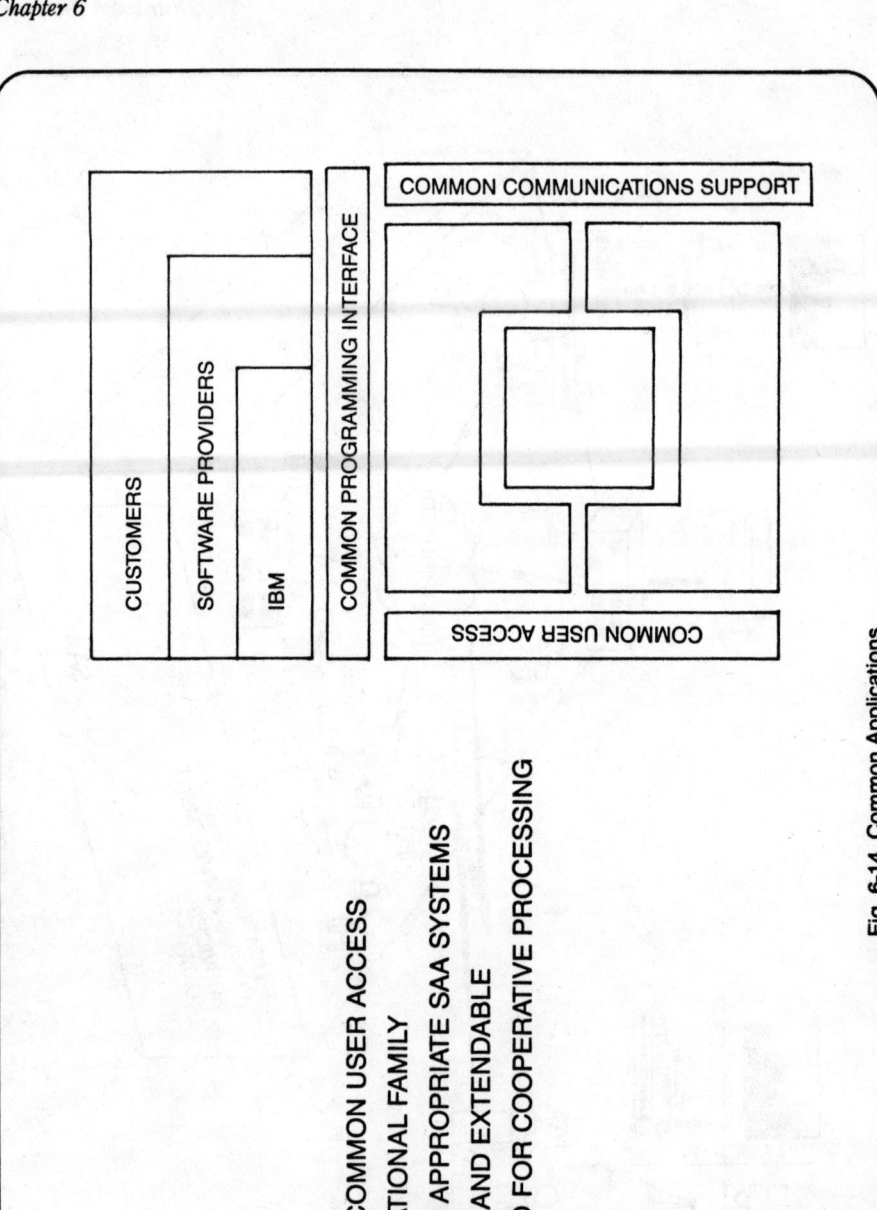

Fig. 6-14. Common Applications.

- ADHERE TO COMMON USER ACCESS
- UTILIZE RELATIONAL FAMILY
- EXECUTE ON APPROPRIATE SAA SYSTEMS
- INTEGRATED AND EXTENDABLE
- STRUCTURED FOR COOPERATIVE PROCESSING

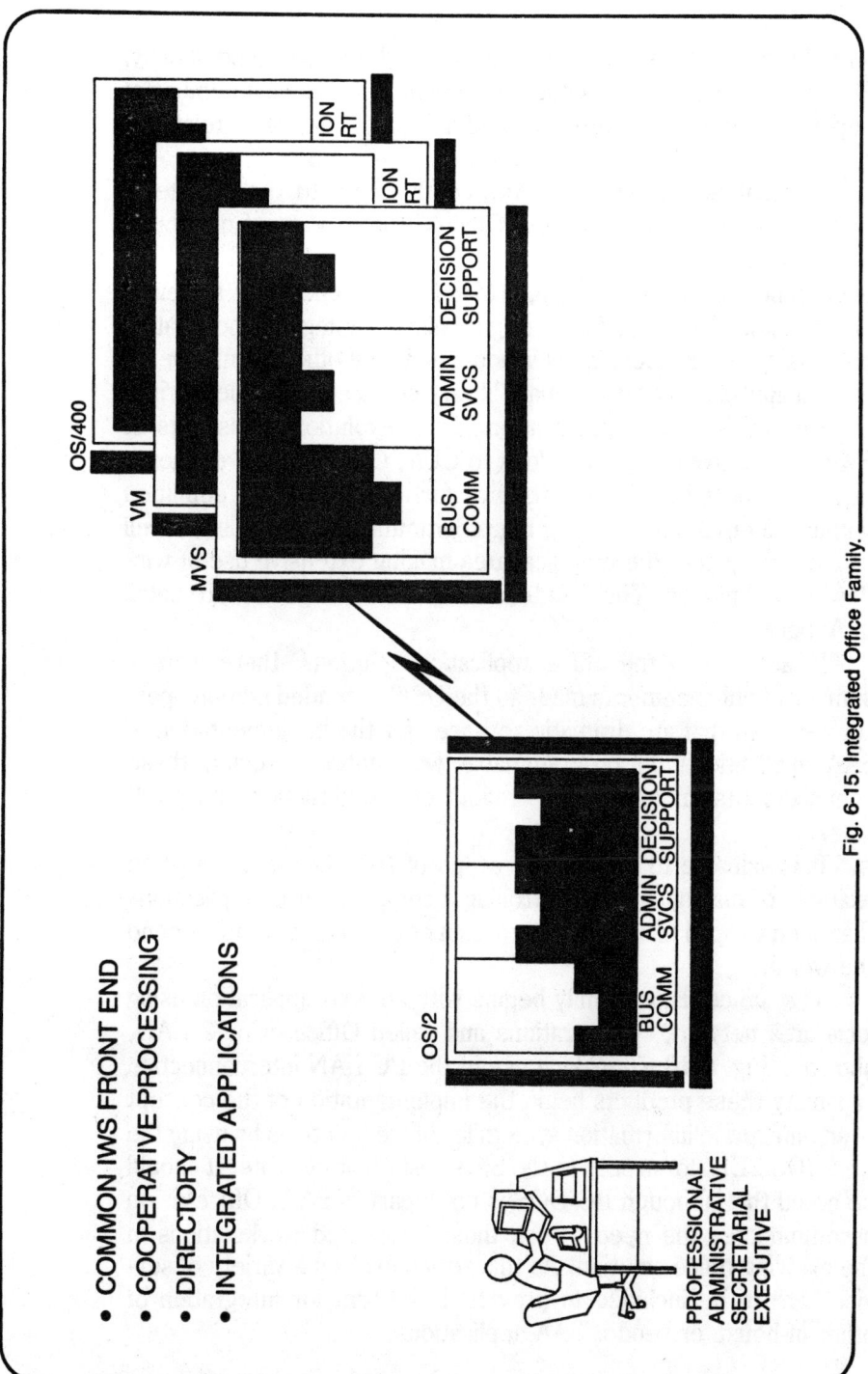

Fig. 6-15. Integrated Office Family.

ways beyond the new office offerings as will be discussed shortly. However, pausing on the OfficeVision Family content, a number of important statements are included in that event that relate to IBM's SAA.

First, it demonstrated IBM's commitment to the long term underlining investment in SAA. OfficeVision is a set of new business solutions, a set of SAA applications that include all the SAA environments: OS/2, OS/400, VM and MVS operating systems. Second, it is the first IBM offering to take advantage of cooperative processing design techniques in addressing the office requirements in such application areas as mail, library services, and calendaring.

Finally, it is a demonstration of the evolutionary aspects of SAA, as it introduced extensions to CUA, CPI and CCS elements of SAA. The CUA extensions give further clarity and definition within the environment using nonprogrammable terminals, as well as extensions into the graphical area making extensive use of windowing techniques. These extensions are described in more detail in Appendix D.

In addition to the office application solutions, there were a number of enhancements made to the OS/2 extended edition operating system that are dramatic advances for the implementation of SAA applications on programmable workstations. Again, these enhancements underscore the rollout of SAA function into products.

It is valuable to look at the scope of IBM OfficeVision as an example of managing and controlling a complex set of applications that need to span many users across an enterprise, perhaps around the world.

The OfficeVision Family begins with an SAA application using local area network configurations and called OfficeVision/2 LAN, shown in Fig. 6-16. In making use of the PC LAN interconnection capability these products begin the implementation of the concept of an enterprise information system for office functions by using the PS/2 (OS/2EE) for access to the SAA host environments. It should be noted that although PC/DOS is not a part of SAA, OfficeVision accommodates the need to use those supported workstations in the evolving office solution. As this series evolves a variety of services are to be included to provide a platform for integration of other in-house or vendor SAA applications.

- NEW LAN-BASED OFFICE
- RICH NEW FUNCTION
- STRONG CONNECTIVITY TO ALL ENVIRONMENTS
- IBM DOS PARTICIPATES

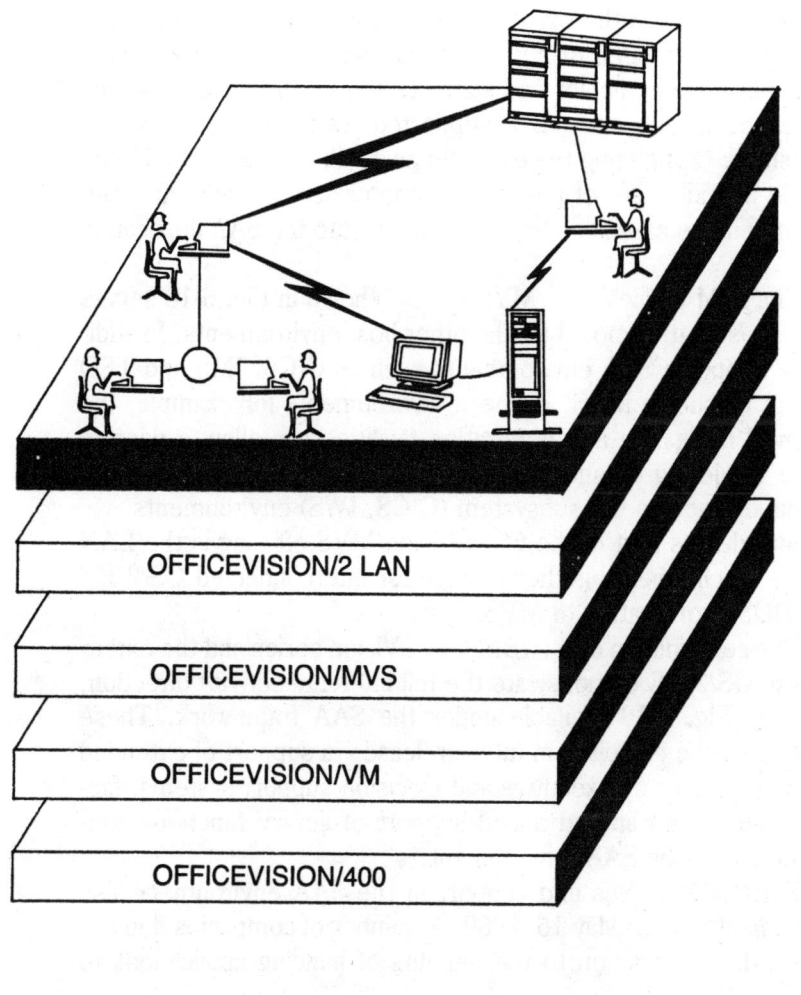

OFFICEVISION/2 LAN

OFFICEVISION/MVS

OFFICEVISION/VM

OFFICEVISION/400

Fig. 6-16. IBM OfficeVision/2 LAN series foundation.

The first release, shown in Fig. 6-17, of the IBM OfficeVision/2 LAN includes integrated tools for communication and document processing. These tools provide access, in a cooperative processing fashion, to such applications as electronic mail, address books and telephone auto-dial functions. In addition a variety of document processing tools will become available to the end user to enable the composition of notes and documents.

Future releases will include new editors featuring an easy-to-use capability in composing complex documents that include text, graphics and images. A new relational library will be made available that can be used on the LAN or in a central facility. Included in the early support are decision support tools such as query, report writers and business graphics and statistics tools. The full calendaring and scheduling support is to be supported in a cooperative processing fashion. Completing the early support will be a set of tools that provide a flexible set of programming interfaces to help integrate new or in some cases existing applications into the SAA application set.

The IBM OfficeVision/MVS series, shown in Fig. 6-18 serves as a representative model for the other host environments. In addition, it supports SAA environments such as CICS, IMS and TSO that are unique to MVS. In these environments for example, the improved navigation and integration facilities can allow a user to have a single log on and single view into the office and business applications across the subsystem (CICS, IWS) environments.

Included as part of the OfficeVision/MVS offering is the LAN series, which when together provide for interconnected OS/2 EE (and DOS) workstation to MVS.

The combination of the IBM OfficeVision series and the extensions to OS/2 EE demonstrate the full interconnectivity direction, shown in Fig. 6-19 available under the SAA framework. These facilities will be exploited in future releases in support of extended SAA applications of Executive and Decision support systems, facsimile integration and advanced support of library functions consistent across the SAA environment.

Further examples and support in the SAA environment also were announced on May 16, 1989. A number of companies demonstrated their conviction to the benefits of building applications to

- MAIL
- ADDRESS BOOK
- TELEPHONE AUTODIAL
- COMPOSITE EDITOR
- RELATIONAL LIBRARY
- INTEGRATED DECISION SUPPORT
- CALENDAR
- APPLICATION INTEGRATION

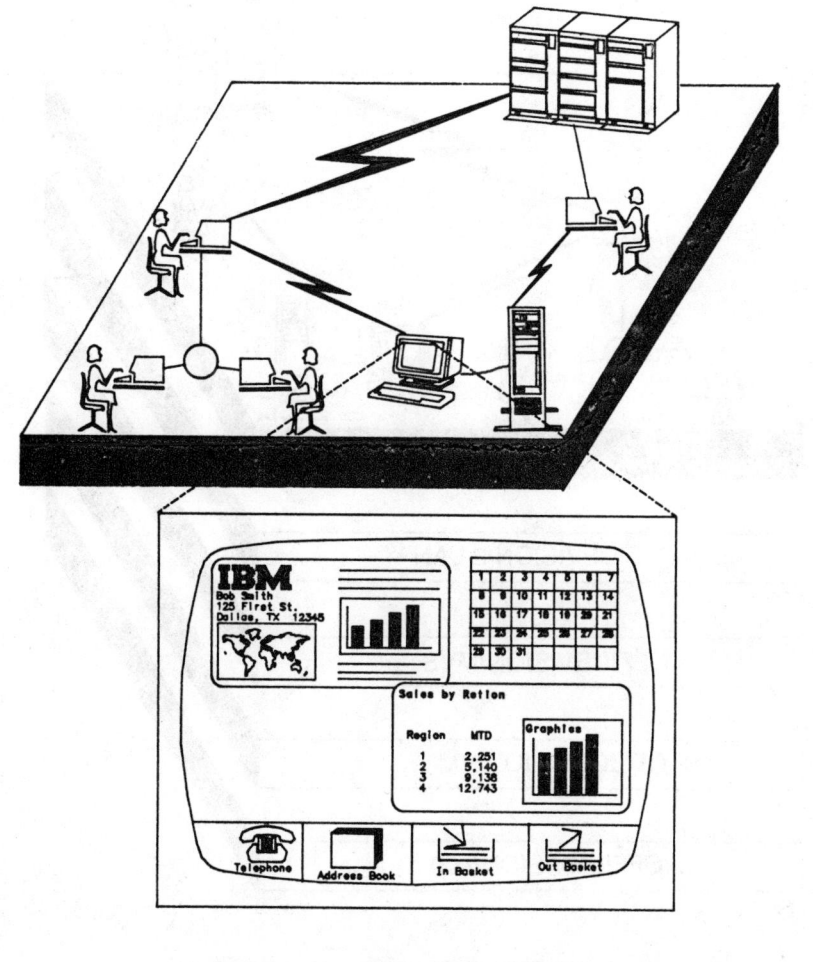

Fig. 6-17. IBM OfficeVision/2 LAN series options.

81

- RICH OFFICE FUNCTION
  - —MAIL
  - —ADVANCED EDITOR
  - —LIBRARY
  - —PERSONAL FILE CABINET
  - —DECISION SUPPORT
  - —INTEGRATED CALENDAR
- INTEGRATION WITH CICS APPLICATIONS
- POWERFUL CONNECTIVITY

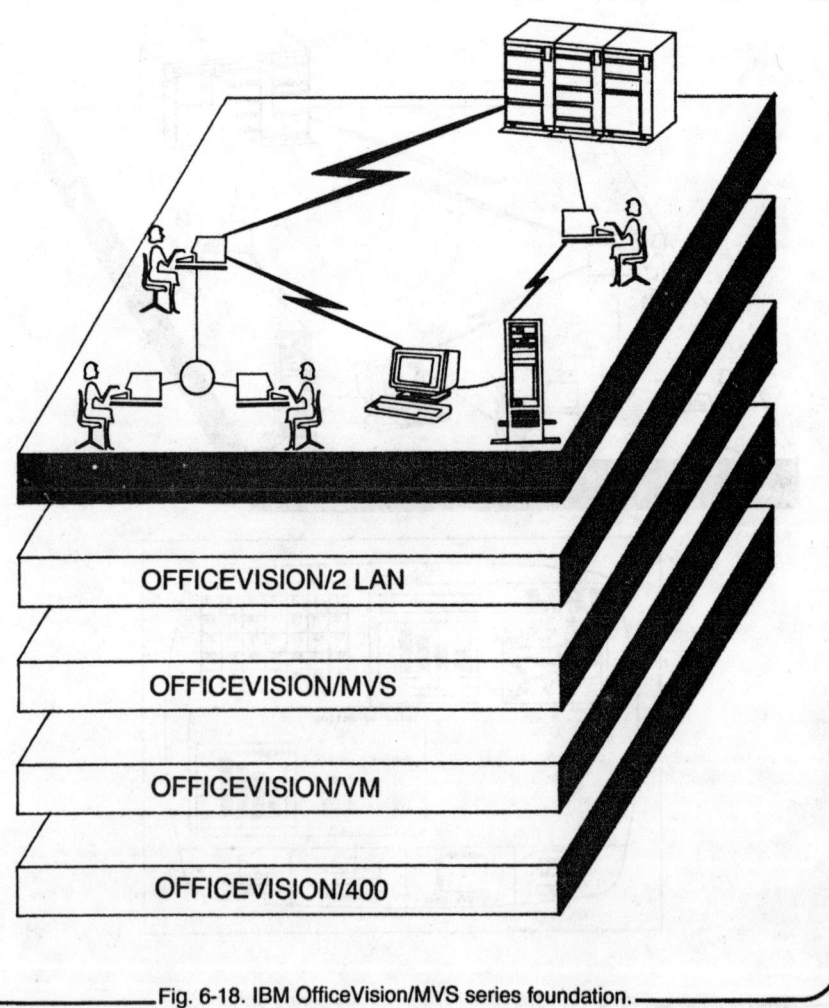

OFFICEVISION/2 LAN

OFFICEVISION/MVS

OFFICEVISION/VM

OFFICEVISION/400

Fig. 6-18. IBM OfficeVision/MVS series foundation.

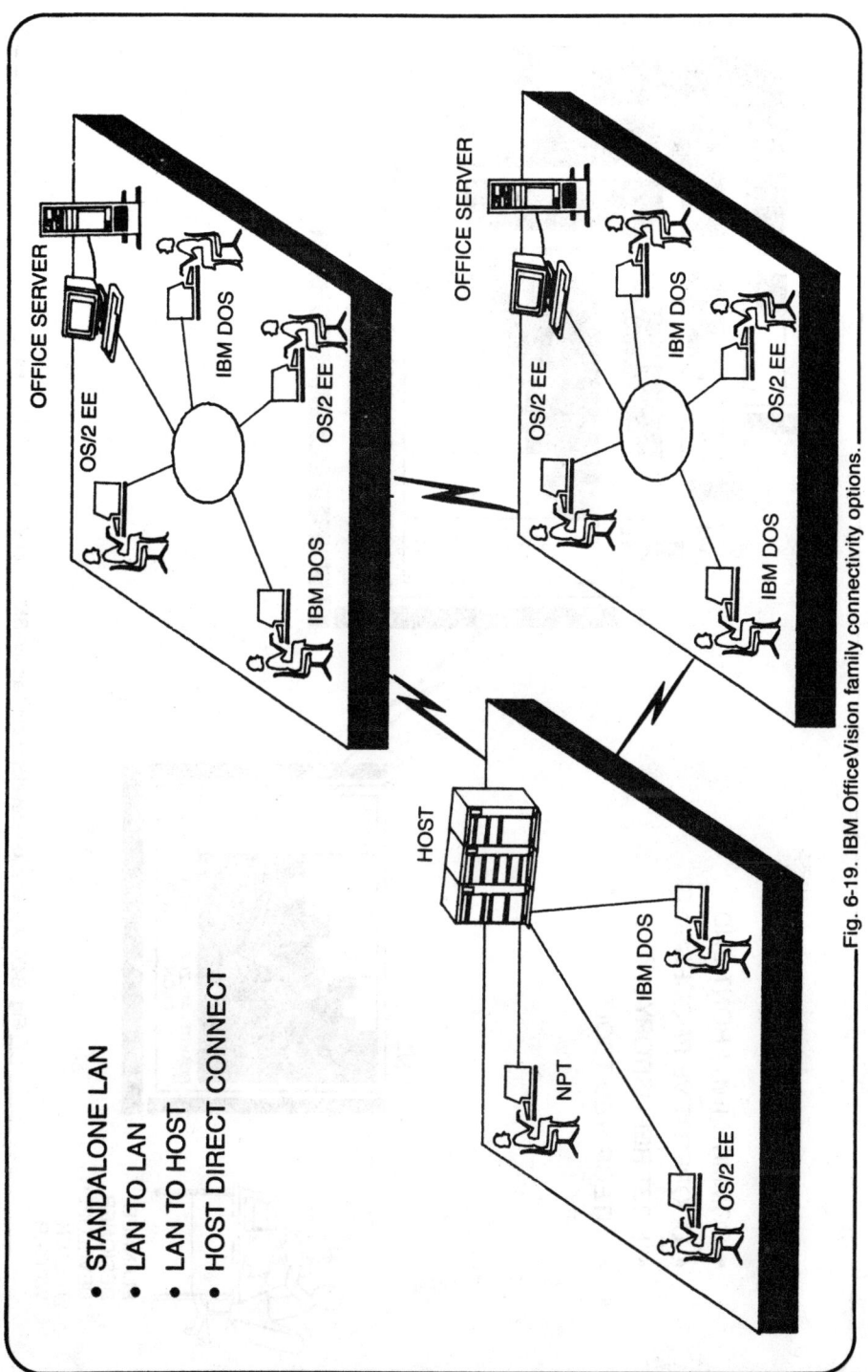

Fig. 6-19. IBM OfficeVision family connectivity options.

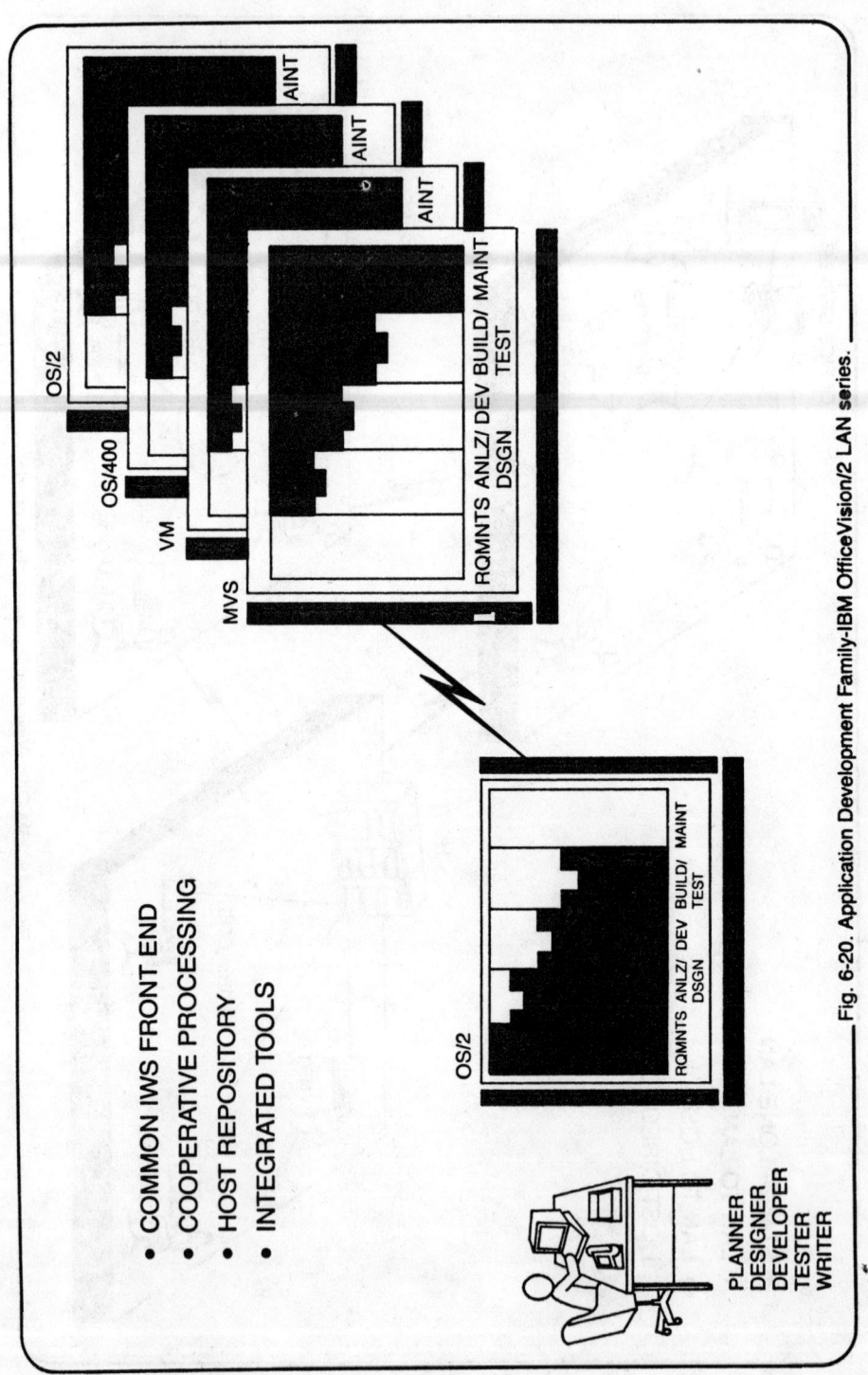

Fig. 6-20. Application Development Family-IBM OfficeVision/2 LAN series.

conform to SAA. These companies are identified in Appendix E and address a broad range of industry needs.

The future design and implementation of SAA applications will be performed within the fast evolving IBM application development environment. The evolution of IBM's CASE (Computer Assisted Software Engineering) will be an extremely important phase of the SAA story.

The IBM Application Development Family of offerings will be an SAA application set of its own, as shown in Fig. 6-20. The following chapter is a descriptive look at the IBM direction for application development and its integration into the SAA scenario.

7
Application Development

The Application Development Environment (ADE) is commonly referred to as Computer Aided Software Engineering (CASE). The latter term suggests the broad engineering disciplines that are applicable to the development of software systems. The development of this field is intended to provide an engineering discipline for software developments, the maintenance of the resulting systems and the project management facilities to guide the development managers.

In addition to the disciplined approach, this fast evolving field includes structure methodologies to be applied to the programs. A vast array of tools are being made available that can be used at the different phases in the life cycle of a program. Future application development environments will be offered within a system framework that integrates these tools and methodologies in a "seamless" fashion. That is, the results of the completion of one of the tools becomes available to be used by a subsequent tool or related tool transparent to the end user. The motivating drive behind the evolution is development productivity. It is envisioned that software development teams who use an advanced ADE will:

- Be able to create and maintain more applications than with classical methodologies.
- Create and maintain more complex applications.

- Achieve higher levels of quality.
- Provide greater ease of use to end users.

ADE or CASE changes the nature of the work in software development. Figure 7-1 illustrates the future direction of this change. Today's dominant methodologies require 60% of the effort to be expended in the laborious and error-prone steps of programming and testing of the application and 40% of the effort in defining the requirements of the application and laying out the systems design.

Structured programming techniques, a step in this evolution can begin to shift the focus and effort on the front end stages of development. ADE technologies provide a dramatic shift to 80% of the effort in defining the problem and 20% in creating and testing the actual application coding. Associated with this shift is a collapse of overall time. A typical development process today is represented in Fig. 7-2. The business requirements are generated from meetings and discussions and passed on through written documentation and more meetings with the systems designers. These iterative stages result in the manual preparation of specifications for the function needed, how the display screens are to be stored and manipulated, and all of the logic necessary to propose the program. These documents are passed to the programmer who decides how he will lay out the detailed steps of the program.

The following steps of coding are accomplished usually on a terminal, interacting with a high-level language such as COBOL. And so it proceeds through the life cycles. The larger or more complex the application, the more people to be involved, the more complex the planning, scheduling, coding, integration testing, documentation, and prototypes before the final product is ready for live data.

ADE introduces a number of key automated elements into this environment, including the use of graphics technology by all the tools. Diagramming and specification tools would be used during the design phases and by the management tools used across the life cycle. As the design progresses, incremental design checkers and analyzers are used to shape the design and check the logic and interactions at a very early stage. Once the specifications are completed and automatically filed the application is generated directly from the specifications. At the heart of the system is a Repository

	CLASSIC	STRUCTURED	CASE
BUSINESS MODELING	20	30	40
SYSTEMS DESIGN	20	30	40
PROGRAMMING	20	15	5
TESTING	40	25	15

Fig. 7-1. Development Discipline.

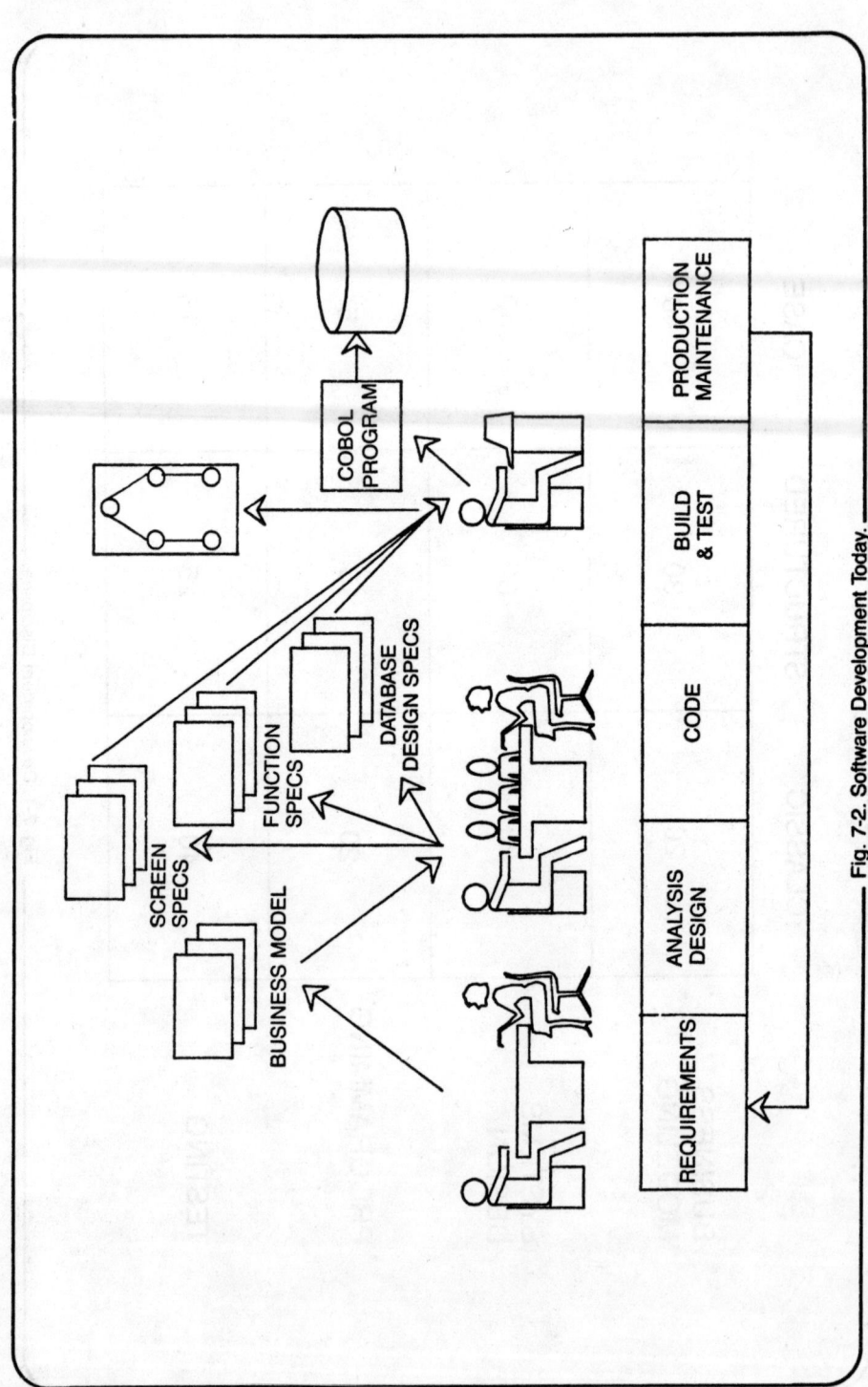

Fig. 7-2. Software Development Today.

shown in Fig. 7-3, that interfaces to the tools used in the front end of the process to the completion at the back end.

The productivity benefits of such a system as described above varies from a 25% to 50% increase over some of todays development methods on some applications and to hundreds of times increases in productivity in other applications.

The IBM direction is to structure a modern ADE that will increase productivity by addressing each of the following requirements:

- Provide an integrated application development environment.
- Expand the coverage of the application development life cycle.
- Protect the customer's current investment.
- Support new application development technologies.
- Provide portability across SAA systems environments for development and execution of the application.
- Provide migration and coexistence with current tools from multiple sources.

The overall objective is to give MIS directors the strategic base to evolve their application development environments and to apply these tools to realize the enormous productivity benefits.

The IBM direction for ADE begins at the intelligent workstation, shown in Fig. 7-4. The OS/2 extended edition operating system will be the common end use platform for using the system. The system design philosophy is one of cooperative processing (see Chapter 5) and the introduction of a powerful software technology called a Repository. This approach brings to the application developers all the power of IBM's software direction.

This system structure, shown in Fig. 7-5, provides IBM and its customers the opportunity of an integrated interface to the end user while allowing all the supporting systems structures and tools to evolve asynchronously. As we will see, IBM's SAA software strategy and components are an integral part of this direction.

At the same time IBM has provided the flexibility of open architectures that allow CASE tool vendors to integrate into the

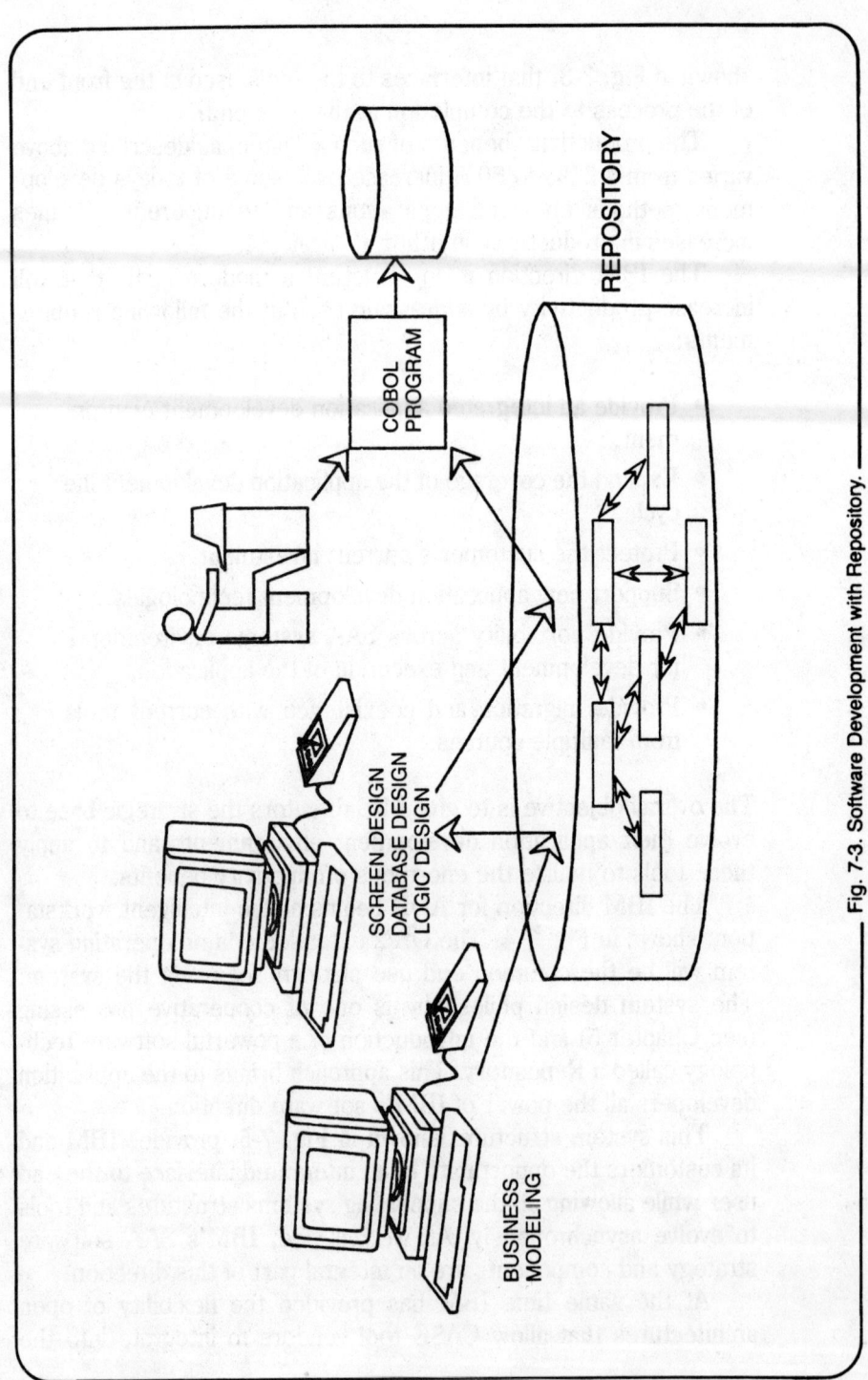

REPOSITORY

COBOL
PROGRAM

SCREEN DESIGN
DATABASE DESIGN
LOGIC DESIGN

BUSINESS
MODELING

Fig. 7-3. Software Development with Repository.

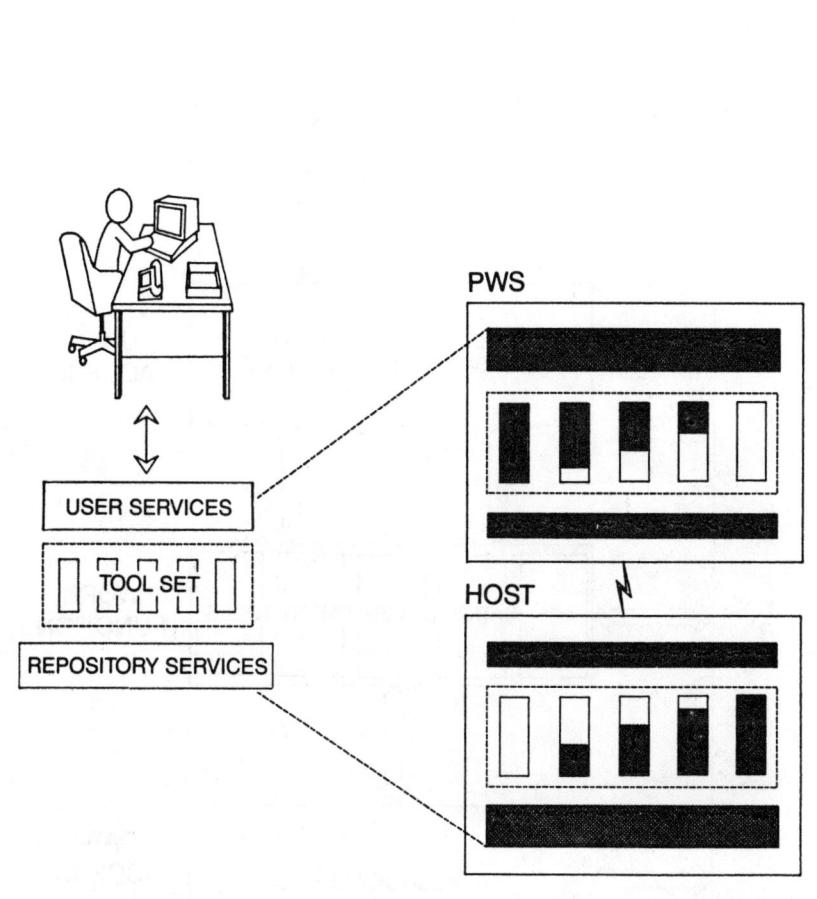

PWS

HOST

USER SERVICES

TOOL SET

REPOSITORY SERVICES

- PS/2 BASED FRONT END
- HOST BASED REPOSITORY
- COOPERATIVE PROCESSING TOOLS

Fig. 7-4. IBM ADE Direction.

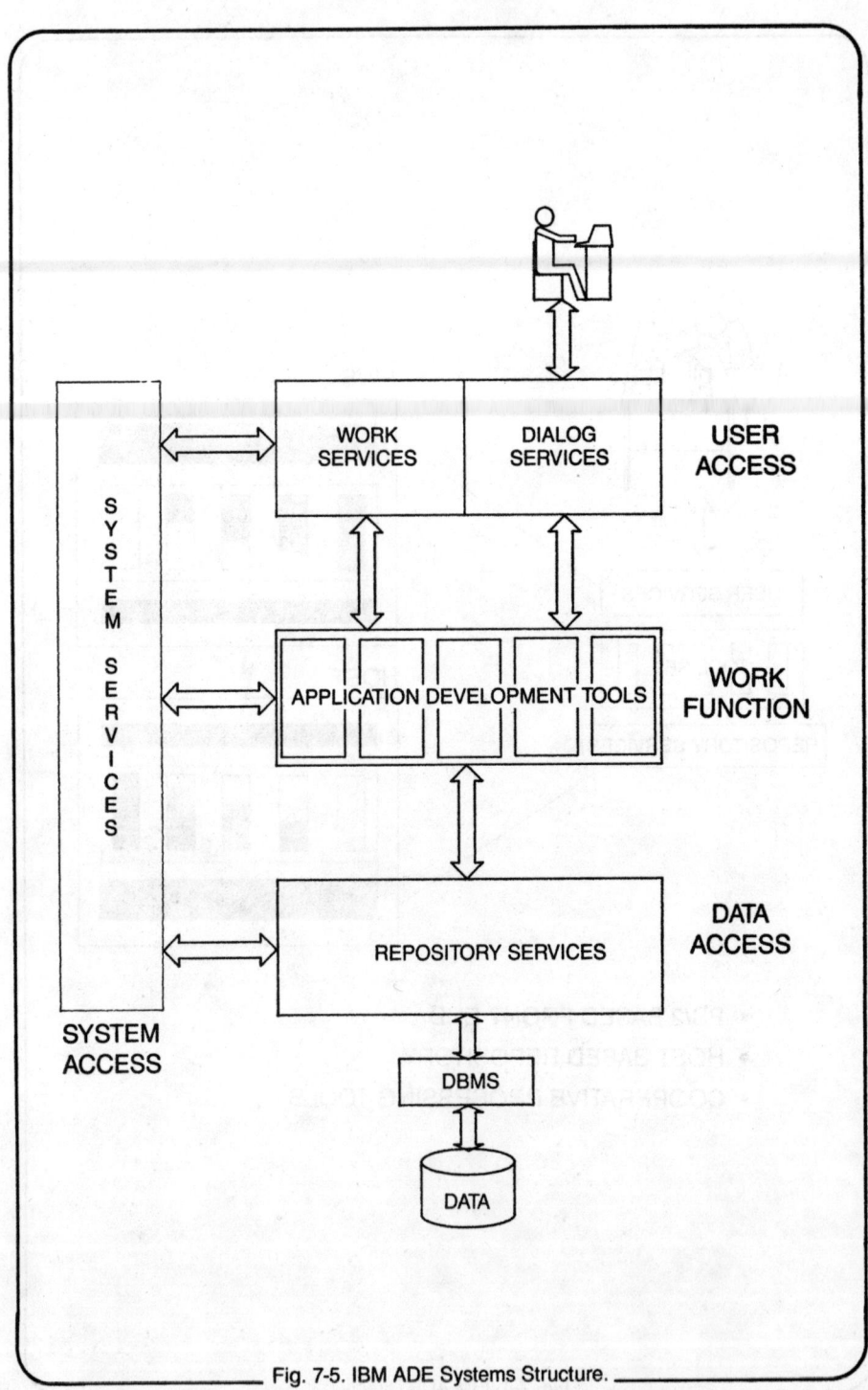

Fig. 7-5. IBM ADE Systems Structure.

IBM SAA systems structure. The IBM ADE SAA direction, shown in Fig. 7-6 allows applications being developed on one system environment to be executed in another SAA system environment. It is not hard to imagine the enormous flexibility that this target will give the IBM customer as he evolves his applications and system environments.

Overall, IBM has set a course that provides the opportunity of the best of worlds for all participants, their customers, tool vendors and of course IBM.

You cannot go much further in the discussion of IBM's ADE strategy without stopping and discussing a Repository (Fig. 7-7) for this is the heart of a SAA ADE system. As the application developer calls into play all the various tools to define, design, develop, test, maintain and manage the life cycle of his application it is the Repository that allows the definition of parts of his program (objects) and their relationships to other parts. The Repository becomes a single point of control, allows data-sharing among the tools within the phases of the process.

This includes a capability of having multiple views of the data as required by the use, the tools and the system database support and security services. In and of itself, the Repository has its own set of management functions that define and maintain the various data models created by the tools. It supports the services needed to enter data, maintain it, create reports, provide security, access control, and ensure the overall integrity of the information. This support is key to an important function of versioning. It is the *versioning function* that allows the programmer to keep track of the different levels of his application. This of course is critical during development, maintenance and distribution and updates to users, particularly if an application supports hundreds or thousands of users.

The model description of IBM's ADE tool direction is shown in Fig. 7-8. The IBM ADE plan is to provide full application development life cycle coverage. The plan is to achieve this through the open architecture approach of SAA that will allow the participation of IBM products, vendor products and the customers' own development tools. The challenge will be to provide the technical interface information in such a way that accelerates the use of the system structures that support a fully integrated application development approach.

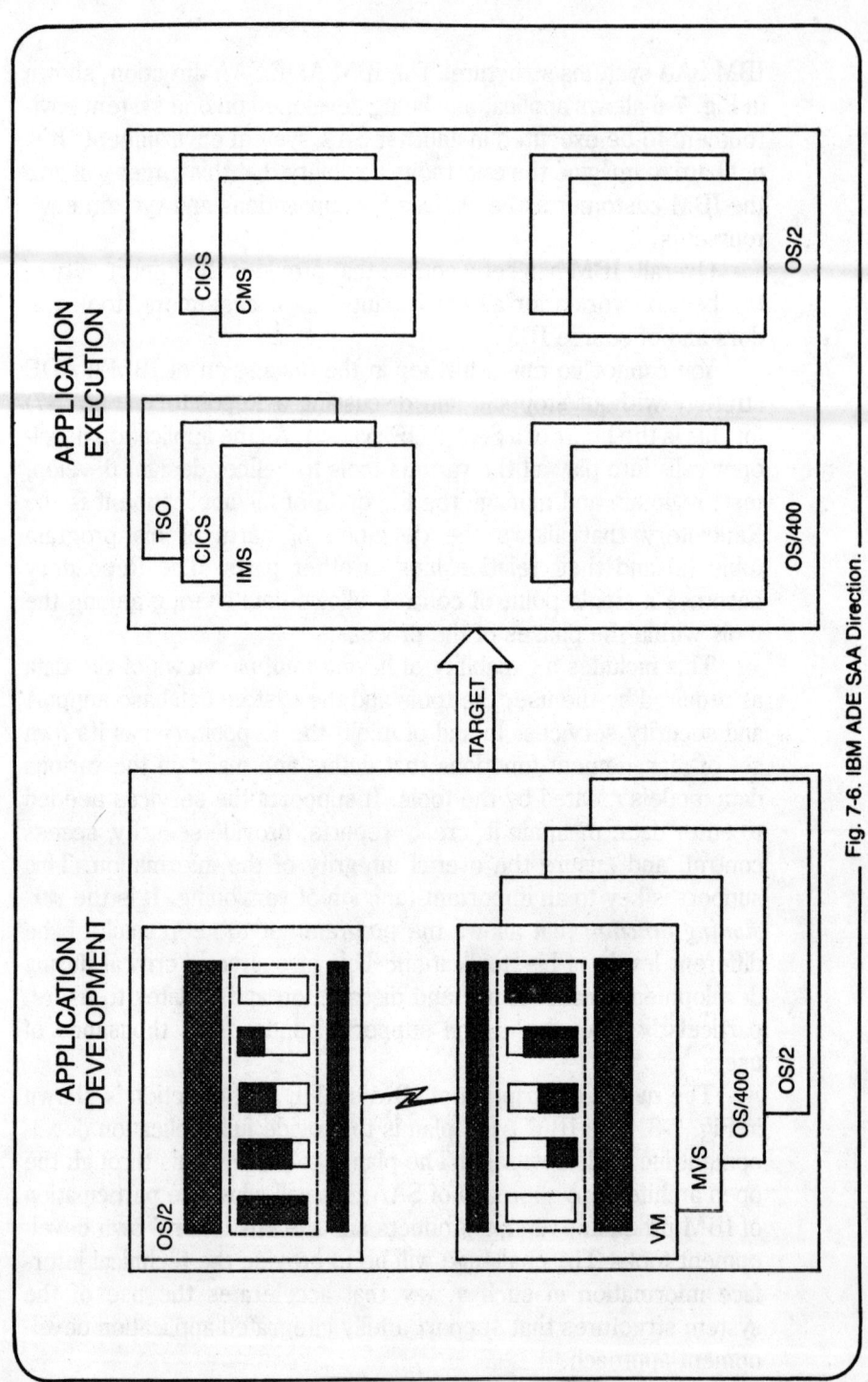

Fig. 7-6. IBM ADE SAA Direction.

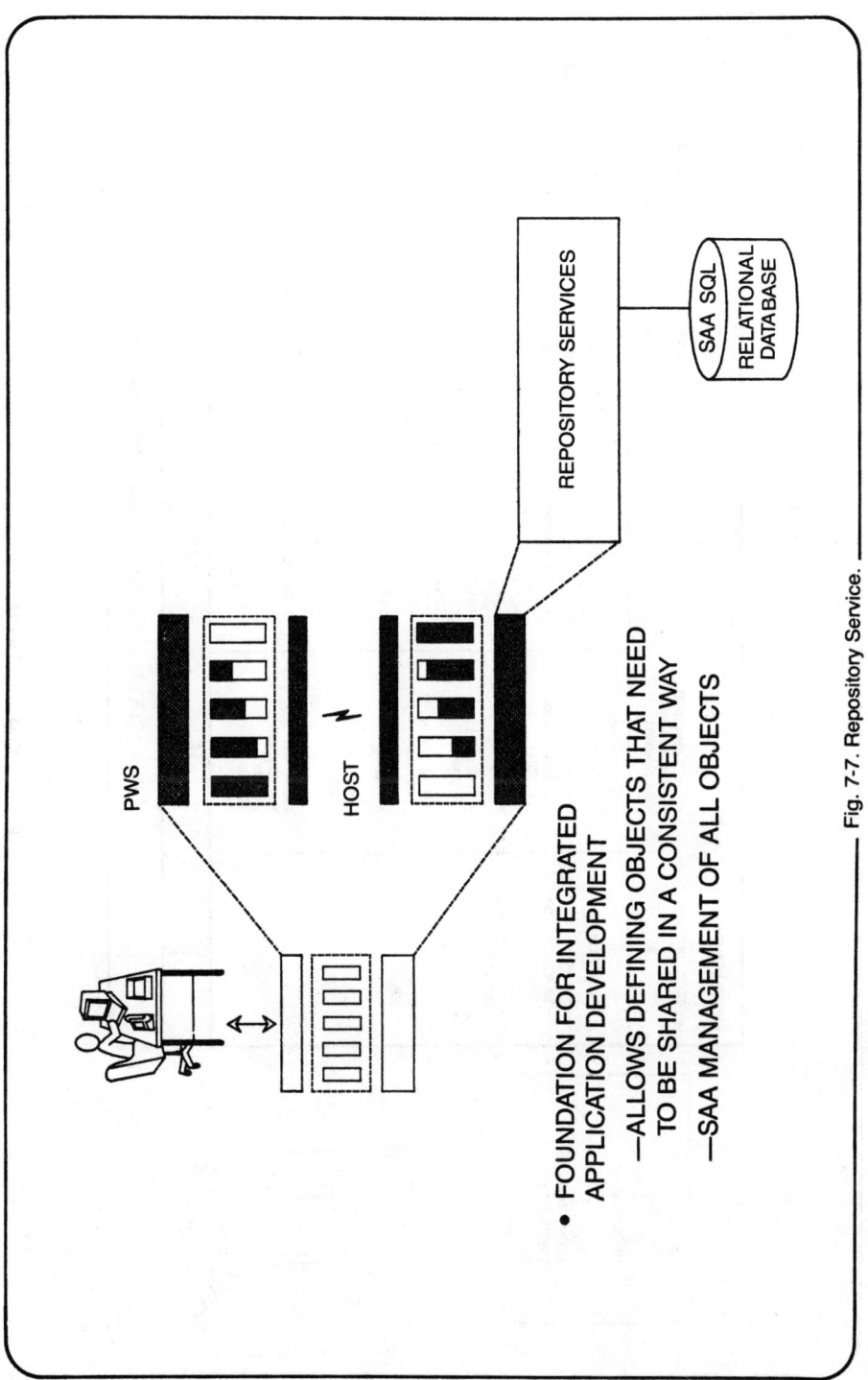

PWS

HOST

REPOSITORY SERVICES

SAA SQL

RELATIONAL DATABASE

- FOUNDATION FOR INTEGRATED APPLICATION DEVELOPMENT
  —ALLOWS DEFINING OBJECTS THAT NEED TO BE SHARED IN A CONSISTENT WAY
  —SAA MANAGEMENT OF ALL OBJECTS

Fig. 7-7. Repository Service.

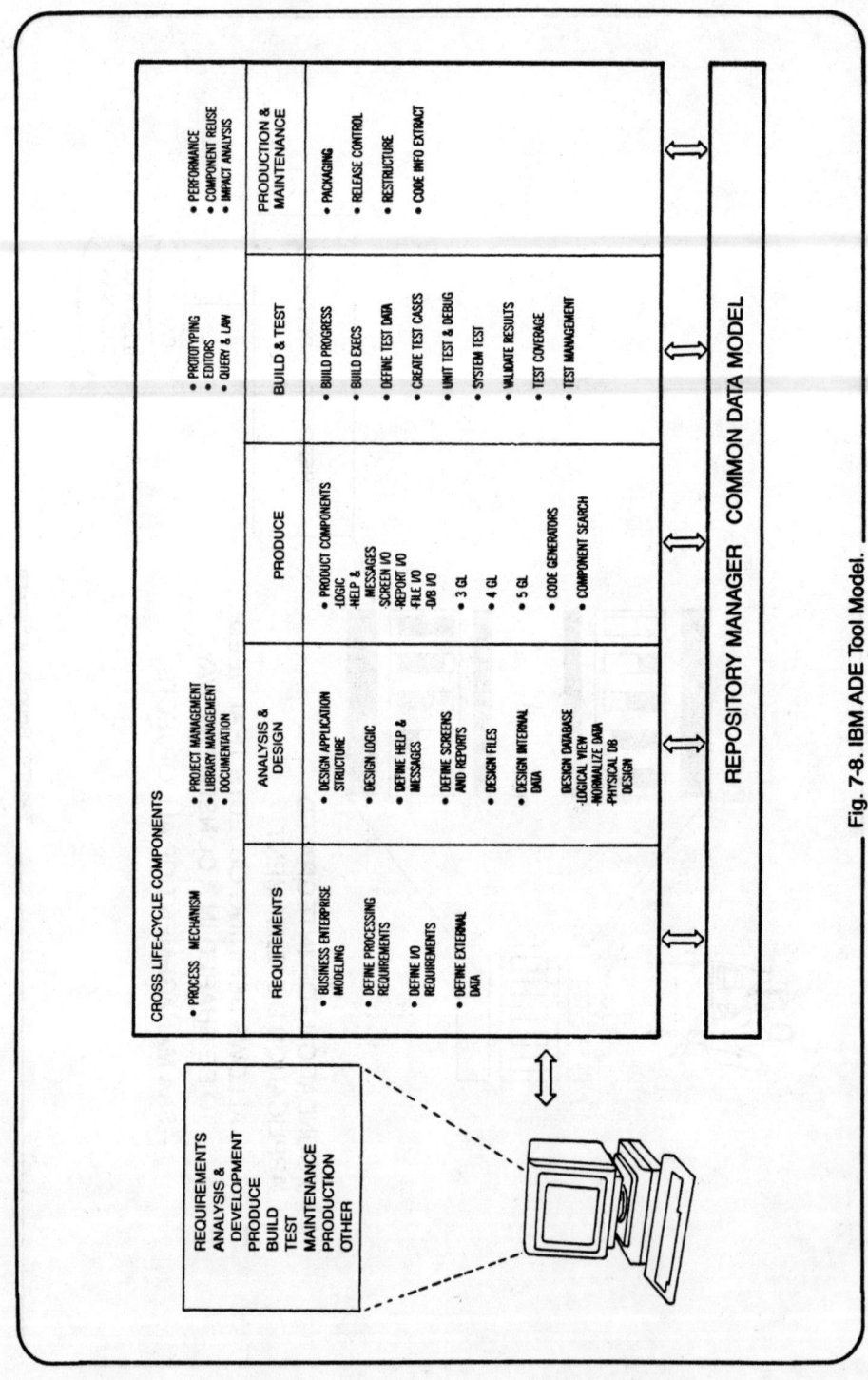

Fig. 7-8. IBM ADE Tool Model.

ADE MARKET RESEARCH

One of the conclusions of the market research studies conducted by IBM was that customer requirements could be categorized into six major cells, as shown in Fig. 7-9. A general description of the differences found follows:

Cell #1: Extensions to CASE   Companies in this category are industry leaders in the use of CASE technology. They share a number of important characteristics:

- Top management understanding and involvement in the use of modeling and decision tools.
- Installed tools successfully used in pilot projects and being expanded to use across the development projects.
- A strategic plan incorporating the needs for education, new CASE tool usage, systems support, workstation transition, etc.
- Close technical relationships with system vendors and CASE tool vendor.
- Requests of early versions of Repository and tool functions. Allocate part of their resources to advanced technical planning.

Cell #2: Committed to CASE   Companies in this category are much like those in cell #1, the principal difference being timing and experience.

Cell #3: Understanding CASE   Companies on cell #3 are actively studying their needs for CASE. They generally have a good understanding of product availability but have not reached the point of developing their plan or strategy nor have gotten top management involvement. There may be some experimentation with CASE technology and pilot projects being planned or underway.

Cell #4   Companies or installations in this category have needs or desires that are primarily focused on programmer productivity at the language level. Their immediate needs do not include a

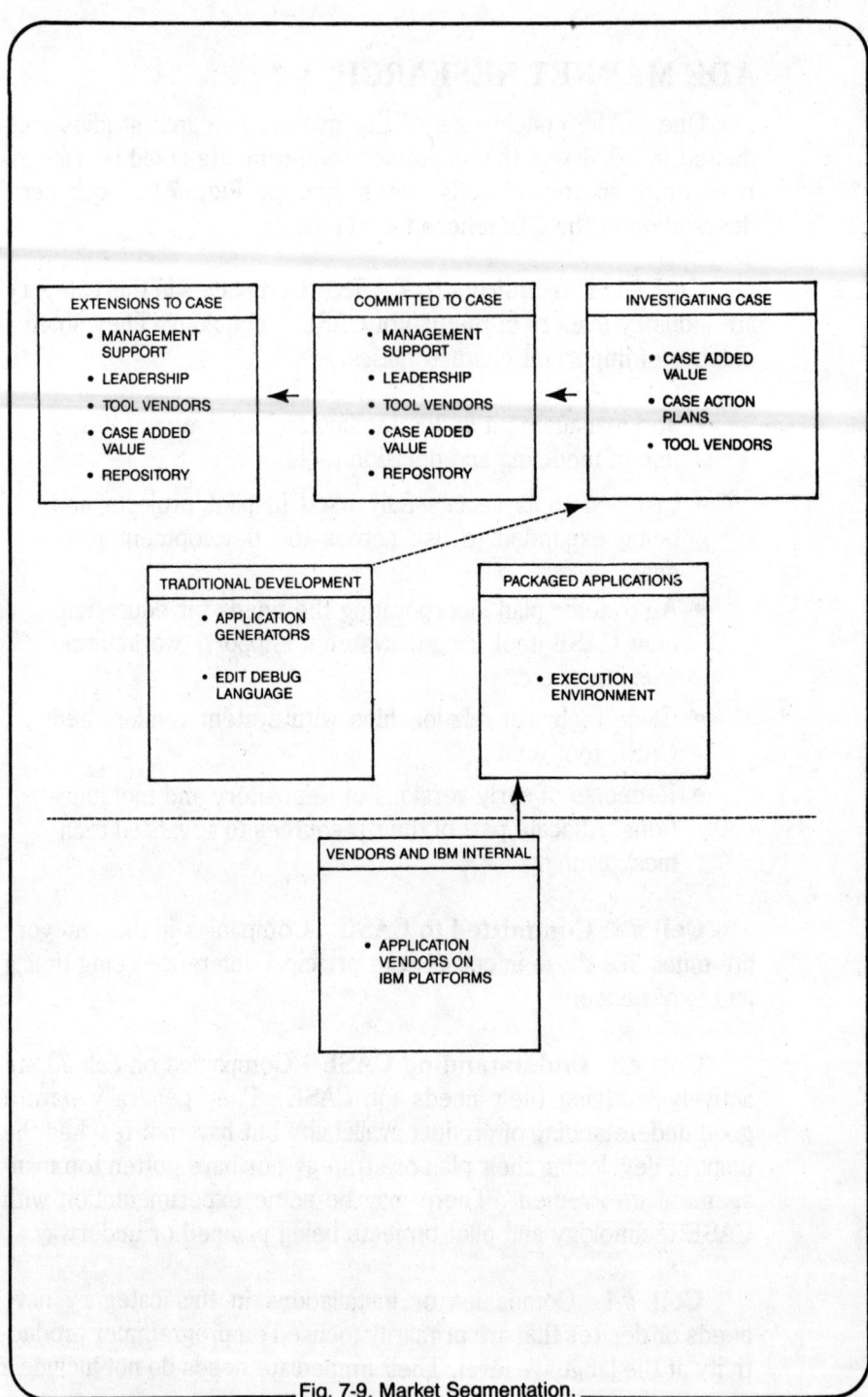

Fig. 7-9. Market Segmentation.

full life cycle strategy of front end tools, modeling etc. The next step for many of these installations is expanded use of workstation critical edit and debug facilities and the use of application generators.

Cell #5 Applications Provided   This cell represents those companies or installations that have little or no programming development capability. Applications are purchased and supported by third-party vendors, systems houses, or centralized development in this firm. They may be the use of ADE facilities in the execution mode.

Cell #6: Application Vendors   The characteristics of cells 1, 2, or 3 may apply to the third party vendors and systems houses that are segmented separately from the users of the applications.

The above structuring provides a means to continue focus on different customer needs and provide a basis for planning future products, introduction timing, education, and marketing support that more closely aligns itself with customer characteristics.

AD/CYCLE

On September 19, 1989, IBM made a worldwide introduction of its SAA ADE direction. This event included a description of IBM's strategic direction, the announcement of a number of products including the MVS version of the Repository. The announcement also stated that several selected vendors' CASE products are to be an integrated part of the IBM solution.

The eight major building blocks of AD/CYCLE are shown in Fig. 7-10. Across the life cycle of software development are the tools to be used for process management, project management and documentation aids.

The tools for modeling business organizations, business functions and processes as well as related data is represented by the Enterprise Modeling block. Next in the development process are the analysis and design tools to be used to describe the logical steps of an application, related input data and service and report format. There are also powerful data design tools used for organizing and describing a database structure. The objective is for the

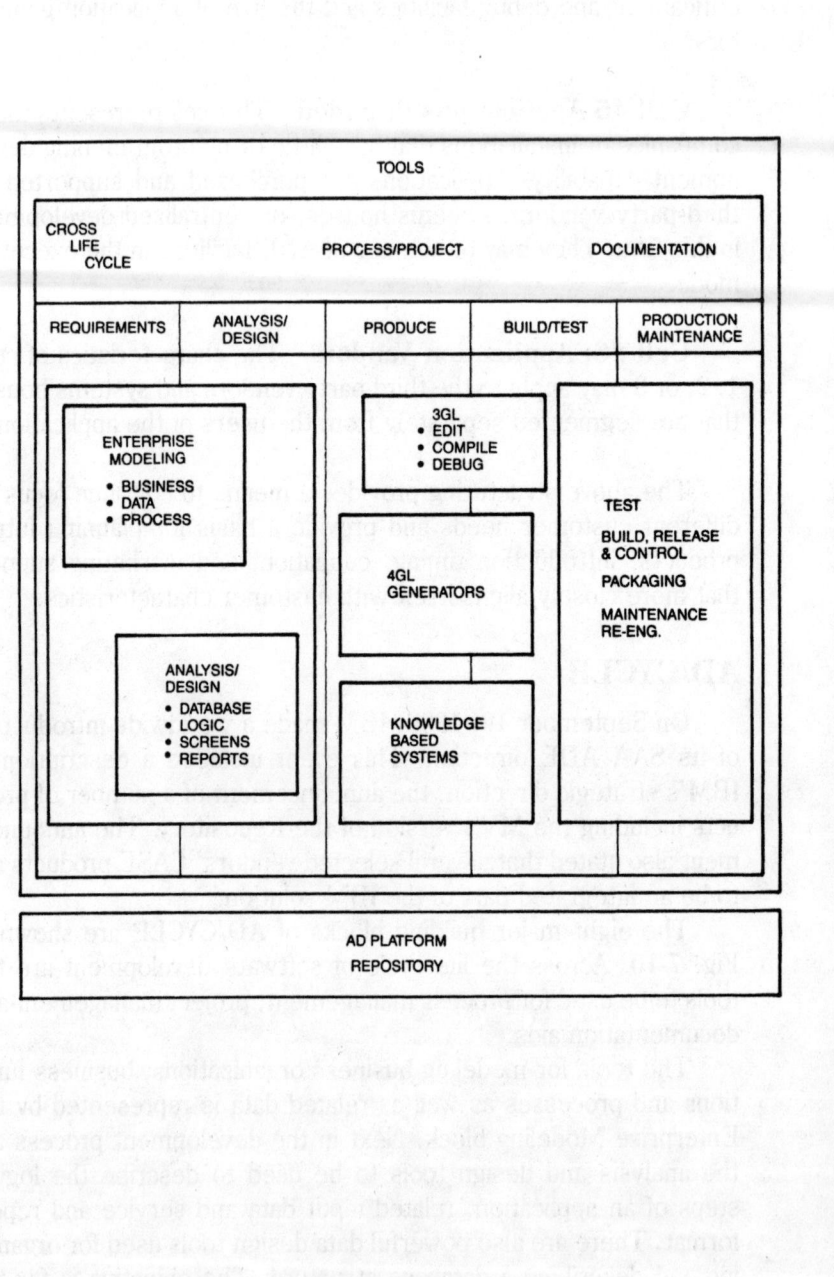

Fig. 7-10. AD Model.

output data of the modeling phase to feed into the systems design and analysis phase. The information from the first phase is stored in the Repository in a standard format and becomes accessible by the design/analysis phase.

Next in step are those languages and generators used to create the program. The so-called third generation language (3GL) compilers such as COBOL, Fortran, C, and PL/1 would be positioned here along with the editing and debugging aids used with those languages. (4GL-machines language, 2GL-symbolic languages).

Fourth generation languages (4GL) are referred to as "application generators." The input to the 4GL facilities are very high-level statements that describe the application input, output and logic. The generators create an executable series of steps that are interpreted by an "interpreter" in the execution environment.

Alternatively, generators output a series of COBOL language statements that are passed to a COBOL compiler. The result of this latter phase being an application that is executed with better/faster performance than can be achieved by an interpreter.

The fifth generation languages are those facilities that incorporate the technologies being developed called artificial intelligence, expert systems, or knowledge based systems.

Again, the output of the previous plan of analysis/design is the input to the above mentioned languages directly or via the Repository function creating a "seamless" flow through the process.

In the final block of the AD Model are positioned the tools used for testing, maintenance, and re-engineering of applications.

In the IBM model, the Repository is shown as part of the AD Platform. Included in this platform is the AD Information Model, the Repository services, tool services workstation navigation facilities and the Common User Access elements. The Repository will be described in more detail later in this chapter.

You can now view Fig. 7-11 and imagine the appropriate parts of the AD Model residing in the workstation with complementary portions in the host environment. The output of course to be executed in one of the SAA environments.

IBM has selected three leading CASE tool vendors and has positioned them in the AD/Cycle model to be a part of the IBM solution for application development. These companies are Bachman Information Systems, Index Technology Inc., and Knowledge-Ware. In general the CASE tools of these vendors are positioned in

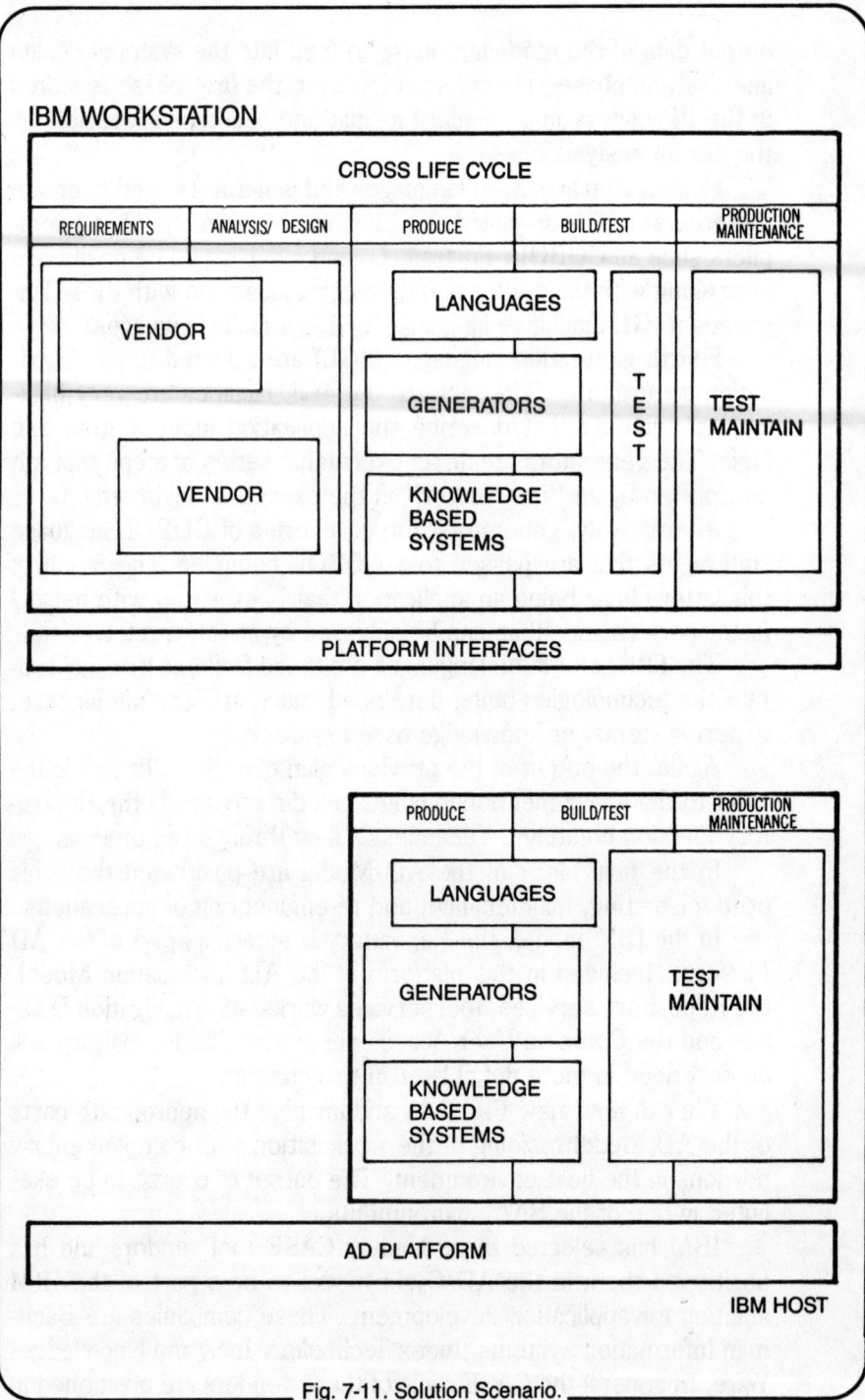

Fig. 7-11. Solution Scenario.

the requirements and analysis/design phases of AD/CYCLE. In fact, the companies product lines extend beyond these boundaries and include or interface to application generation capability and re-engineering facilities.

AD/Cycle has been declared an "open-architecture" system and a major application element of Systems Application Architecture. This means that various systems interfaces will be architected and made public with an intent that customers and vendors who build tools and applications that comply to the interfaces will have access to the IBM supplied systems resources in a consistent fashion. AD/Cycle has the potential to create a profound change in the information systems industry. It will effect change to IBM's future software development, customer's and IBM's relationships with software vendors, and for customers, a shift in the culture of the information systems departments and the way they perform their mission. It is clear that IBM will try to orchestrate this strategy to be a win-win-win for customers, vendors, and IBM.

Let us take a look at the elements of this announcement as each represents a major strategic commitment on the part of IBM. The major elements are:

- An *open application development* architecture that is part of SAA.
- *Vendor tool offerings* stated as part of the IBM solution where IBM has taken equity positions, established development contracts and worldwide marketing arrangements with the vendor companies.
- The announcement that over thirty *other CASE tool vendors* have committed their product lines to AD/Cycle.
- A new set of *consulting services* and offerings by the IBM Systems Integration Division teamed with selected service vendors.
- A set of application *development tools and software services* that conform to SAA standards.

These elements promise to bring new levels of quality, productivity and efficiency to the increasing challenge of application development. Let us further describe and comment on each of these strategic elements:

Open Architecture

Clearly this represents an opportunity to create and evolve an industry standard (or group of standards), which can give customers great flexibility, wide choices and foster creativity to improve programming. One cannot help but think of the explosion in the PC industry that occurred as a result of IBM's open architecture approach.

Vendor Tool Offerings

KnowledgeWare's IEW/Planning Workstation, IEW/Analysis Workstation, and IEW/Design Workstation provide an integrated expert systems approach to enterprise modeling and design and analysis function. The products provide extensive realtime error checking and full use of advanced graphics techniques for the ease of use of the analyst/programmer. The product line is committed to OS/2EE, interfaces to IBM's Cross Systems Product and over time will further integrate through use of the IBM Repository.

Index Technology's product line PC Prism, Excelerator I/S, Customize for DB/2, and Excelerator for CSP/AD also provide business modeling and analysis/design capability. The product design philosophy of Index is to provide capability to customize offerings for various customer and market needs.

Bachman provides a full range of product offerings focused on database design, building and maintenance. They forward engineer or re-engineer DB/2, SQL and IMS databases, assist in migration to DB/2 from other databases. Their tools are built on an expert systems base and provide guidance and assistance to the user upon demand.

IBM views these partners as close members of their development team and as a long-term asset in the AD/Cycle strategy. Although the product offerings overlap it is believed that the differences among them will be important to their customers as they propose an IBM solution.

Tool Vendor Commitments

During the early development of AD/Cycle IBM held meetings in its laboratories at which they disclosed to selected vendors the status of its design of the Repository and other AD/Cycle elements. The vendors who were part of the disclosures were asked by IBM to sign agreements that they would build their CASE tool products to conform to SAA's CUA, and run under OS/2EE. There were other agreements to interface to CSP, support national languages and to integrate over time using the Repository in exchange for these agreements. IBM would disclose early design information to help these companies plan their future products. Now over thirty of these companies have stated their intent to integrate into the IBM AD/Cycle architecture.

To the extent that companies like McDonnell Douglas, Texas Instruments, Andersen Consulting and others fulfill this intent there will be a major unifying force in the industry. (See Appendix E).

IBM understands that some of its customers may want their AD solution to contain products from these companies. Although IBM does not market the product lines it is clear that it intends to keep these vendors up to date by inviting them to continue to attend seminars and workshops on new developments. Also, when a customer has made a final selection of the tool set other than one of IBM's partners, the marketing force is being instructed to cooperate with the customer in getting his AD solution installed.

Consulting Services

IBM's System Integration Division (SID) formed out of the Federal Systems Division has gained extensive experience in development systems working with the U.S. government and plans to leverage that experience and skill base with offerings in support of AD/Cycle. A new direction was also set in this arena as SID announced it intended to have complementary working relationships with four service companies—Computer Task Group (CTG), Computer Power Group (CPG), Cap Gemini, and GE Consulting— giving them a combined resource potential of over 20,000 people.

IBM Tools and Services

The offerings from IBM are promised to evolve over time and to become more integrated and to conform fully to SAA. In that sense they can be viewed as the harbingers of where IBM will make its' product investment. Their relative positioning in AD/Cycle is shown in Fig. 7-12.

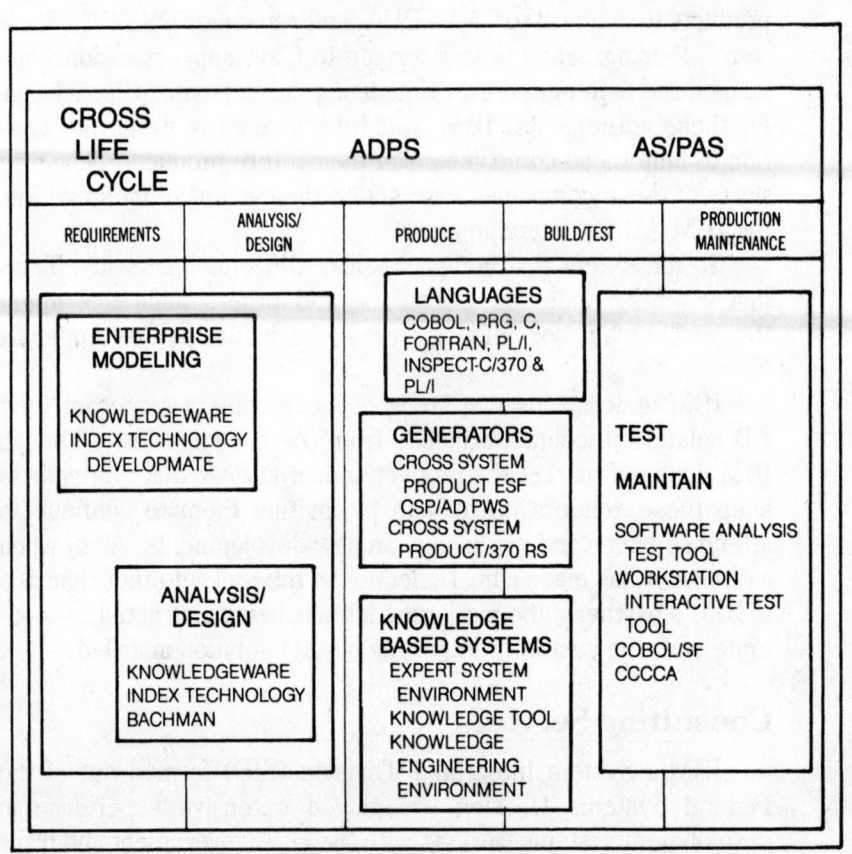

Fig. 7-12. AD/Cycle Model.

REPOSITORY

The MVS version was the first IBM Repository Manager to be announced. It has a mid-1990 shipment date. Typically, IBM will begin shipments six months before a "general availability" date. Two dozen or so customers around the world will work closely with IBM during an "early shipment program" intended to test the software in a real working environment.

The motivation in providing a common Repository in the application development environment is to provide centralized storage of certain kinds of information that is used by the various tools during the stages of development. Through this common storage comes the ability to integrate tools operating over the life cycle in a "seamless" fashion. This information is referred to as *objects*. How the data is stored in an object is called a *data model* and is to be described in IBM's "common data model."

Associated with an object such as a module of source code or object code is *header* information, which contains information about the object such as its relationship to other objects. The Repository manages these relationships and their abstractions through another model form called the *entity—relationship (ER) model.*

With this concept in mind one can see how a Repository manager can store all levels of data from business model output forms, specifications, panel designs, source code, test plans, test cases, procedures, libraries, reports, etc. Each object can contain common identifier information in the header.

In the IBM offering what is commonly called a Repository is contained under the definition of the IBM AD Platform and is a combination of the Information Model, Tool Services and the Repository. In addition the Common User Access rules and the workstation implementation on OS/2 running under OS/2EE will be enforced through the AD Platform definition.

The structure and format of the data/objects discussed above is described in the *Information Model*. In addition to the model for data/object storage additional services and definitions will be provided to support library functions and to extend the usability for tool builders.

Tool Services provide common operations to manipulate information defined by the information model. These include standard functions such as copy, delete and store. Extended functions such as verifying and configuration-control will be provided in library management functions.

The AD/Cycle *Repository Manager* provides the single point of control for the application development environment. The interface to the Repository allows tool builders to extend services provided by the Information Model and Tool Services. An example of this is the Dictionary Model Transformer. This IBM tool works in conjunction with the Repository and helps users OS/VS DB/DC dictionary to move their data to the Repository. Another example is the IBM Query Management Facility that provides the user the capability to retrieve information from the Repository and create customized reports. It is this central control function that is the core of AD/Cycle.

PROCESS/PROJECT MANAGEMENT

IBM's direction in these important management functions is represented by the introduction of Application Development Project Support (ADPS), AS and Personal AS as part of AD/Cycle. ADPS can be used in the definition and enforcement of the development model defined by the installation and can multiply concurrent projects. AS and Personal AS are used to control and manage project resources using traditional project management techniques. Both sets of products will go through an extensive evolution as they broaden their functional control and conform to SAA standards.

PROTOTYPING

The IBM AD solution is dependent on the product offerings from Bachman, Index Technology and KnowledgeWare. However, IBM has introduced a prototyping tool called DevelopMate that complements those vendor offerings by refining the output of the business models and providing the ability to prototype an application and to share its results with other tools

LANGUAGES

Users can expect a continuing evolution of language support from IBM. This will include, 32-bit compilers, extensions to the

Cross System Product, integrated edit, compile and debug features on the workstation, and a full upgrading and expansion of their expert systems—knowledge based systems offerings into a workstation format with open interfaces. All of these will continue to be important components of the AD/Cycle.

TEST, MAINTENANCE, REENGINEERING

Most large information systems executives will state that 60% to 80% of their resources are devoted to maintaining current applications and that their backlog of new applications is in the range of 1 to $2^1/2$ years.

IBM has introduced several tools that have proven themselves in their internal development projects.

Software Analysis Test Tool (SATT) performs measurement on the coverage of PL/I and COBOL II application in test. The Workstation Interactive Test Tool (WITT) provides the ability to create test inputs and provides records of the test sessions. The COBOL Structuring Facility (CSF) restructures COBOL source code to well documented views of the program. The COBOL and CICS/command-level conversion aid convert macro level source and copy members to a command panel.

These products together with the Bachman product line for database provide a power set of tools that cover the major components of the maintenance challenge; i.e., process (Cobol), data (DB/2), and test.

PRODUCTIVITY

A discussion of application development is incomplete without addressing the potential productivity gains. The value of the information systems investment required to implement AD/Cycle in the cost of high function workstations, repository software tools, training and management focus and time commitment is extensive. For many it is intuitive that the industry must go forward and that these new technologies have already given us a glimpse enough of their potential value. Certainly the commitment of IBM to direct its attention to software arena is an important backdrop in that potentially billions of dollars will be spent improving programmer productivity.

A lot must be done in the field of metrics, the measurement of software costs and programmer productivity. New approaches are being discussed and explored but to date hard data remains anecdotal. However, even this data is impressive. What is missing of course is a predictive model that can be used for a particular installation, application or investment decision.

Most of the time, and rightly so, the answer to the question of "how much productivity gain can I expect?" begins with "it all depends!" and so it does. Some approaches identify 20 to 30 different variables to be examined. Some of these can be quantified, others are subjective.

One of the benefits of the advent of AD/Cycle will be to force these questions on value to be addressed with more precision and hopefully encourage work by vendors, customers, consultants and academia that will result in more usable guidance.

Following are some guidance factors gleaned from vendors, customers, internal users and various reports. Although they are useful, please imagine every conceivable caveat of "it all depends," and that actual experience will vary considerably.

In general, the data should be considered as the effect of using the associated tool technology in a single instance, for example a single application. In addition, a judgment is shown as to the effect of that technology on the overall life cycle. The results are summarized in the table below and in Fig. 7-13. The following table shows a 50% decrease in effort is a 100% increase in productivity or a productivity measure of 2:1 over traditional methods, i.e. Cobol:

AD Component	% decrease effort component	% decrease in overall life cycle
Cross life cycle	8-25	8-25
Enterprise Modeling	20-30	20-30
Analysis/Design	30-50	10-20
DB Design	50-80	5-10
Languages	0	0
Edit/Debug	40	20
Generators	80-90	40
Knowledgebased*	V.High	V.High

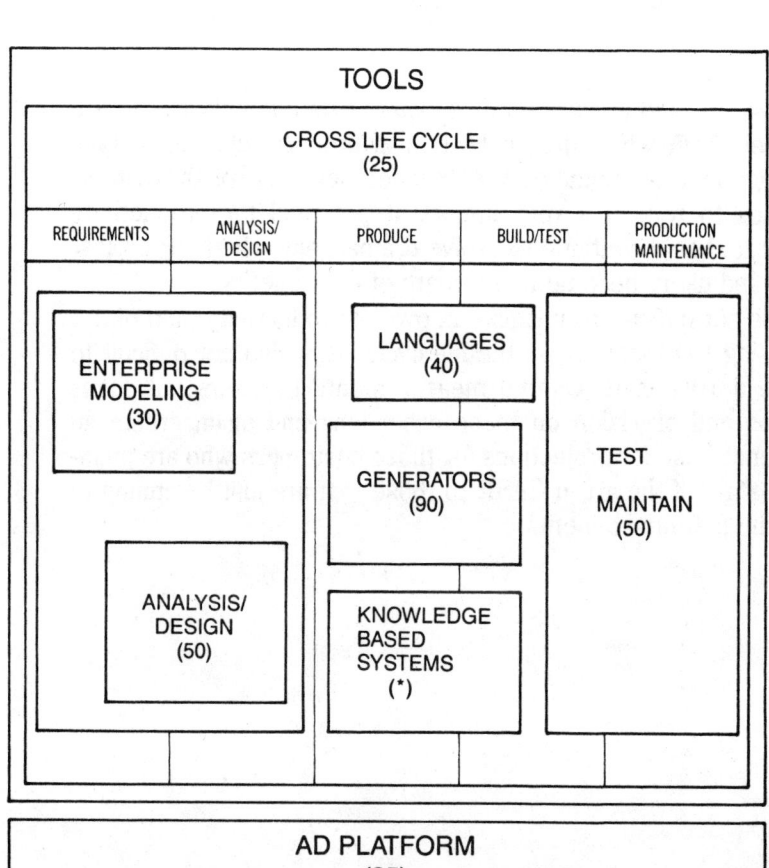

Fig. 7-13. AD Model Productivity Potential.

AD Component	% decrease effort component	% decrease in overall life cycle
Test	25-50	5-10
Reuse/Re-Eng	20-50	20-50
Repository	25	25

Knowledge based application development productivity claims are extremely high when the application is properly chosen to take advantage of this technology. A broader base use of these tools continues to remain a very important potential for productivity gains that should continue to evolve dramatically when DP professionals and users become more aware of the benefits.

It is not difficult to imagine an overall productivity gain of 2:1 from using AD tools across the life cycle. It is also not difficult to imagine a 10:1 gain. Careful measurements by users will focus attention and precision on these assertions and again create an experience base for projections for those customers who are pushing the state of the art in CASE to those that are just beginning to study the potential benefits.

8

IBM Management System for SAA

Michael Killen is a consultant to industry on information systems industry and the author of a book called *IBM: The Making of the Common View*. He says "many people believe that great creative accomplishments take place in an unstructured environment. I don't think that's true. They just can't see the structure in which the genius works."

IBM's worldwide hardware and software development activities and structure involves 27 laboratories in North America, Europe and Asia. The focal point for this mission is centered in the IBM United States organization located in Purchase, New York, structured as shown in Fig. 8-1. In addition to the U.S. Marketing and Service organization and supporting staff functions, IBM U.S. has organized the product development operations into six lines of businesses (LOBs) which have revenue and profit and loss accountability to the IBM Corporation. These lines of business, each headed by an IBM Vice President, follow with their key product responsibilities:

LOB	Responsibilities
Enterprise Systems	IBM System/370 high-end processors and related operating systems such as MVS. ES also produces IBM's high-volume printers.

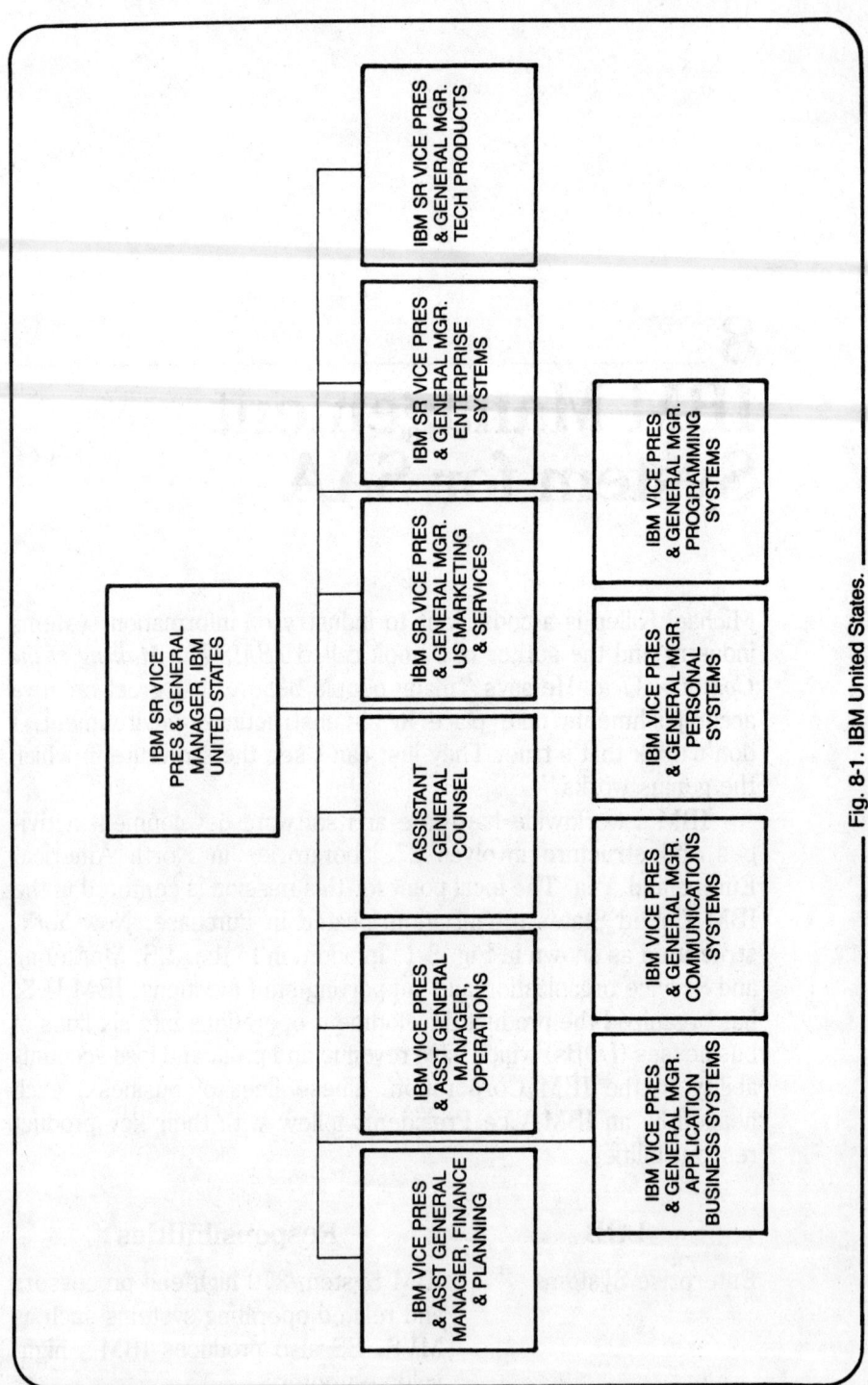

Fig. 8-1. IBM United States.

Application Business Systems	The midrange processors such as the AS/400 system, System/36, System/38 and their operating systems. ABS also develops storage devices for IBM's mid-range and PS/2 product families.
Personal Systems	IBM desktop systems such as PS/2 and Operating System/2. PS also oversees the typewriters, displays, and low-end printer businesses for IBM.
Communication Systems	IBM Telecommunications hardware and software products including controllers, modems, and SNA.
Technology	IBM logic and memory technologies and the electronic packaging used in the IBM product line.
Programming Systems	IBM data management software, programming languages, application development software, and SAA.

The Programming Systems LOB, with development missions from Systems Application Architecture to data management software, affect every major product in the corporation. The core of the operation of the LOB takes place in three laboratories.

The Santa Teresa Laboratory located in San Jose, California has worldwide responsibility for Systems Application Architecture, the CPI architecture and data management software including DB/2, IBM's relational database important to a customers' SAA system. In addition the Information Management System (IMS) product, the Query Management Facility (QMF) and with the Cary Laboratory is responsible for CASE. Santa Teresa also has corporate responsibility for most programming languages such as COBOL, Fortran, PL/1, BASIC, C, and APL.

The software development laboratory at Cary, North Carolina, is 19 miles from Raleigh's Research Triangle Park facility which is where Communications Systems develops much of IBM's communications software products. The Cary laboratory develops products and software tools used by application programmers and in systems performance products. As already mentioned, Cary develops CASE tools used to simplify application development. One of these, Cross System Product (CSP), is an important part of IBM's ADE plan.

The Toronto Laboratory has grown from 300 people in 1980 to over 1300 today and is still growing. In addition to having developed key products for OS/400, Toronto is responsible for SQL/DS, the relational database for the VM operating system. One of Toronto's newest projects involves the development of a standard dictionary function for use in SAA networks and exchanging messages and data files across different SAA systems. Toronto also has responsibility for development of several key languages including C, RPG, and ADA. ADA has become a standard in working with the U.S. government and has an interesting footnote. It is named after Lady Augusta Ada Byron Lovelace, the daughter of Lord Byron, said to have been the first programmer in history!

Several other locations work very closely with the Programming Systems LOB in carrying out its SAA mission. This includes the Austin, Texas laboratory with responsibility for the PS/2 product family and the OS/2 operating system. The Rochester, Minnesota laboratory responsible for OS/400 software; Hursley, England laboratory responsible for CICS a popular transaction management system; Vienna, Austria laboratory develops a variety of CASE tools and the Menlo Park facility which is working in the field of expert systems and artificial intelligence.

It is the genius of the designers and programmers in the above facilities that has been charged with making SAA a reality. The original "management structure" to guide SAA development was a closely knit committee that met once a month under the direction of Earl F. Wheeler, IBM Vice President and, at that early time of SAA, in charge of IBM's small corporate function overlooking software activities for the corporation.

When the Programming Systems LOB was formed in April of 1988, Earl Wheeler moved quickly in defining how he would direct the resources and manage the responsibility of SAA, now deemed critical to IBM. The first step was to define the value of SAA in terms of the customer, to the application vendors and to IBM and to get agreement in the operating units for the value statements, shown in Fig. 8-2. The objective was to get the customers needs

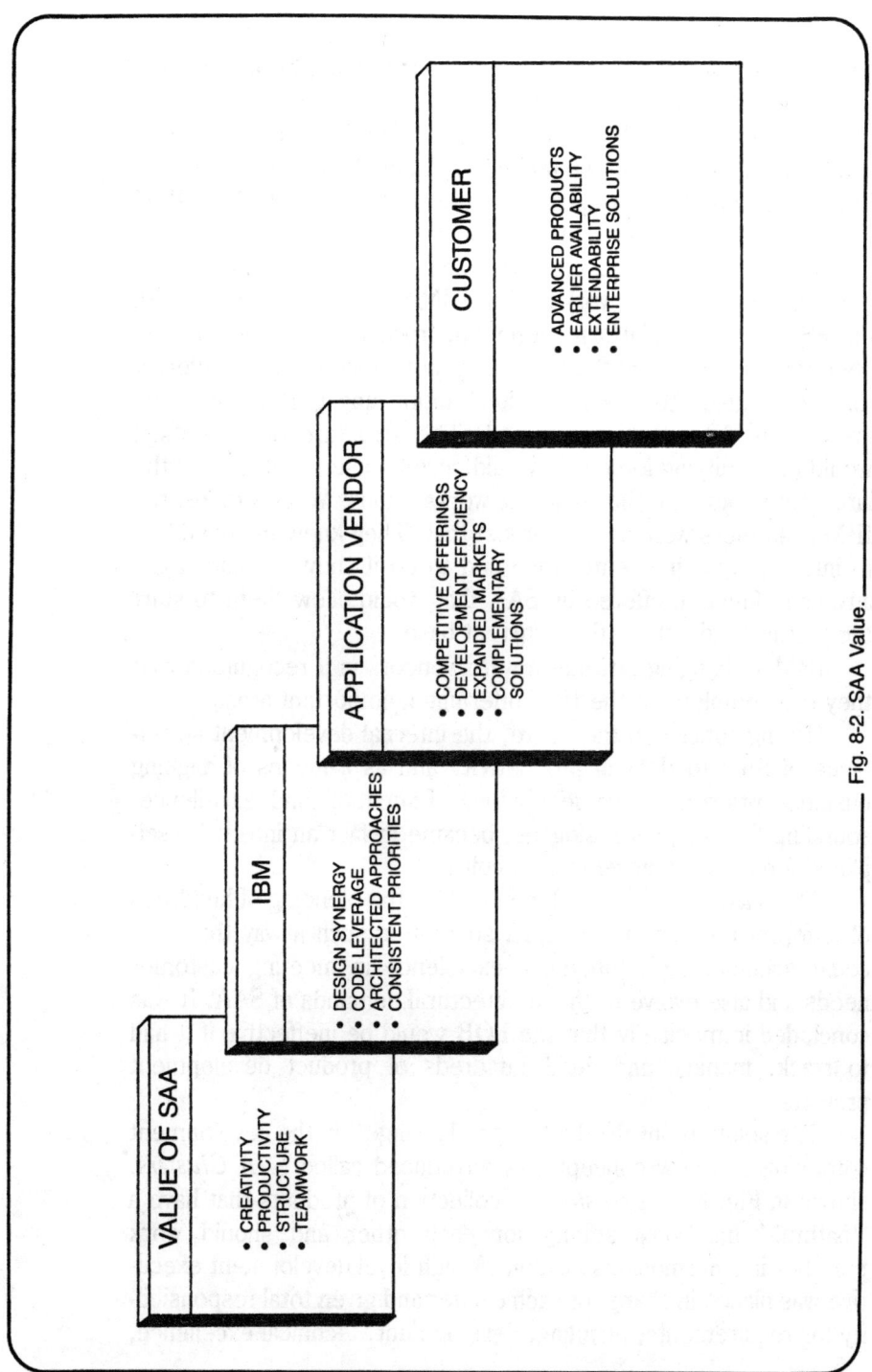

Fig. 8-2. SAA Value.

directly in front of the technical teams so that it was clear that what was to be done was for the customer!

From that point, the other values would flow to the vendors and to IBM, all rooted in the technology benefits promised by SAA. In the decision of declaring the value of SAA is embodied the IBM business strategy. The software technology would provide the basis for unprecedented creativity and productivity through the emerging power of the workstation. IBM has positioned itself with the PS/2 hardware platform with its microchannel architecture and operating system (OS/2) as the only personal computer offering that could give the customer the multitasking performance and growth the future would demand. The structure of SAA itself would be a unifying force that would permit customers to build the large networks with thousands of workstations. What's more, the IBM customers were asking for just that. They knew the need was to interconnect their enterprise and to do it they demanded the advanced function offered by SAA that would allow them to start the journey and extend their current base.

IBM's changing attitude toward vendors is a recognition that they can complement the IBM offerings in important areas.

Having concluded the above, the internal development advantages of SAA to IBM in productivity and as a means of aligning business priorities became obvious. Execution and excellence, sounding like shopworn slogans, became in fact an internal disciplined force on the development culture.

The success of SAA is dependent on the blending of hundreds of different products in the SAA solution in such a way that they could maintain their functional excellence in meeting customer needs and also evolve to the architectural demands of SAA. It was concluded immediately that the LOB would be ineffective if it had to track, manage and audit hundreds of product development projects.

The solution, involved a "cultural change" in the development community. A new concept was introduced called *SAA Clusters*, shown in Fig. 8-3. A *cluster* is a collection of products that have a "natural" functional affinity for each other and should work together in a harmonious fashion. A high-level development executive was placed in charge of each cluster and given total responsibility for requirements, planning, development, technical excellence,

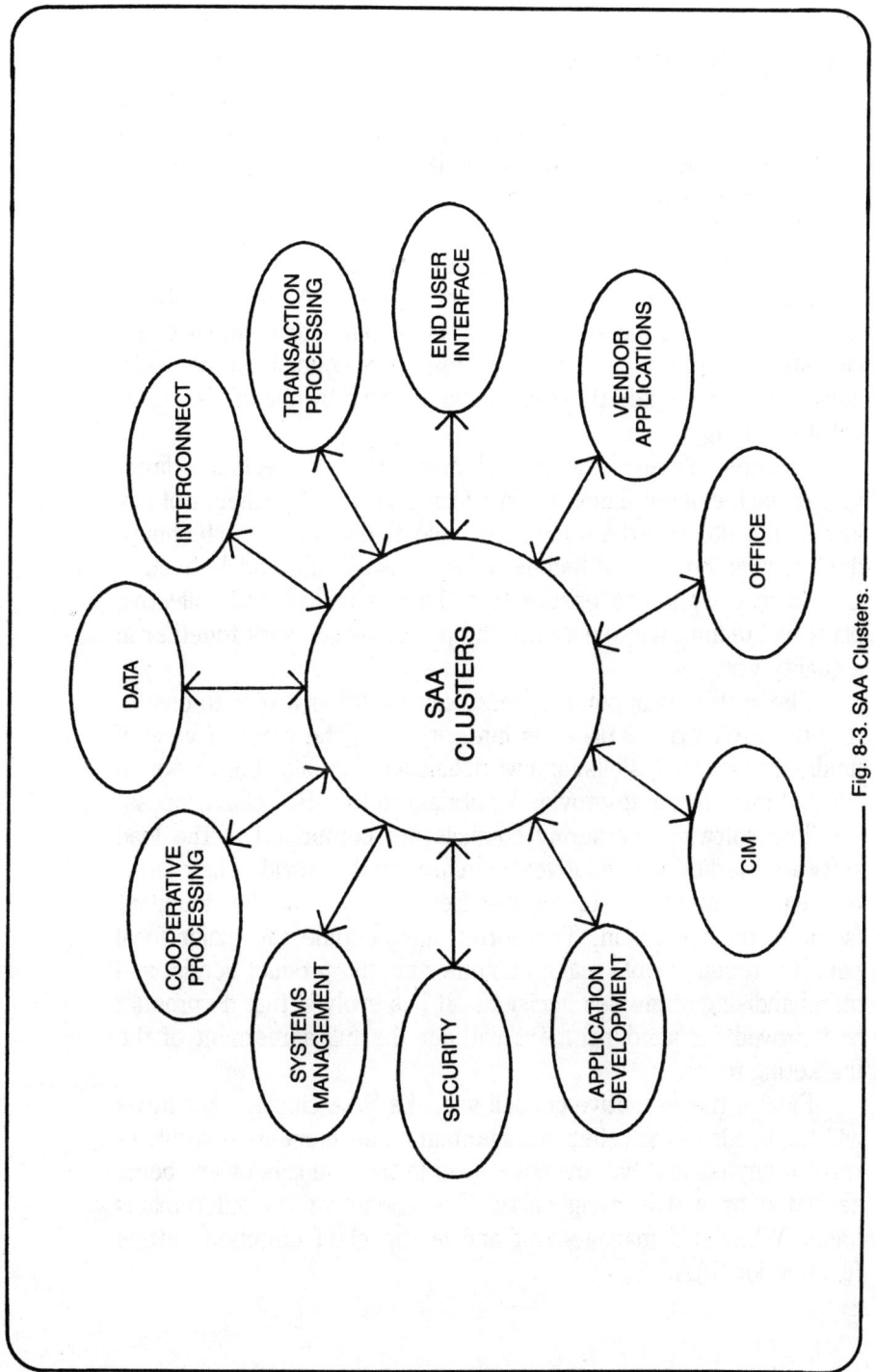

Fig. 8-3. SAA Clusters.

and timeliness of their cluster. This would require a level of unprecedented teamwork, coordination, and interdependency since not all the development resources working on the cluster components would report direct to the executive. It would be an ongoing test of matrix management techniques.

Having defined the fundamental value system and the technical development directions, Earl Wheeler announced how he planned to manage the effort in the new line of business. Above the laboratory level he announced the formation of four management councils, shown in Fig. 8-4, including an executive council that he would personally chair. The others would be directed by one of his assistant general managers.

The design council meets each month with the technical directors of each cluster. They would inform the other members of any key issues affecting the others and collectively define the technical directions and make the technical decisions affecting SAA. In addition, it is their job to ensure that their individual and collective plans had technical integrity i.e. the pieces would work together in a quality way.

The system plan council meets several times a year to ensure that the SAA master plan has integrity from the point of view of funding, resources, skills, and work balance. It is also the responsibility of this council to provide input data to the IBM plan process.

The software marketing councils are comprised of the lead software marketing executives from around the world. Their job is to ensure that the customer requirements remain the dominant factor in the SAA plan. This forum has become the major focal point for requirements major customer needs, product needs, and merchandising strategies decisions. It has evolved that no product is approved for announcement without the full agreement of the marketing team.

Finally, the executive council with the SAA cluster executives and the heads of the other management councils meets monthly to resolve any issues that are not solved in the councils or are being escalated by a dissenting party. The executive council remains under Wheeler's management and is the chief direction setting function for SAA.

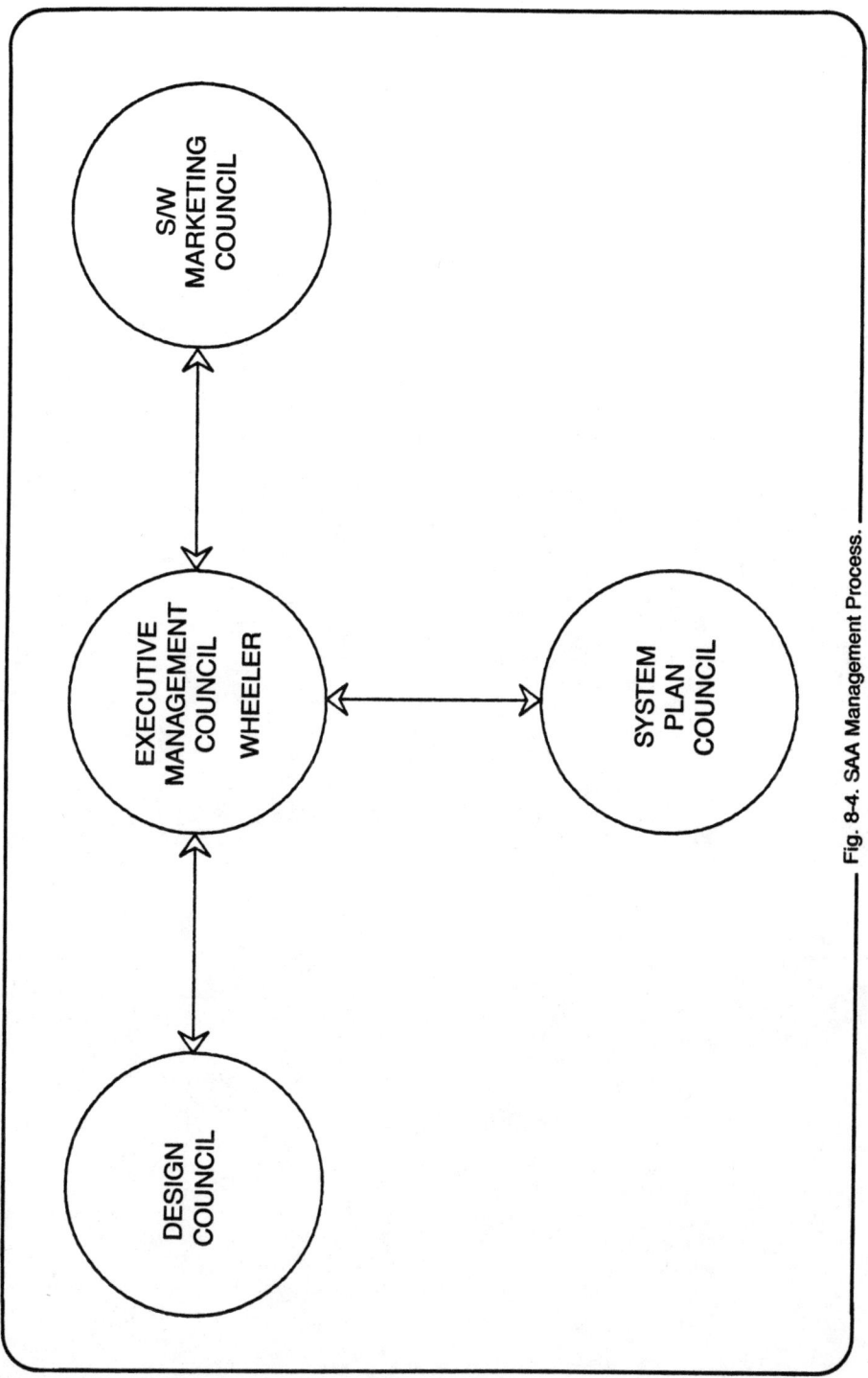

Fig. 8-4. SAA Management Process.

9
SAA and UNIX

The UNIX operating system was developed by the Computing Science Research Group at Bell Laboratories in the late 1960s to create a computing environment for programming research. This initial need still characterizes the fundamental strength of the operating system. It contains many tools that are useful in developing software, producing documentation and a flexible file system for processing.

UNIX has continued to evolve as an operating system where today there is estimated to be over 100 different versions and several base standards being installed on thousands of systems. Industry estimates project that by 1992 UNIX operating systems will be running on 18% of the worldwide shipments of computer systems. That compares to an estimated 9% in 1988.

Several of the characteristics of the UNIX system explain its attractiveness. It is an interactive system, responding to the user commands. It is multi-tasking, therefore capable of executing several tasks at one time. It is a *multi-user system*, allowing more than one person to use it at one time. Finally, the easy, low cost availability of the programming code to the many microcomputer and minicomputer manufacturers has caused the spread of its adaptation for their use.

Enthusiasts for UNIX will argue its virtues versus SAA for as long as one cares to listen and the opposite is equally true. The marketplace fact is that customers are buying large numbers of systems using UNIX and in order to share in that opportunity IBM developed its own version called AIX.

AIX is a family of operating systems that runs on the Personal System/2, the RISC System/6000 and the System/370 systems, as shown in Fig. 9-1. AIX supports the several UNIX standards and offers additional features that make it the most powerful UNIX operating system available. A unique advantage of the IBM approach is that they can offer a customer systems performance growth of over 600 times measured from the high end PS/2 models to the IBM 3090 model 600. Other manufacturers of UNIX are limited to their workstation implementation or a significantly limited growth path.

IBM's strategy is to offer SAA systems and AIX systems that can work together as members of the customers enterprise solution. In order to clarify its position on the relationship of its two operating systems families, IBM recently made the following statement:

"IBM will respond to customer needs with SAA and AIX platforms which are considered superior to comparable offerings.

SAA is based on our customers' requirements and provides the broadest range of applications and functional capability. SAA is built on the platforms of IBM's major operating systems and is tied to industry standards with published interfaces and protocols.

AIX is built on UNIX-based standards and specifications such as Posix and X-open. It will include open software foundation offerings and added support tailored to the strengths of IBM computing systems.

The determination of which IBM solutions are proposed or developed, SAA, AIX or both will be based on factors such as customer preference, function, price/performance, and application attractiveness and availability. In general, where a solution currently exists, extensions and enhancements will be made on the same operating system base.

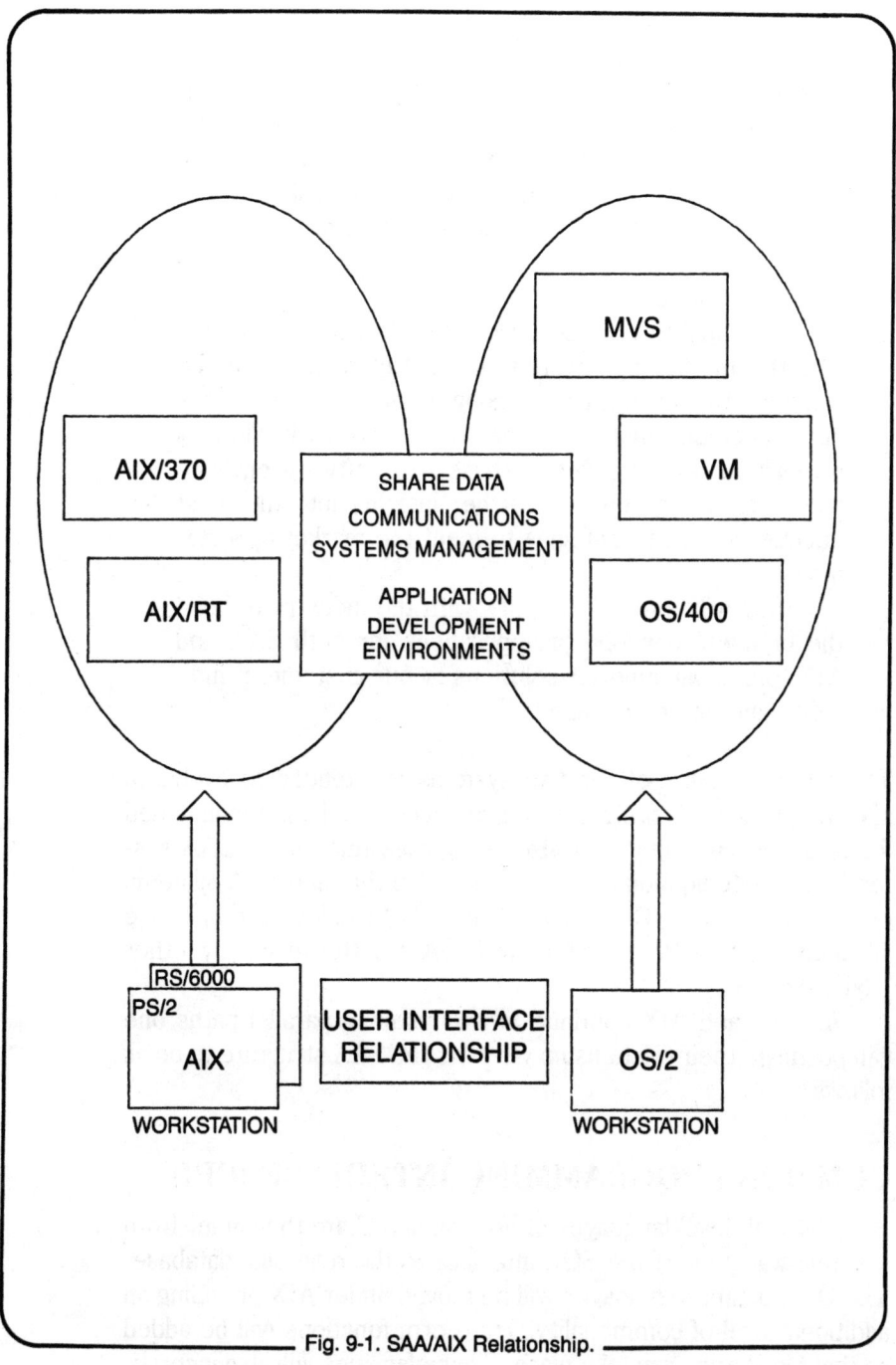

Fig. 9-1. SAA/AIX Relationship.

To support customers choosing both SAA and AIX to meet their application needs, IBM will link these environments and allow data to be shared between them. We will implement a consistent set of data and communication capabilities, such as relational database and OSI, and provide our customers with application development capabilities that include consistent tools where appropriate, such as Fortran and C.

Additional work is underway to more discretely analyze the market opportunity and better understand the elements that discriminate among market segments. It is our expectation that the results of this work will allow us to position, in more detail, these two software environments as well as give us further insights into the most effective solution strategies to meet the market opportunities.

IBM will continue to work with the industry to build the broadest portfolio of applications for both SAA and AIX, providing superior solutions to our customers' individual and enterprise needs.''

The interoperability of the two systems is intended to evolve in such a way that the standards and character of AIX are maintained for that user community. It also recognizes that as the SAA systems became ubiquitous it will be essential that non-SAA systems operate with them. Clearly, IBM intends to enjoy a competitive advantage with AIX operating with SAA better than any other UNIX system.

As SAA and AIX continue to evolve along parallel paths one can postulate their relationship vis-a-vis the SAA structure to be as follows:

COMMON PROGRAMMING INTERFACE (CPI)

The high-level languages of Fortran and C are the same. Both systems will support the SQL interface to the relational database. The OS/2 database manager will be moved under AIX providing an additional level of commonality. Transform functions will be added so that file sharing can take place. These facilities will also incorporate many of the distributed services functions being developed under SAA.

COMMON COMMUNICATIONS SUPPORT (CCS)

There are three sets of protocols supported in SAA. These are SNA, OSI, and TCP/IP. The latter is a high-performance protocol system popular in many airlines and banking applications. Over time all of these protocol systems will be able to request or respond to any of the other protocols in such a way as to partition the application from these specific communication functions.

COMMON USER ACCESS (CUA)

IBM will continue to promote its CUA definition and attempt to influence industry standards as well as customers. Guidelines and software tools will be developed that will tend to highlight the similarities of the various standards. One-time customer frustration and influence will begin to dictate a single standard.

APPLICATION DEVELOPMENT ENVIRONMENT (ADE)

A variety of different tools will be available in the SAA and AIX environments. IBM's priority is to be competitive in each of these areas. This of course translates to differences in structure, tools and timing. Much work remains to be done by IBM, its customers and the industry to fully understand the requirements. In the meantime pursuing common languages, data movement, and interconnection provides a starting point.

Figure 9-2 is a comparison of the operating systems structures of SAA and UNIX and demonstrates that you can view these two systems as having a common layered structure.

Some objectives of each system are the same, such as consistency across different hardware systems and portability of software. UNIX systems have shown great virtuosity in acceptance and systems adaptation. This has resulted in thousands of applications available to be run on an apparent common systems structure. SAA, however, is a proprietary set of offerings from IBM only.

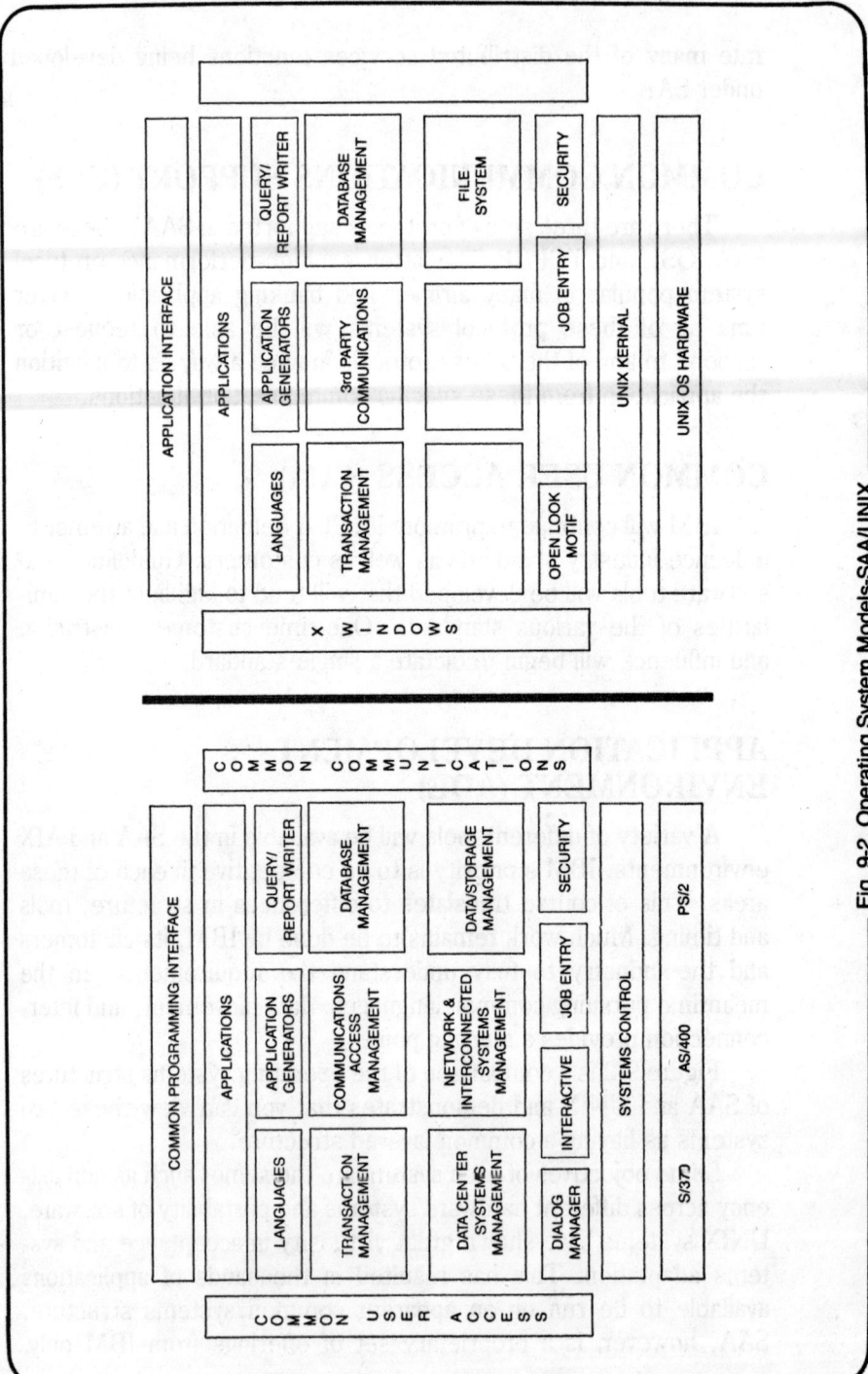

Fig. 9-2. Operating System Models–SAA/UNIX.

However, as SAA unfolds and documented interfaces are published, SAA becomes more open on its standard bases. In the future, there is more similarity than might be immediately apparent. As different manufacturers adopt UNIX to their hardware system and introduce new functions the "standard openness" of UNIX starts to become unique to that manufacturer.

There are general and specific similarities and commonality between SAA and UNIX. However, there are important differences in the following areas:

- Application interfaces
- Data management
- Storage management
- User interface
- Communications support
- Network management

It is ironic that just as IBM has organized a full-scale solution to provide a common operating system structure across its diverse hardware platforms that yet another common operating system family arises in popularity in the marketplace. It is not a question of a win or lose strategy for IBM, but one of balanced investment strategy that gives IBM the opportunity to make one plus one add up to more than two for their customers.

From an SAA point of view, there will continue to be the challenge of fully embracing UNIX system into the SAA enterprise. The implication on the host side will be to have access to data residing on the UNIX system and to incorporate that host-to-host access into the SAA concept of distributed data (warehouse). The other vantage point is from the workstation side of the equation and that is to provide for a UNIX workstation to pipe into the SAA data (and application).

Whatever the bias or technical approach, it is clear that customers will have both environments in their enterprise and will want a meaningful way for them to coexist as a total enterprise-connected resource.

10
The Future Direction of SAA

The future direction of Systems Application Architecture as we move into the 1990s will be determined on one hand by a number of current issues and requirements that are well understood today and not yet satisfied, and on the other hand by the technological evolution of computing systems defining new and more challenging software requirements.

The former observation is evidenced in the Common User Access, shown in Fig. 10-1 which has gone through a rapid evolution of definition and product capability. This has resulted in a span of interface function from straightforward representation of lists and menu functions that have been familiar on the nonprogrammable terminals to the sophisticated graphical capability of the new personal computers, including manipulation of multimedia devices, high-speed animation, and high-resolution image data.

As the 1990s evolve, the technology and functional enhancements to the CUA component will be optimized to the programmable workstation, as shown in Fig. 10-2. There will be, in effect, a cap put on the CUA support of the nonprogrammable terminal.

However, even at the "capped" level, a user will have enhanced capability of significant function consistent with the PWS including the use of action bars and some windowing function. The determining factor on use will be end user demand of applications that provide significant increases in information contact for the end

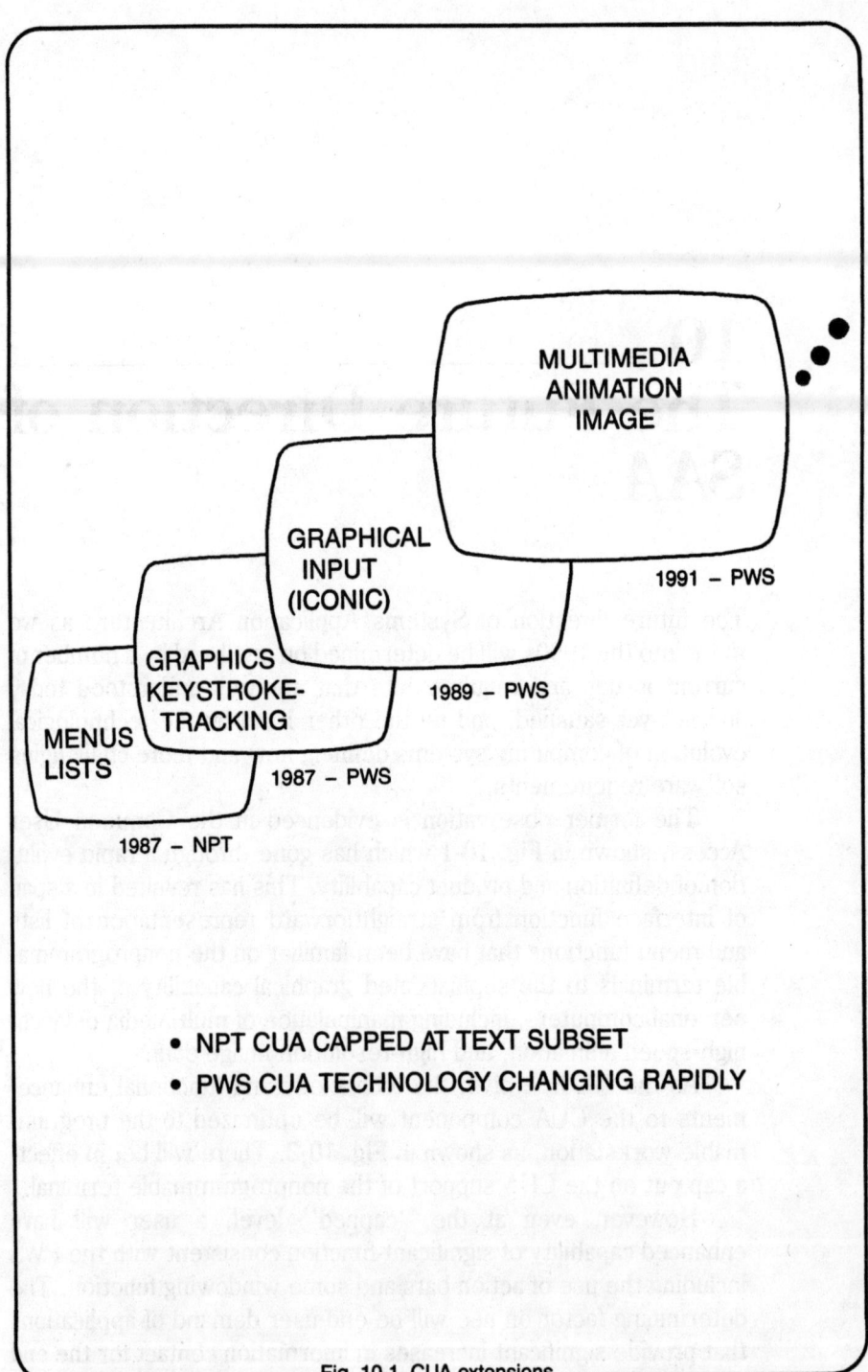

MULTIMEDIA
ANIMATION
IMAGE

GRAPHICAL
INPUT
(ICONIC)

1991 – PWS

GRAPHICS
KEYSTROKE-
TRACKING

1989 – PWS

MENUS
LISTS

1987 – PWS

1987 – NPT

- NPT CUA CAPPED AT TEXT SUBSET
- PWS CUA TECHNOLOGY CHANGING RAPIDLY

Fig. 10-1. CUA extensions.

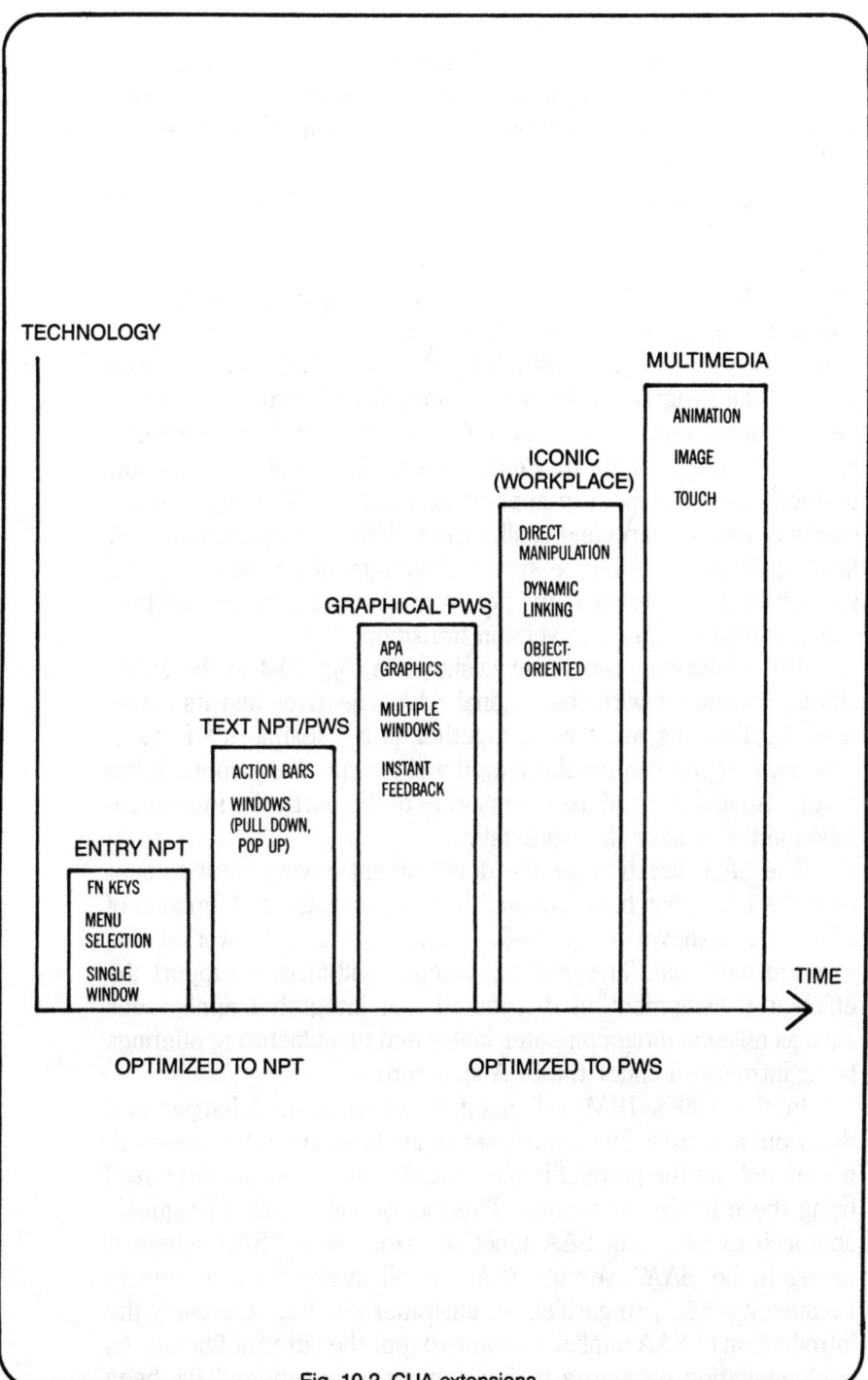

Fig. 10-2. CUA extensions.

user and still remain easy to use. It is in anticipation of those applications that will be implemented using graphical output, and compound documents including voice and images that the new levels of CUA will be designed to address.

During the 1990s we will begin to experience the mass upgrade of applications and the creation of new applications that will provide more information integration across the enterprise, as shown in Fig. 10-3. These applications will require relational database technology distributed among a variety of computer systems with different design points, all interconnected and accessed through the programmable workstation. As this evolution occurs, SAA products must provide for a function that allows the coexistence of the old with the new and the migration of programs, data, protocols into the modern application versions. The key requirements of this scenario and challenges to IBM in its providing SAA function across the multiple-system environments is the continuing support of such devices as the nonprogrammable terminal and providing software version to version transition.

The application users' view, shown in Fig. 10-4 in the 1990s will be consistent with the original SAA objectives and its evolution. Applications must work together in a "seamless" fashion. That is, function can be distributed and executed anywhere in the enterprise and the end user is unaware of the particular implementation in the host or the workstation.

The SAA direction for the development environment to support the 1990s has been outlined by the principles and function of AD/Cycle as shown in Fig. 10-5. Again, the role of the workstation is a dominant one. The evolving function will further support the efficient development of distributed and integrated applications such as office and the computer integrated manufacturing offerings being introduced under the SAA structure.

In the 1990s IBM will need to adopt a model-structured description of SAA function. A set of application models needs to be defined and the product implementation managed and optimized using these model definitions. This can be viewed as a pragmatic approach to providing SAA function. More of a "SAA where it needs to be SAA" versus "SAA in all systems environments because it's SAA, (regardless of customer needs)." Certainly the introduction of SAA implied to some extent the latter definition. As implementation became a reality, legitimate questions have been

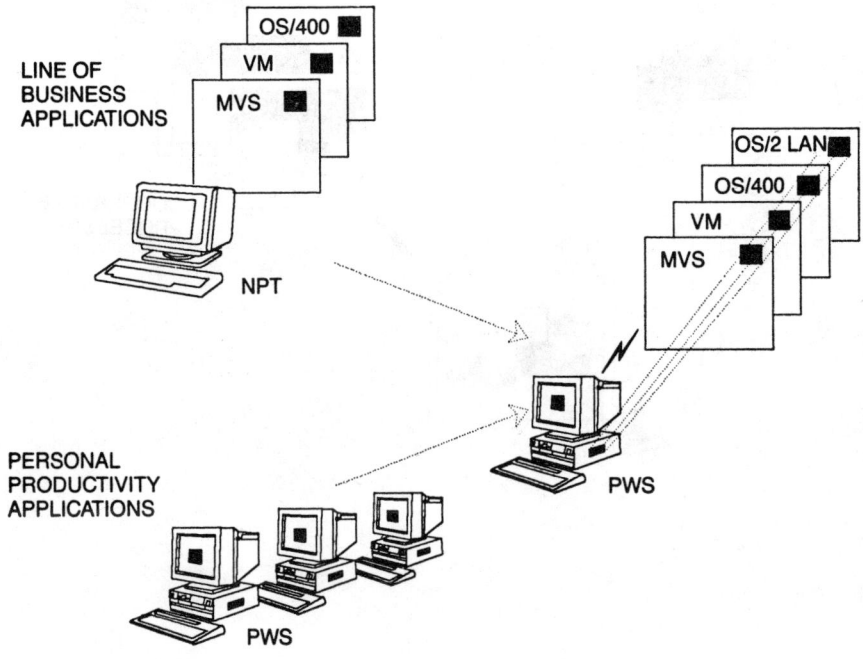

TODAY'S APPLICATIONS   COOPERATIVE APPLICATIONS

- BUILD APPLICATIONS TO TAKE ADVANTAGE OF
    - HOST TECHNOLOGY (RDB)
    - WORKSTATION TECHNOLOGY (CUA, LOCAL PROCESSING)
    - MULTIPLE SYSTEM DESIGN POINTS
    - INTER-SYSTEM TECHNOLOGY (CONNECTIVITY)

Fig. 10-3. Enterprise applications.

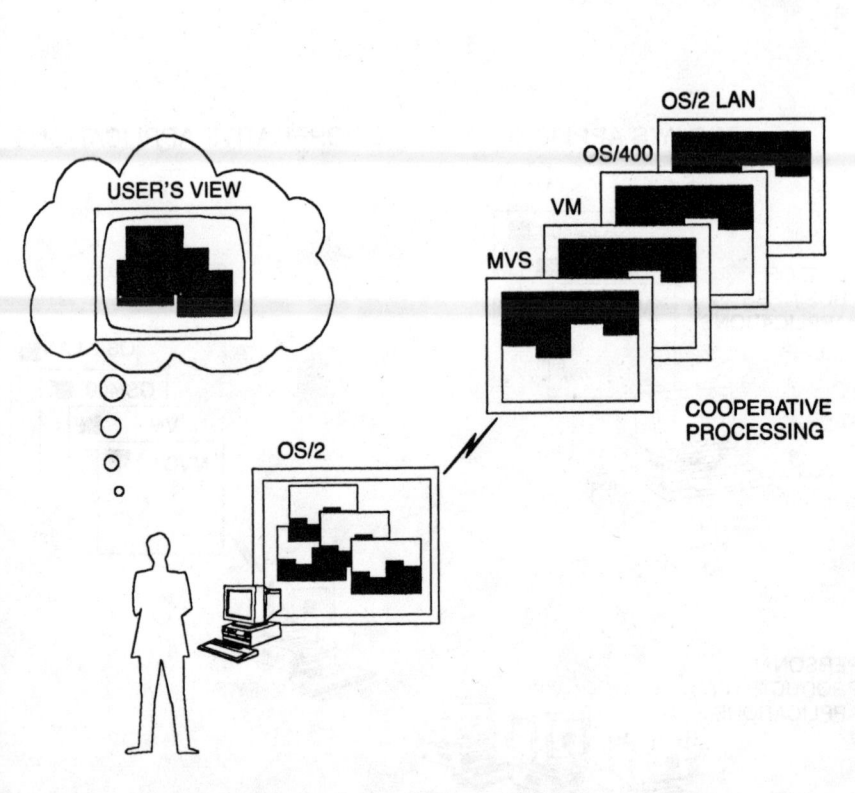

- ENHANCED PRODUCTIVITY THROUGH USER INTERFACE AND SEAMLESS VIEW OF APPLICATIONS
- DISTRIBUTION OF APPLICATION FUNCTION TRANSPARENT TO USER
- COMBINES STRENGTHS OF WORKSTATION AND HOST CAPABILITIES

Fig. 10-4. Cooperative applications from the application user's view.

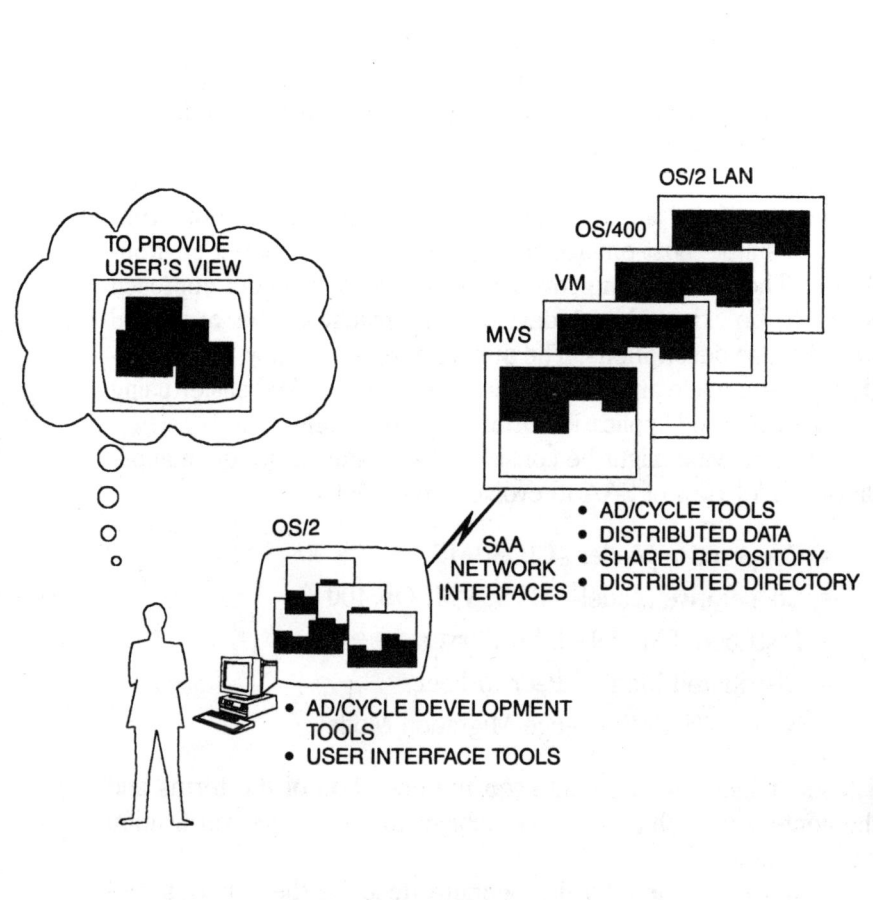

Fig. 10-5. Application developer's view.

• UNIFORM PWS WORKBENCH

• GENERATE APPLICATION FUNCTION WHICH SPANS PWS AND HOST

• INTEGRATE WITH SAA APPLICATIONS (OFFICE, CIM, . . .)

raised on the need and value of an "all things to all systems" approach.

In a simple example, is there really a significant customer demand for PL/1 on the AS/400? Some would say no, yet, IBM is providing the capability to be consistent with the SAA definition. The whole question of what needs to be built as an SAA component, available in all environments, gets to be much more complex as you move from language components to local applications running in a simple host environment to complex distributed environments. Therefore, some form of an application model approach needs to be adopted and development plans will be organized around these descriptions. The purists may be unhappy, faster progress will be made and mid-course corrections will be easier using a well-understood application-oriented base of reference.

The following might be considered as a starter set of an application model view of SAA to evolve in the 1990s:

- Cooperative Model—CICS/IMS
- Cooperative Model—MVS, VM, OS/400
- Distributed Model—LAN Server
- Distributed Model—Peer to Peer
- NPT/PWS CoExistence Migration Model

These "might be" because even the definition of the terms and the context of such models are subject to debate and verification with customers.

In any case, the following sections describe the kind of structure that is being considered and tested as requirements for specific SAA implementations.

Cooperative Model (CICS)

Figure 10-6 shows the key SAA components of the (CICS) model. The PWS operates with a local version of CICS running under OS/2. The application CUA support is provided by a combination of the Dialog Manager, Presentation Manager and an enhanced version of the EASEL facility.

In addition to the APPC and CPI-C interconnection, the model would require a remote procedure call and efficient messaging facility.

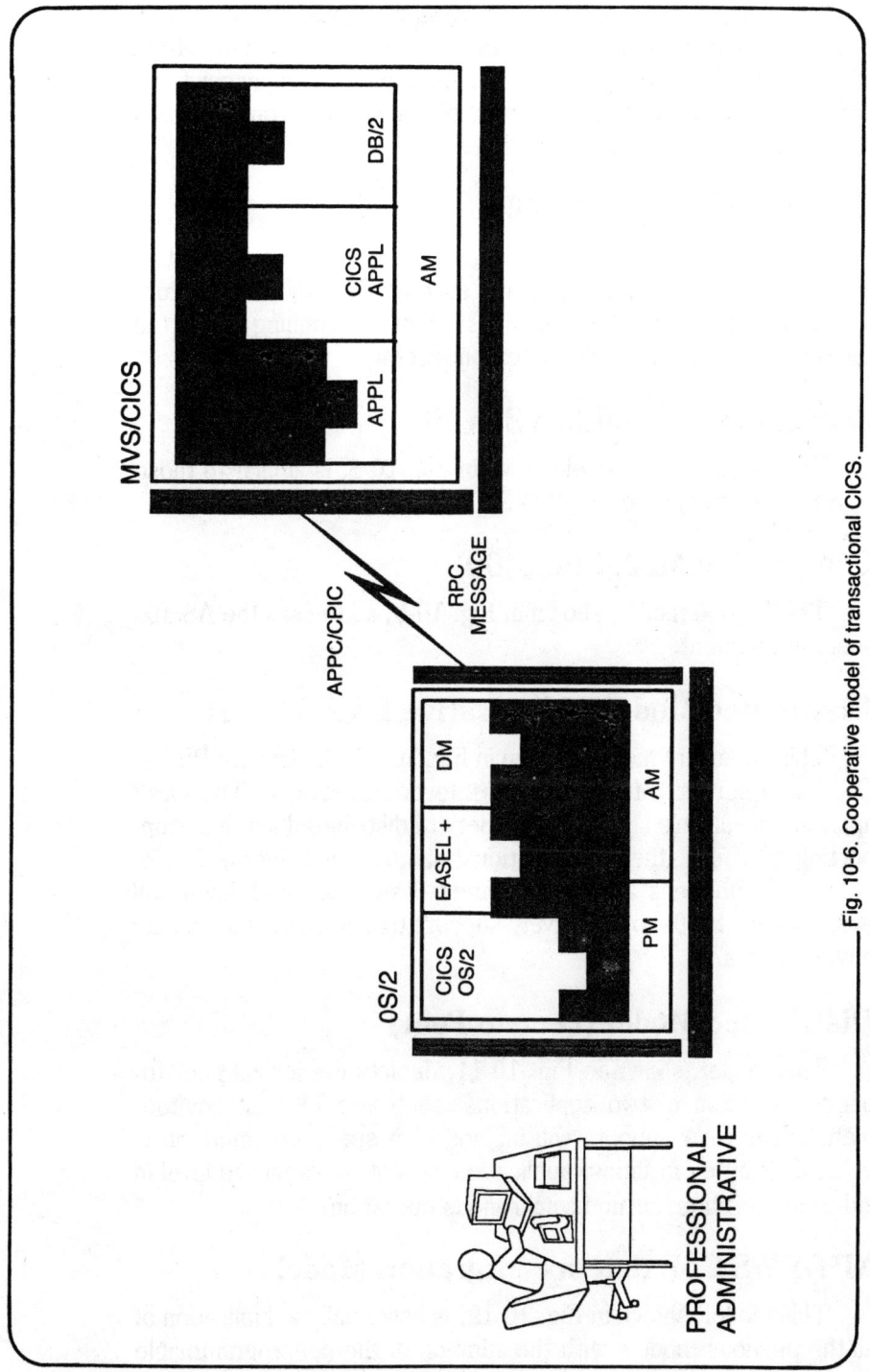

Fig. 10-6. Cooperative model of transactional CICS.

The host system, MVS in this example would run the CICS application which would be running in conjunction with the IBM relational database member (DB/2). An application manager function must also be part of the model to provide the transition and control functions for application flow.

Cooperative Model (IMS)

The (IMS) model shown in Fig. 10-7, is similar to the CICS version and adds some components such as VTRAN which is running to interface to IMS. Also, LU2 is shown as running support in addition to the LU6.2/APPC interconnection.

Cooperative Model (MVS, VM)

The (MVS, VM) model shown in Fig. 10-8, is similar to those above and encompasses the MVS/TSO and VM environments.

Cooperative Model (AS/400)

The AS/400 model, shown in Fig. 10-9, addresses the AS/400 host environment.

Distributed Model (Cooperative LAN Server)

This important model, shown in Fig. 10-10, depicts the PS/2—OS/2 as a server gateway to the enterprise network. The OS/2 application will have access to a variety of distributed services supporting data files, the IBM relational database managers, distributed print functions and a distributed directory. OS/2 itself will evolve in the 1990s to effectively support this and the other model environments.

Distributed Model (Peer-to-Peer)

This model, shown in Fig. 10-11, depicts the logical peer-to-peer connection of two applications, each in SAA host environments. The SAA support will include high speed communication links, distributed facilities, application calls at the language level in either synchronous or nonsynchronous operation.

NPT/PWS CoExistence Migration Model

This model, shown in Fig. 10-12, is essentially a duplication of all the previous models with the addition of the nonprogrammable

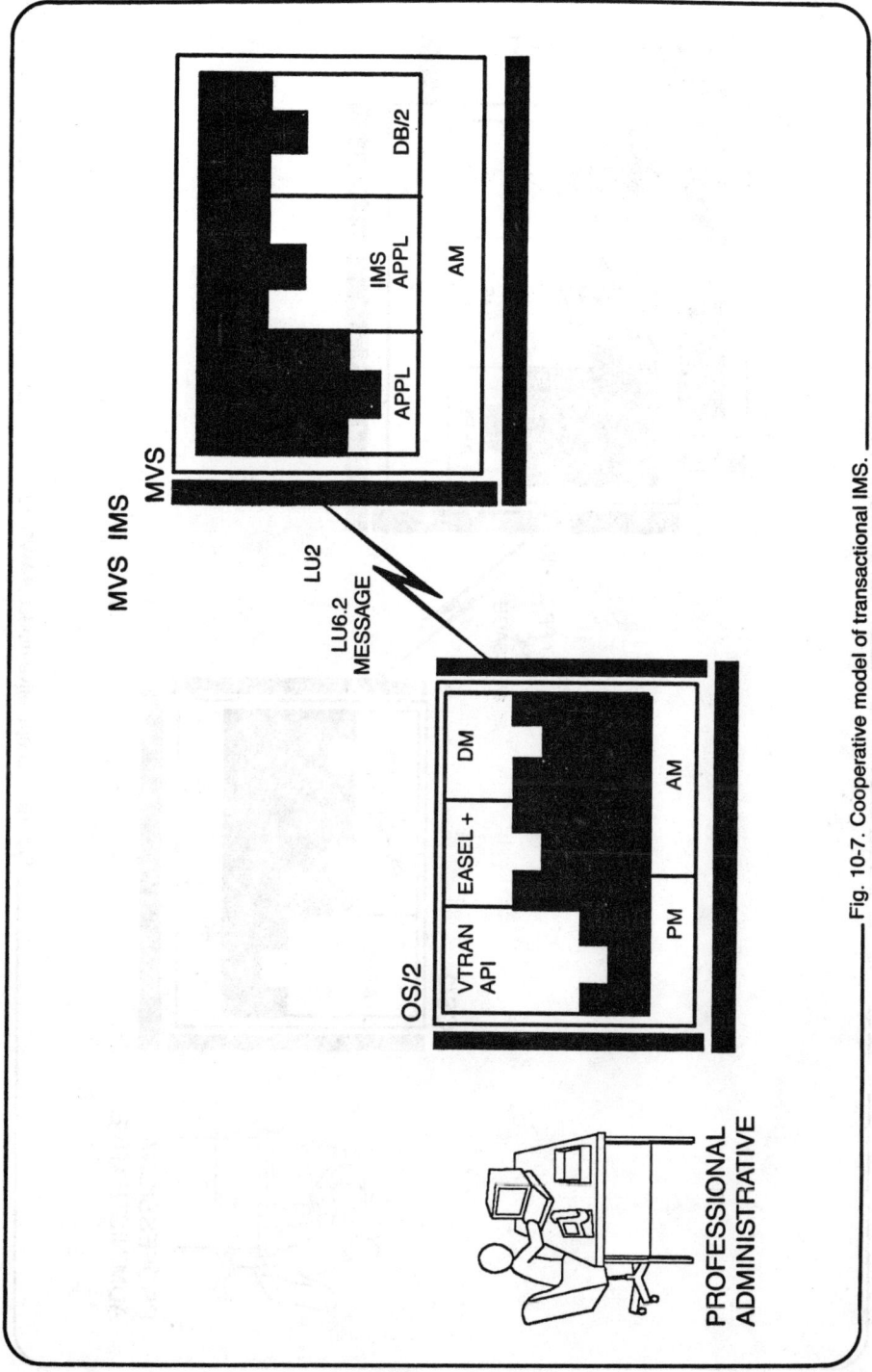

Fig. 10-7. Cooperative model of transactional IMS.

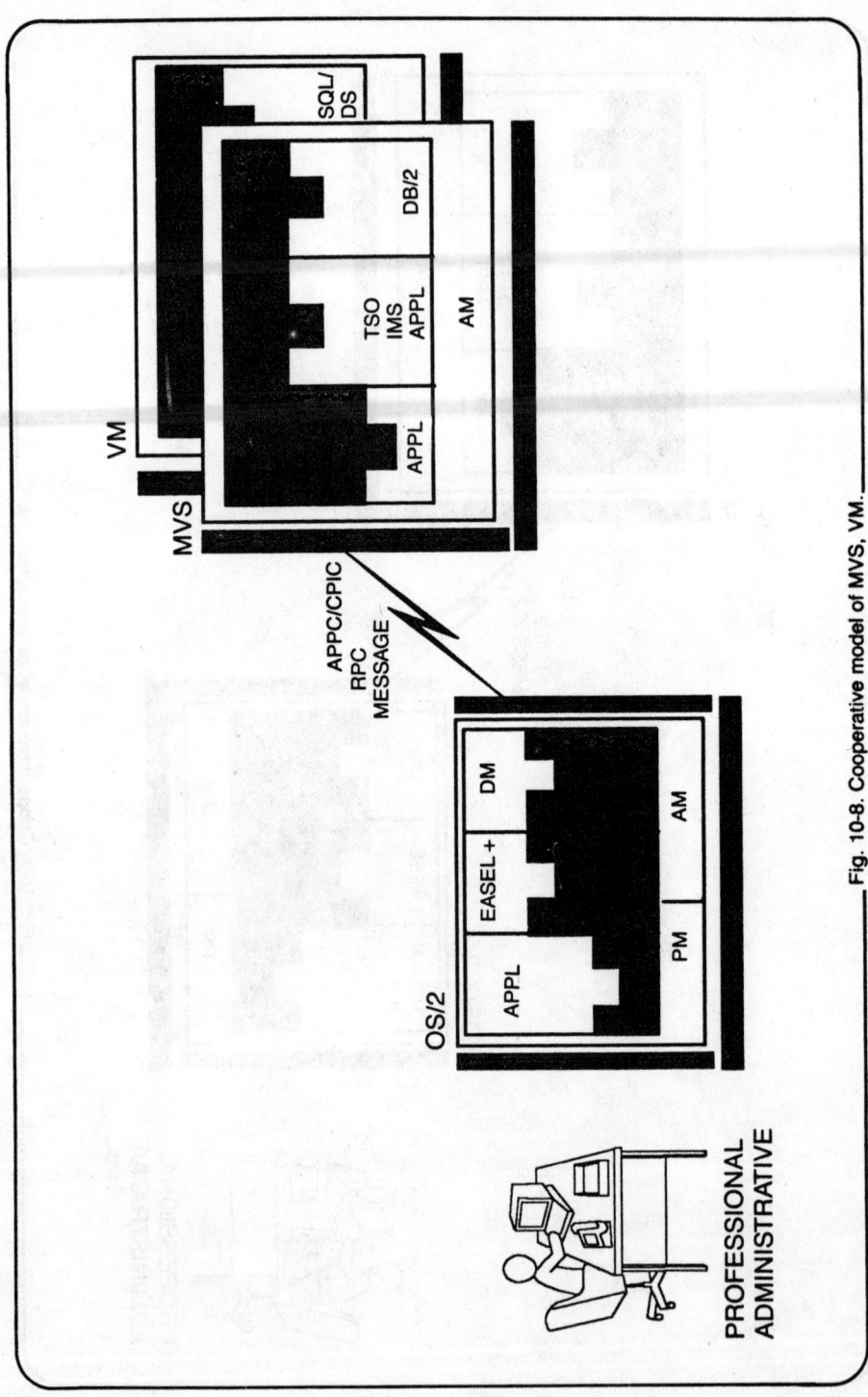

Fig. 10-8. Cooperative model of MVS, VM.

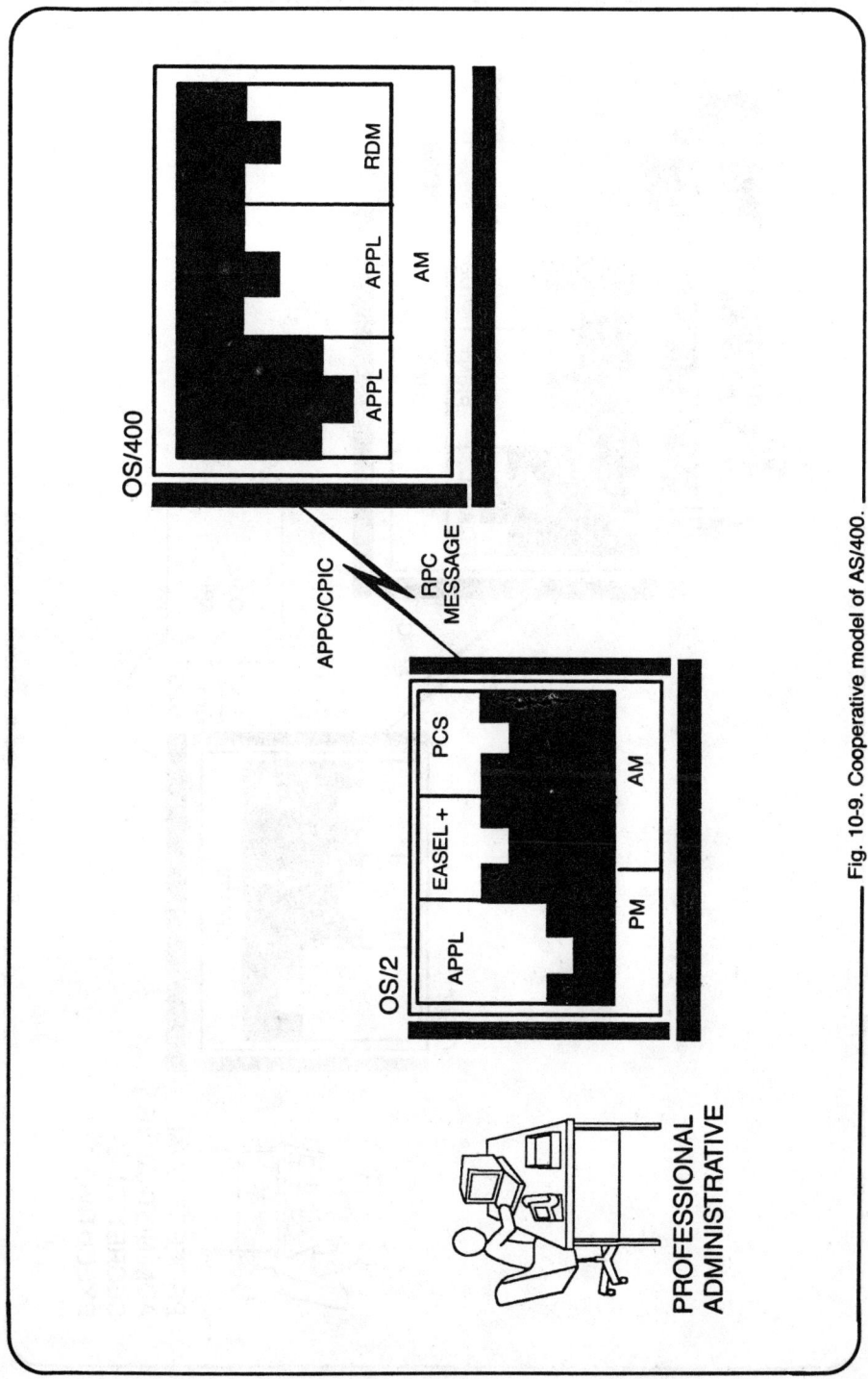

Fig. 10-9. Cooperative model of AS/400.

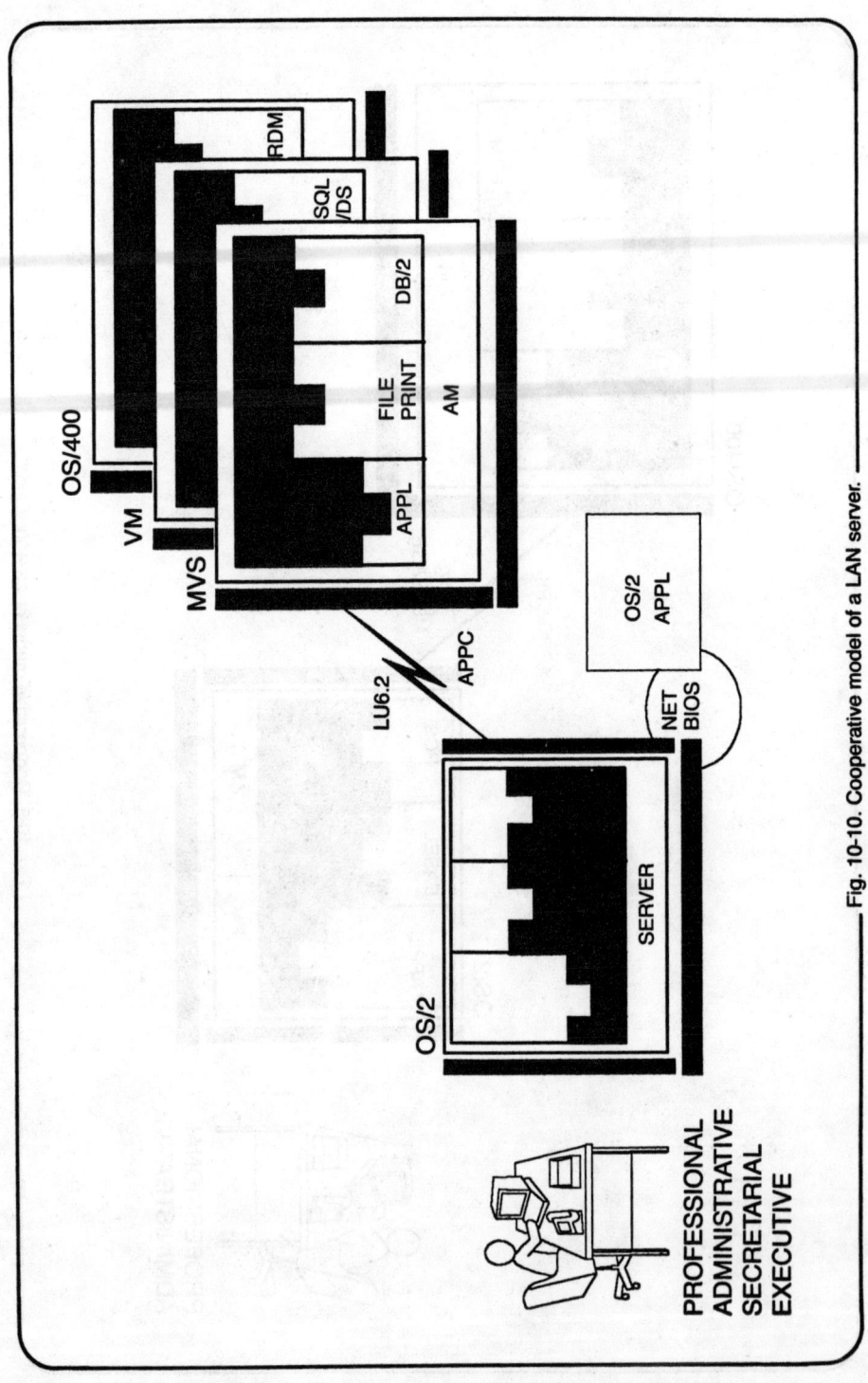

Fig. 10-10. Cooperative model of a LAN server.

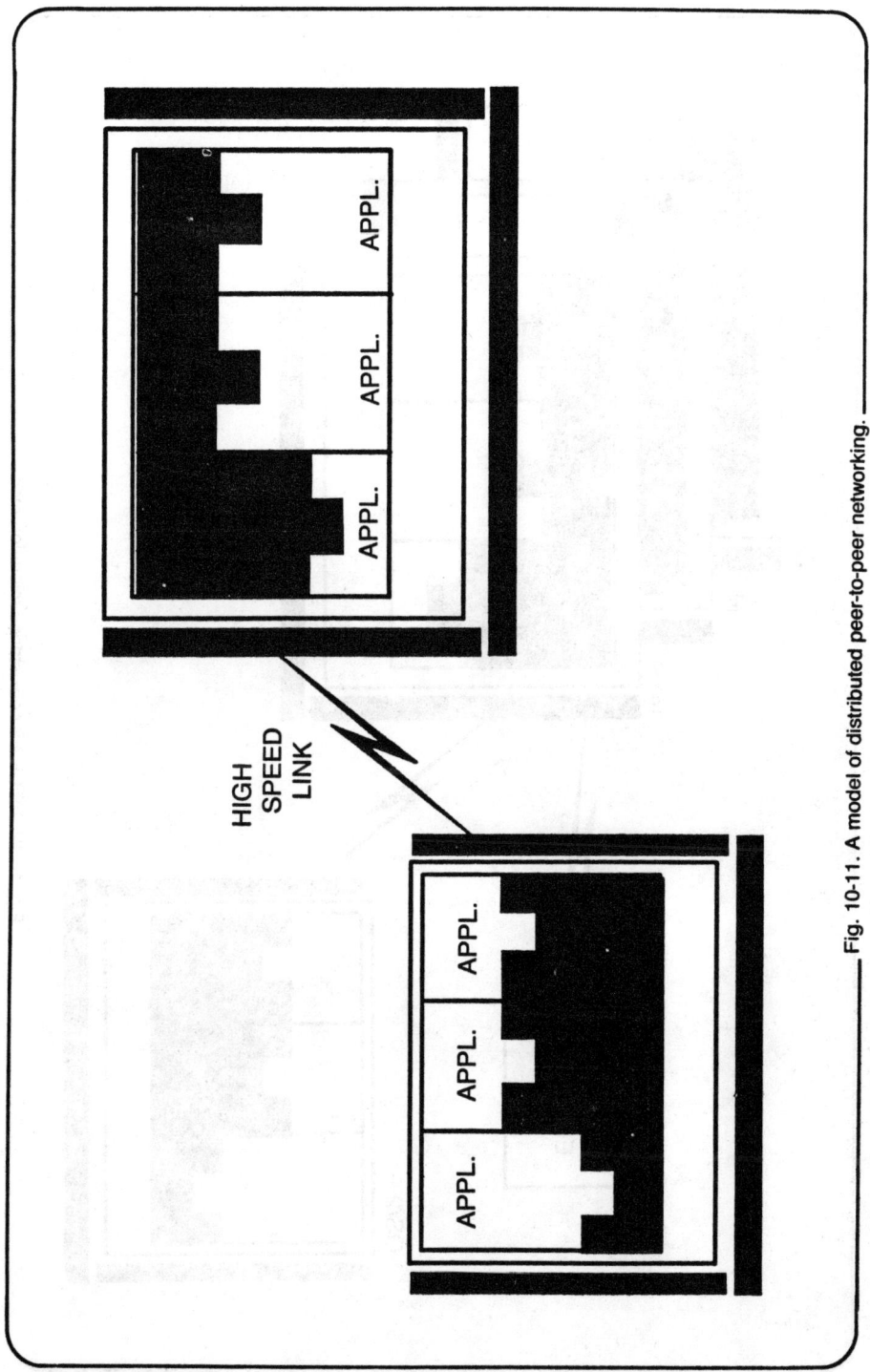

Fig. 10-11. A model of distributed peer-to-peer networking.

HIGH SPEED LINK

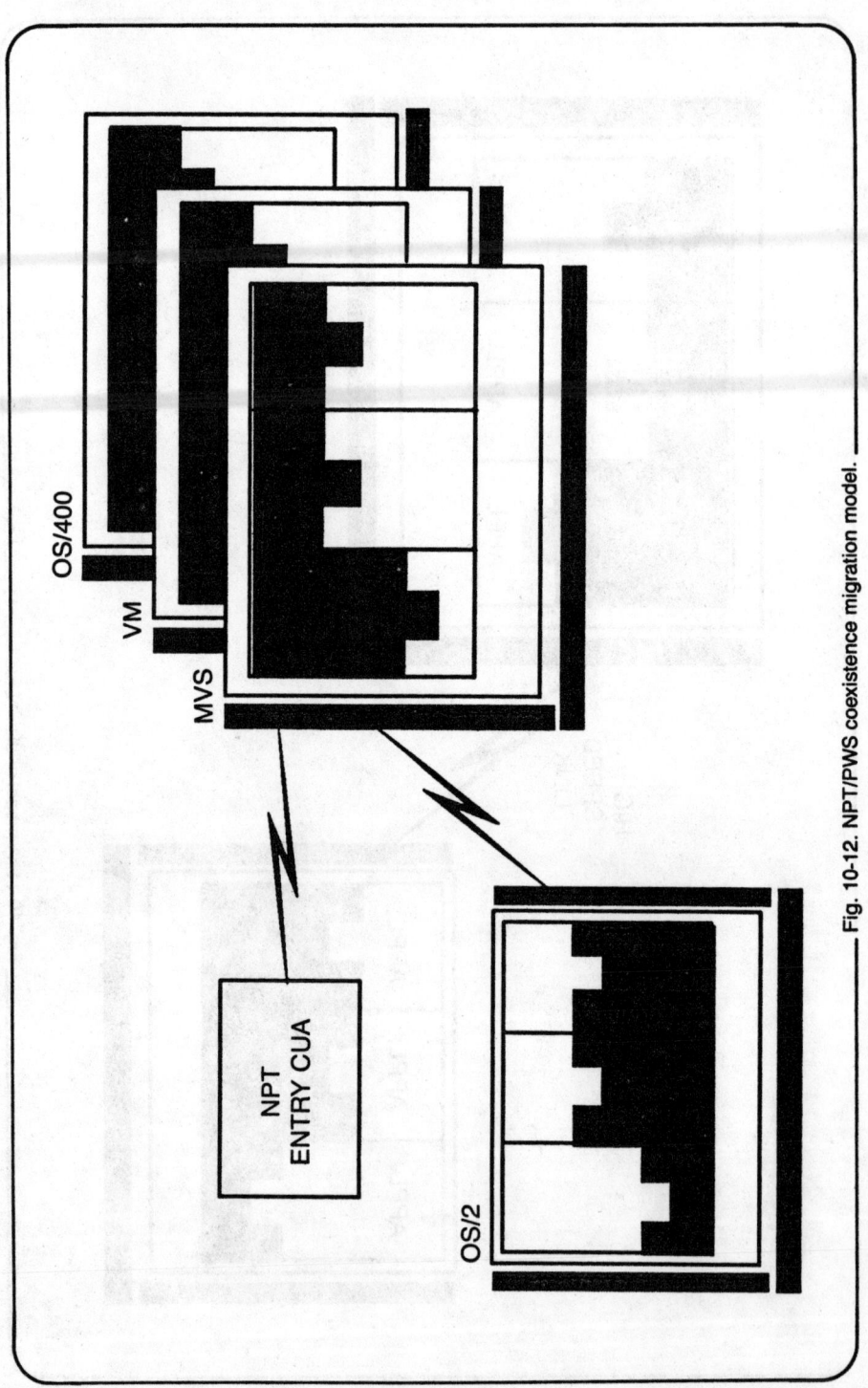

Fig. 10-12. NPT/PWS coexistence migration model.

workstation and its support functions as part of the application scenario. Its inclusion in the SAA model spectrum is to reinforce the requirement of new SAA functions to provide coexistence of current applications that use NPT.

Again, the model examples above are all representative of an approach to have all the functions committed and positioned as part of SAA. Additional work must be done with customers in a variety of industry applications areas to confirm this direction and view of SAA.

All that has been done to date in SAA has been necessary. As these architecture components have now been rendered specific, the next step in the evolution is to position SAA components in the context of application development (AD) and application execution (AE) environments as described above.

A resulting "matrix" can be envisioned of the AD and AE models versus the SAA clusters as shown in Fig. 10-13.

One of the potential benefits of this declaration will be the "openness" of the SAA architecture rendered explicit. The advantage of this is that it will allow the positioning of many IBM and vendor software tools to be SAA. Beyond this, it will allow clear articulation on such issues as the "SAAness" of other operating systems such as VSE.

As this scenario suggests, a customer can now design a SAA enterprise that includes the earlier defined SAA operating systems environments and embraces other operating environments in a specific way.

As the attributes of SAA clusters such as data, vendoring, communications, and application development are rendered explicit for each model there will be additional clarity in understanding and building SAA systems in the enterprise. This will be true from the point of view of development platforms and tools as well as the various execution environments.

It is clear to me that the 1990s will not be a "cold and dry" spell for SAA. New systems "clouds and trees" will be defined and supported within Systems Application Architecture and provide more coherency in system design, installation and management.

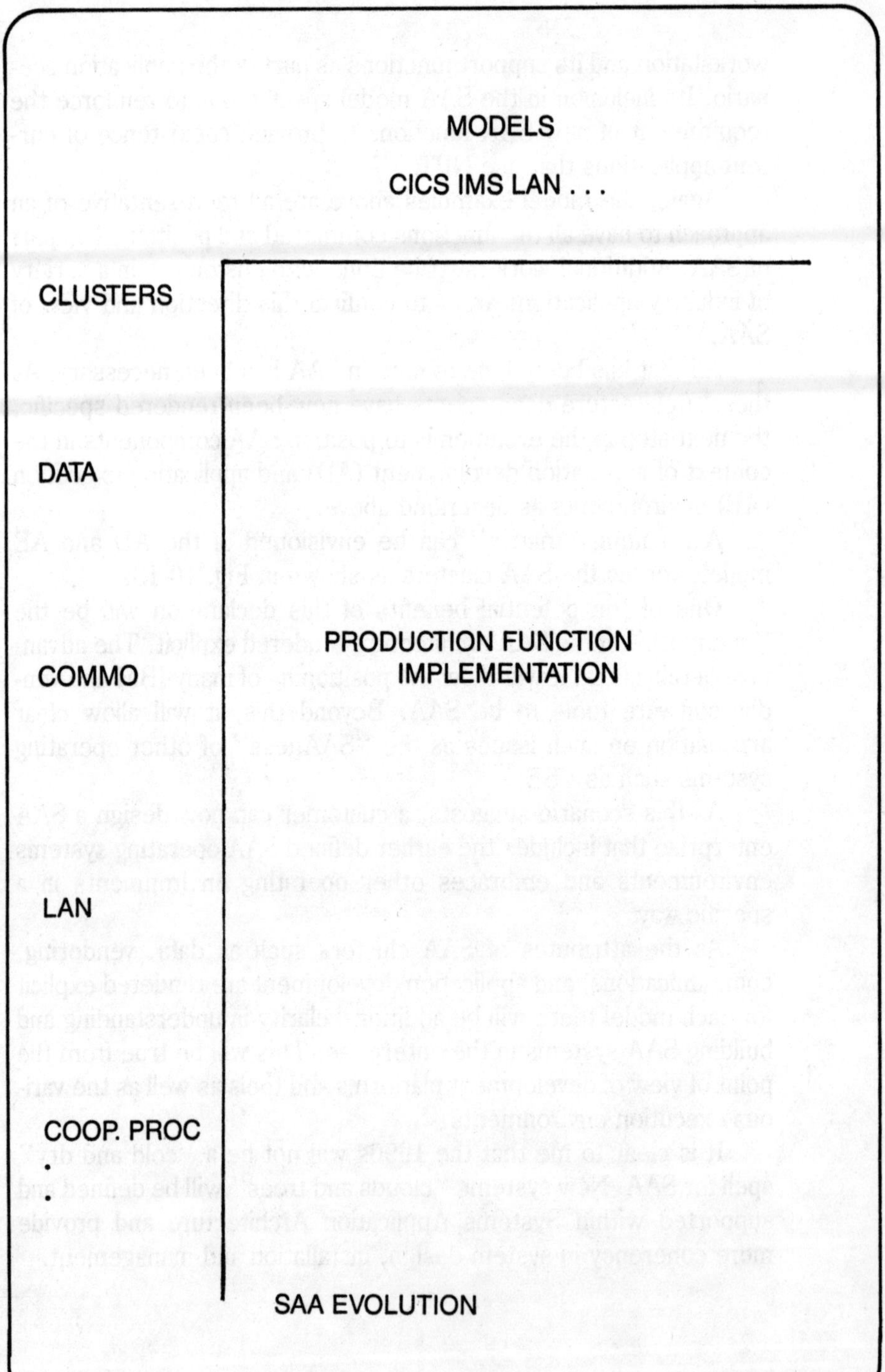

MODELS

CICS IMS LAN . . .

CLUSTERS

DATA

COMMO

PRODUCTION FUNCTION
IMPLEMENTATION

LAN

COOP. PROC

SAA EVOLUTION

Fig. 10-13. The evolution of SAA models.

11
SAA Assessment

On what basis do you make a judgment on the potential success of IBM's SAA strategy? IBM's worldwide revenues for 1988 were $59.6 billion of which $9.9 billion was from application and systems software products. The software segment of the information technology industry is projected to be one of its fastest growing at a compounded growth rate of approximately 20%. For the IBM company to grow, its software revenues must grow.

In an answer to a question in the January 9, 1989, issue of Computerworld; "What are the two or three technologies that you think will have the most impact on your largest customers, and Computerworld readers in the next five to ten years?" John Akers replied:

> "I would say Systems Application Architecture is one. I'm not being facetious. If you ask the pros in computing what they'd like to do that they can't do today, what they need is productivity enhancements in software development, continuity in terms of people dealing with computers and screens and enhanced connectivity. That is precisely what we're trying to give them."

Given the sign of the revenue importance of software to IBM and the strategic priority given to SAA by John Akers it is fair to conclude that IBM is dedicated to making SAA a success.

Mr. Akers adds emphasis to the importance of the SAA strategy in his letter to the stockholders as printed in the IBM 1988 Annual Report.[21]

"Our range of operating system software provides a platform for customers to plan their growth into the 1990s. Key to that growth is IBM's Systems Application Architecture (SAA), which will allow users to look at and work with applications across IBM's product line."

Reports in the trade press, consultants reports, customer testimonials, technical articles and business analysis reports range from the most positive comments on SAA to predictions that the next chairman of the board of IBM will abandon SAA and adopt a totally new (and unexplained) direction. The internal IBM evidence of success of SAA is starting to show positive results. This is based on the increasing acceptance and positive response of its customers to several key SAA products, around the world. These include DB/2, CSP and the SAA languages. The second major indicator is the large number of customer projects involving SAA directions and the increase of requests for early product information. Although it may be too early to declare total success; IBM management could conclude that they are clearly going in the right direction from their customer's point of view but they (IBM) has much work to be done.

The following sections examine the key elements of SAA from a point of view of what IBM is trying to do, an examination of the risks and potential consequences. Because SAA and its impact on IBM's software products is such a dominant factor to IBM's overall success, extending into virtually every one of its product lines it will be somewhat straightforward over time to measure success. It can be measured on the year-to-year growth of the IBM company.

The key underlying SAA components that will be assessed are the architectures, cooperative processing, distributed processing, application development, and the impact of UNIX.

SAA ARCHITECTURE

CCS is perhaps the best defined and most predictable aspect of SAA. The basic protocols will continue to evolve, heavily influenced by industry standards and user groups. IBM will continue to achieve a very high level of interconnectability of its product lines and minimize the criticisms of product mismatches in this area.

There are two areas of high risk that fall into this general discussion area. The first is the support of local area networks (LAN) in the SAA products. The second is the support of the communications networks with management, security and recovery facilities in support of the SAA distributed data strategy.

IBM's limiting factor is not technology in either case. It will be its ability to decide on the best technical solution for its customer and successfully manage a coordinated set of products to the marketplace. The Common Programming Interface (CPI) will continue to be expanded over time with new interfaces defined for such functions as the repository and security. There will be challenges in meeting industry standards from time to time on some SAA products which may lag demand. This will not be a major impact area. There will also be demands for new SAA function under the CPI, such as the ADA languages. In general, these demands will be satisfied by IBM.

The arena of the Common User Access (CUA) will continue to be a major source of controversy in the industry. Debates are "X windows" interface and that provided by the Presentation Manager (PM) will continue over the next several years. Although irritating criticisms will appear this situation will not present a major business impact to IBM. They will, over time, converge the SAA interfaces to include evolving standards and provide tools to support a variety of approaches. Although there are some isolated risks in the base architecture evolution of SAA it appears to be on a substantially sound base with the major challenges being customer and internal management driven and not technology driven. IBM should be able to meet the fundamental objectives of SAA in providing consistency across the SAA operating systems family.

Cooperative Processing

The popularity of the personal computer and its acceptance as a fundamental tool in business operations is well established in the western world markets. As technology has brought the cost of these powerful workstation configurations to below $10,000 the economic justification has been made easier. IBM's cooperative processing strategy is intended to continue to exploit this trend by bringing more of the power of the workstation to the end user.

IBM faces significant technical challenges in providing the software products to support the host-workstation cooperative processing environments. However, it appears certain that by the end of 1990 all of these necessary products will be available.

The major acceptance factor on this key strategic element of SAA is economic, whereas customers are relatively comfortable in purchasing personal computers for today's application needs at costs of $5000 the effective SAA workstation cost can appear two or three times higher. In order to address this inhibitor IBM must quickly provide demonstrable applications that demand the use of all the positive attributes of cooperative processing and be able to convert the costs into realizable benefits to the customer.

Toward this end, IBM has established programs to encourage hundreds of application software companies to convert their most successful applications to PS/2 using the OS/2 EE operating system. In addition, IBM's Office System offerings will exploit the OS/2 technology while allowing migration from existing terminals and PC-DOS operating system-based PCs.

At risk is the future base of its 1988 workstation revenue which was in excess of $11 billion. On the other hand, the combination of PS/2 with its proprietary micro channel architecture in combination with its new OS/2 operating systems can represent a new horizon of revenue opportunity as these rich function workstations become an integral part of the envisioned enterprise system.

Many may disagree, but it is this aspect of the SAA strategy that will have the most fundamental effect on IBM future growth and ultimately the "success" of SAA. It is interesting to note that many architectural and functional elements of SAA in the support and accommodation of display terminals and the PC-DOS operating systems are intended to allow customers coexistence and orderly migration to a full SAA system. Facilities such as the Easel Workstation editor provide a customer with the capability to have applications that were previously generating NPT dialogs become SAA and CUA conforming. At the same time, he/she can begin an evolutionary approach to cooperative processing applications. Therefore, the area that might contain the highest technical risk and highest marketplace acceptance risk seems to have that risk moderated by a product plan that can support a more evolutionary or conservative approach of the customer base.

Distributed Processing

Distributed Processing is the dimension of SAA that contains all the dependencies and risks described in the previous section, and includes the development of the functions to support distributed databases. Although the latter represents a significant technical challenge, it lies in an area of IBM technical strength. DB/2 is becoming established as the premier worldwide relational database and the ability for DB/2 and SQL/DS to connect to each other is already available. Future extensions to these concepts should be substantially fulfilled by the end of 1990.

Application Development

There are major risks facing IBM in providing an integrated application development environment. The first is the development of the repository products and platforms on a timely basis. The second is the success of business partnerships with CASE tool vendors in the integration of their products to the IBM Repository. Customer acceptance with managed expectation of this evolving technology in a meaningful way must be counted also as a risk. Many companies with vision have already made a commitment and are receiving benefits in the short term as they work on the long term solution.

The IBM Repository is certain to go through an evolutionary process of functional enhancements and acceptance over time. The dedication of the vendors and customers to use the early revisions, provide feedback and demands on IBM for improvements will be essential to establish this technology.

The initial reception will be apparent by the end of 1990 and the level of exploitation of the integration potential should be understood by the end of 1991.

SAA represents a major strategic variable in the information technology industry that will effect billions of dollars of business decisions and purchases. IBM is investing hundreds of millions of dollars in SAA to give IBM a competitive position and to be the preferred solution provider. The implementation of this direction is a balance of technical, marketing, and business risk that IBM appears to be in a position to execute.

Appendices

A
Customer Value Categories

Customer value categories describe how significant areas of a business are supported through appropriate *software product value categories* (the functions and/or capabilities of a software product).

Business Solutions A software solution that supports customer business goals; enhances company productivity; improves decision making; and integrates business systems.

Growth Enabling The extent to which a product supports application development and growth, while removing inhibitors; fast response to customer, and business requirements.

Protection of Investment Provision of a manageable rate of software product change, within an evolutionary strategy; minimizing the cost to the customer of skills, applications, system software and hardware.

End-User Productivity Increased user performance while rework is reduced; improved availability and access to data; and the enabling of personal computing.

System Management Extent to which a software product reduces personnel downtime and training through reduction of complexity; improvement to operational productivity, adequate security, auditibility, accounting, administration, and integrity.

B
Product Value Categories

Product value categories describe the functions and/or capabilities of a software product.

Functionality   User-initiated product function enabling the performance of a task.

Capabilities   Features supporting the use of functions:

- *Usability*: The "ease of use" attributed that allow the user to effectively interact with the product to do productive work intuitively.
- *Performance*: Speed and efficiency with which product executes its functions; speed, response time, and resource utilization.
- *Reliability*: Frequency, number, and seriousness of incidents and program errors. Recoverability attributes.
- *Installability*: Ease of installing and initializing the software.
- *Maintainability*: Error diagnosis; response time and quality of program error fixes; manageability of maintenance and installability of service.

- *Documentation*: Accuracy of information presented; format; understandability; thoroughness and completeness; ability to find information, appropriate for intended audience.
- *Adaptability*: Designed for modification and enhancement; modular, flexible, configurable, with user exits.
- *Exploitation*: Optimum utilization of hardware and software system components.
- *Standards and Architectures*: Conformance to industry and international standards: provision for portability, compatibility, connectability and national language support.

C
SAA Products and References

COMMON PROGRAMMING INTERFACE (CPI)

In the following tables, the availability (AVAIL) column indicates the SAA product that delivers the CPI for that platform. A product name and number in parentheses indicates a non-SAA product that can implement a subset of that CPI.

The information in the announcement (ANN'D) column indicates one of two conditions:

(1) IBM has indicated its intent to supply the CPI in the referenced announcement letter.

(2) A product name, number and date in the announced column indicates the product that will deliver the CPI and its planned availability date.

Following the *SAA Products - Common Product Interface* tables are two reference tables; *SAA - CPI Languages/Services Cross Reference* and *SAA - CPI Languages/Services Availability*.

SAA Products—Common Programming Interface

SEE NOTES (pg 167)	MVS TSO/E		VM/SP CMS	
	AVAIL	**ANN'D**	**AVAIL**	**ANN'D**
COBOL	COBOL II R3 5668-958 *(5)*		COBOL II R3 5668-958 *(5)*	
FORTRAN	FORTRAN V2R3 5668-806		FORTRAN V2R3 5668-806	
C	C/370 5688-039		C (PO) 5713-AAH *(1)*	C/370 5688-039 6/89
RPG		Anncmt # 288-336		Anncmt # 288-336
APPLICATION GENERATOR	CSP V3 5668-814		CSP V3 5668-814	
PROCEDURE LANGUAGE	TSO/E 5685-025 *(10)*		REXX VM/SP R3 + 5664-167	
QUERY INTERFACE	QMF V2R3 5668-721 *(8)*		QMF V2R3 5668-AAA *(8)*	
DATABASE INTERFACE	DB2 R3&V2 5740-XYR 5665-DB2		SQL/DS V2R1 + 5688-004	
DIALOG INTERFACE	(ISPF 2.3) (5665-319) *(2)*	(ISPF 3.1) (5685-054) 5/89 *(2)*	(ISPF 2.2) (5664-282) *(2)*	(ISPF 3.1) (5684-043) 6/89 *(2)*
PRESENTATION INTERFACE	(GDDM) (5665-356) *(3)*		(GDDM) (5664-200) *(3)*	
COMMUNICATION INTERFACE		Anncmt # 287-471	VM/SP R6 5664-167 5664-173	
DISTRIBUTED FILE MANAGEMENT		Anncmt # 288-336		Anncmt # 288-336
DISTRIBUTED RELATIONAL DB		DB2 V2R2 5665-DB2 3Q89 *(12)*	SQL/DS V2.1 + 5688-004 *(13)*	

SEE NOTES (pg 167)	IMS/DC		CICS/MVS	
	AVAIL	ANN'D	AVAIL	ANN'D
COBOL	COBOL II R3 5668-958 *(5)*		COBOL II R3 5668-958 *(5)*	
FORTRAN	N/A		N/A	
C	C/370 5688-039			Anncmt # 287-471
RPG		Anncmt # 288-336		Anncmt # 288-336
APPLICATION GENERATOR		Anncmt # 287-471	CSP V3 5668-814	
PROCEDURE LANGUAGE	N/A		N/A	
QUERY INTERFACE	N/A		N/A	
DATABASE INTERFACE	DB2 R3&V2 5740-XYR 5665-DB2		DB2 R3&V2 5740-XYR 5665-DB2	
DIALOG INTERFACE	N/A		N/A	
PRESENTATION INTERFACE	N/A		N/A	
COMMUNICATION INTERFACE		Anncmt # 287-471		Anncmt # 287-471
DISTRIBUTED FILE MANAGEMENT		Anncmt # 288-336		Anncmt # 288-336
DISTRIBUTED RELATIONAL DB		DB2 V2R2 5665-DB2 3Q89 *(12)*		DB2 V2R2 5665-DB2 3Q89 *(12)*

N/A = At this point in time, the SAA CPI has not been announced as part of the environment's participation in SAA.

SEE NOTES (pg 167)	OS/2 EE		OS/400	
	AVAIL	**ANN'D**	**AVAIL**	**ANN'D**
COBOL	COBOL/2 6280207		COBOL/400 5728-CB1 *(9)*	
FORTRAN	FORTRAN/2 6280185			Anncmt # 288-289 *(11)*
C	C/2 V 1.1 6280284			Anncmt # 288-289 TBA 3Q89
RPG		Anncmt # 288-336	RPG/400 5728-RG1 *(9)*	
APPLICATION GENERATOR	EZ-RUN *(7)*		CSP V3 5668-814 *(6)*	Anncmt # 288-289 288-528
PROCEDURE LANGUAGE		Anncmt # 289-217		Anncmt # 288-289 TBA 3Q89
QUERY INTERFACE	OS/2 EE V1.0 90X7933/4	EE V1.2 289-217 11/89		Anncmt # 288-289 *(11)*
DATABASE INTERFACE	OS/2 EE V1.0 90X7933/4	EE V1.2 289-217 11/89	SQL/400 5728-ST1 *(4)*	
DIALOG INTERFACE		EE V1.2 289-217 11/89		Anncmt # 288-289 *(11)*
PRESENTATION INTERFACE	OS/2 EE V1.1 90X7933/4	EE V1.2 289-217 11/89		Anncmt # 288-289 *(11)*
COMMUNICATION INTERFACE		Anncmt # 287-471		Anncmt # 287-471 *(11)*
DISTRIBUTED FILE MANAGEMENT		Anncmt # 288-336	OS/400 5728-SS1	
DISTRIBUTED RELATIONAL DB		EE V1.2 289-217 11/89*(15)*		Anncmt # 288-545

SAA Products—Common Programming Interface—Notes

(1) Although not part of SAA, the C program offering can be used to gain early experience with the C language.

(2) ISPF (V2R3 for MVS and V2R2 for VM) supports a subset of the SAA Dialog Interface. Applications written to the ISPF interface will have to be converted to the SAA Dialog CPI for SAA compliance. ISPF V3 offers support for the SAA Dialog Tag Language (DTL) and an improved user interface featuring pop-up windows, action bars and action-bar pulldowns. A subset of the services of ISPF V3 are functionally consistent with the SAA Dialog Interface. ISPF V3 allows the user to begin using the Dialog Tag Language and CUA Interface elements with ISPF.

(3) SAA Presentation Interface will be supported in a future Presentation Manager. GDDM supports some of the elements of the SAA Presentation Interface.

(4) SQL/400 provides a rich subset of the SAA SQL CPI. Differences between SQL/400 and the SAA SQL will be described in an updated SAA Common Programming Interface Database Reference Manual (SC26-4348).

(5) COBOL II R3 provides full support of ANSI 1985 COBOL for MVS/ESA, MVS/XA, MVS/370, VM/SP and VM/XA. Since this product is a superset of SAA COBOL, a SAA flagging option is included to facilitate ensuring that application source code will be portable to other SAA COBOL implementations. (5668-958, 5688-023, 5688-022)

(6) CSP/AD generation now includes OS/400 in the target system selection. Applications generated with CSP/AD V3.2.1 on a S/370 can be executed on a future release of OS/400 (planned availability in 1989).

(7) EZ-RUN will support CSP V3.2.1 applications in PC DOS or OS/2 execution mode (currently without relational database support).

(8) QMF on MVS and VM adds the prompted query user interface for the host QMF user. QMF V2R3 supports the full SAA Query CPI.

(9) COBOL/400 and RPG/400 deliver many of the elements of these SAA CPIs to the OS/400 environment. These compilers will be the implementing products of the respective SAA CPIs.

(10) TSO/E V2 REXX will be the implementing product in MVS/XA (ESA) for the SAA procedure language CPI.

(11) These SAA CPIs are planned to be available for OS/400.

(12) See Announcements 288-545 and 288-547.

(13) Remote Unit-of-Work is currently available with SQL/DS between VM systems. See Announcements 288-545, 288-335 and 288-548.

(14) Initial distributed file management support will be between OS/400s and between OS/400 and CICS/MVS. See Announcements 288-336 and 288-289.

(15) OS/2 EE V1.2 Remote Data Services will implement Remote Unit-of-Work support.

SAA-CPI Languages/Services Cross-Reference

		OS/2	OS/400	VM/CMS	TSO/E	CICS	IMS/DC
C	PI	XX	—	**	**	N/A	N/A
	DI	*X	—	**	**	N/A	N/A
	DBI	XX	—	XX	XX	*X	XX
	QI	XX	—	XX	XX	N/A	N/A
	CI	—	—	XX	—	—	—
COBOL	PI	XX	—	**	**	N/A	N/A
	DI	*X	—	**	**	N/A	N/A
	DBI	XX	XX	XX	XX	XX	XX
	QI	XX	—	*X	*X	N/A	N/A
	CI	—	*X	XX	**	—	—
FORTRAN	PI	XX	—	**	**	N/A	N/A
	DI	*X	—	**	**	N/A	N/A
	DBI	XX	—	XX	XX	N/A	N/A
	QI	XX	—	*X	*X	N/A	N/A
	CI	—	—	XX	—	N/A	N/A
RPG	PI	—	—	—	—	N/A	N/A
	DI	—	—	—	—	N/A	N/A
	DBI	—	XX	—	—	—	—
	QI	—	—	—	—	N/A	N/A
	CI	—	—	—	—	—	—
PROC LANG	PI	—	—	**	**	N/A	N/A
	DI	—	—	**	**	N/A	N/A
	DBI	—	—	—	—	N/A	N/A
	QI	—	—	—	—	N/A	N/A
	CI	—	—	XX	—	N/A	N/A
APPL GEN	PI	—	—	—	—	N/A	N/A
	DI	—	—	—	—	N/A	N/A
	DBI	—	—	XX	XX	XX	*X
	QI	—	—	—	—	N/A	N/A
	CI	—	—	XX	—	—	—

See p. 169 for explanation of chart symbols.

PI	Presentation Interface	**XX**	Full Support
DI	Dialog Interface	***X**	Planned Enhancement Announced
DBI	Database Interface	*** ***	Partial Support in Non-SAA Product
QI	Query Interface	**—**	Support Planned
CI	Communications Interface	**N/A**	Support Not Announced

SAA CPI Language/Services Availability

	OS/2	OS/400	VM/CMS	TSO/E	CICS	IMS/DC
C	XX		—	XX		XX
COBOL	XX	XX	XX	XX	XX	XX
FORTRAN	XX		XX	XX	N/A	N/A
RPG		XX				
PROCEDURE LANGUAGE			XX	XX	N/A	N/A
APPLICATION GENERATOR	XX	XX	XX	XX	XX	
DATABASE	XX	XX	XX	XX	XX	XX
QUERY	XX		XX	XX	N/A	N/A
DIALOG	*X		—	—	N/A	N/A
PRESENTATION	XX		—	—	N/A	N/A
COMMUNICATIONS			XX		N/A	N/A

XX Product Available
*X Product Announced
— Support Available in Non-SAA Product
N/A Support Not Announced

SAA Brochures

Title	Order No.

SAA BROCHURES

SAA: The Key to Greater Productivity	G580-0853
SAA: On the Job; Software Vendor Solutions (Includes 12 vendors)	G320-6704
SAA: A Guide for Evaluating Applications	G320-9803
SAA Applications—A Value Guide (Insert for G320-9803)	G320-9804
SAA: Framework for an Enterprise Information System	G580-4005

OFFICE SYSTEMS BROCHURES

IBM OfficeVision Family for the Large Enterprise	G520-6593
IBM OfficeVision Family for Your Growing Business	G520-6596
IBM OfficeVision/MVS Series	G520-6599
IBM OfficeVision/VM Series	G520-6608
IBM OfficeVision/400 Series	G520-6607
IBM OfficeVision/2 LAN Series	G520-6606
IBM OfficeVision Family	G520-6598
IBM Data Interpretation System	G320-9814

GENERAL INFORMATION AND GUIDES

SAA: The Framework for an Enterprise Information System	G580-4005
IBM Systems Journal, Vol. 27, No. 3, 1988	G321-0091

SAA Fact Sheets

Title	Order No.
HOST-BASED FACT SHEETS	
IBM AS/400 Business Graphics Utility	G221-2664
IBM Distributed Office Support V3	G221-2658
IBM DISOSS Library Services—Extended	G221-2666
IBM DisplayWrite/370	G221-2650
IBM AS/400 Office V2	G221-2654
IBM AS/400 Query	G221-2672
IBM OfficeVision/VM	G221-2656
IBM OfficeVision/MVS	G221-2657
IBM Query Management Facility V2	G221-2671
IBM PROFS Retention Management System	G221-2673
IBM Storage and Information Retrieval System	G221-2674
DECISION-SUPPORT FACT SHEETS	
IBM Application System V2	G221-2649
IBM AS—Project Management Costing	G221-2663
IBM Executive Decisions/VM	G221-2651
IBM Data Interpretation System	G221-2653
IBM Personal Application System V2	G221-2655
OS/2-BASED FACT SHEETS	
IBM DisplayWrite 5/2 Composer	G221-2660
IBM OS/2 Image Support	G221-2661
IBM SearchVision/2	G221-2693
IBM OS/2 SE 1.2	G360-2735
IBM OS/2 EE 1.2	G360-2833
IBM 3270 Communications Family for IBM Personal System/2 and IBM Personal Computers	G360-2739
DOS-BASED FACT SHEETS	
IBM DisplayWrite 4 V2	G221-2659
IBM Office Facsimile Application	G221-2652
IBM Personal Services/PC	G221-2669
IBM Personal Computer Image Document Utility	G221-2692

SAA Technical Publications

Title	Order No.
COMMON USER ACCESS	
Common User Access: Panel Design and User Interaction	SC26-4351
SAA CUA Advanced Interface Design Guide	SC26-4582
SAA CUA Basic Interface Design Guide	SC26-4583
ISPF Conversion Utility User's Guide and Reference	SC34-4216
What's New in ISPF and ISPF/PDF	GC34-2172-4
Writing Applications: A Design Guide	SC26-4362
SAA CUA Application Design Guidelines for CICS BMS	GG66-3115
COMMON PROGRAMMING INTERFACE	
Application Generator Reference	SC26-4355
C Reference	SC26-4353
C Reference—Level 2	SC09-1308
COBOL Reference	SC26-4354
Communications Interface Reference	SC26-4399
Database Reference	SC26-4348
Dialog Reference	SC26-4356
FORTRAN Reference	SC26-4357
Presentation Reference	SC26-4359
Procedures Language Reference	SC26-4358
Query Reference	SC26-4349
RPG Reference	SC09-1286
Entire SAA Library comprising the above items	SBOF-1240
COMMON COMMUNICATIONS SUPPORT	
Common Communications Support Summary	GC31-6810
SAA Portability Guidelines, Phase 1	GG24-3354
Architectures for Object Interchange	GG24-3296
An Introduction to Programming for APPC/PC	GG24-3034

SAA Technical Publications Continued

SNA Format and Protocol Reference: LU Type 6.2	SC30-3269-3
VTAM Programming for LU 6.2	SC30-3400
SNA Format and Protocol Reference: Type 2.1 Nodes	SC30-3422-1
IBM Synchronous Data Link Control Concepts	GA27-3093-3
Operating System/2 Extended Edition Version 1.1 APPC Programming Reference	90X7790
IMS/VS LU 6.2 Adapter Function and Implementation	GG24-3323
IMS LU 6.1 Adapter for LU 6.2 Applications Description/Operations	SH20-9254
Writing IMS SAA Applications: A Design Guide	GG24-3324
SAA and LU 6.2 Considerations on CICS/MVS Applications	GG24-3295
Token-Ring Network Architecture Reference	P/N 6165877
DDM 2.0 Architecture Reference	SC21-9526-2
The X.25 Interface for Attaching SNA Nodes to Packet Switched Data Networks: General Information	GA27-3761 GA27-3345
OSI within Systems Application Architecture (SAA)	G511-1137

SAA Educational Courses

Course Title	Course Code
SAA INTRODUCTION	
SAA Facilities and Planning	S1000
COMMON PROGRAMMING INTERFACE: LANGUAGES	
APPLICATION GENERATOR	
CSP/AD: Basic Design and Definition	32358
CSP/AD: Further Design and Definition	32359
Application Development Using CSP Version 3	U3910
C	
C Language	32356
COBOL	
Fundamentals Of VS COBOL II Programming	32320
VS COBOL II Data Handling	32330
Advanced COBOL II Facilities	32340
VS COBOL II Programming Case Study	32348
AS/400 COBOL Interactive Programming Workshop	S6016
FORTRAN	
VS FORTRAN Coding	I0114
VS FORTRAN 3.0 Enhancements	32304
PROCEDURES LANGUAGE	
REXX Programming Workshop	S3632
Using The CMS System Product Interpreter	32168
RPG	
RPG II Programming	S2511, 12, 15
AS/400 RPG Interactive Programming Workshop	S6004
Discover/Education RPG Programming Workshop	DE005
COMMON PROGRAMMING INTERFACE: SERVICES	
DATABASE SQL Workshop	U4045

SAA Educational Courses (Continued)

DIALOG

ISPF Dialog Management Services	32302

PRESENTATION

Programming For The OS/2 Presentation Manager	P1011

QUERY

QMF Workshop for MVS	U4050
QMF-SQL/DS-VM For Info. Center Consultants	S2605
OS/2 Query Manager Workshop	P1009
Discover/Education OS/2 Database Manager	DE013

COMMON USER ACCESS

Programming For The OS/2 Presentation Manager	P1011

COMMON COMMUNICATIONS SUPPORT

SAA COMMUNICATIONS—GENERAL

Data Communications Environment	G3645
AS/400 Networking	S6021
AS/400 System And System/3X Networking	S6024
AS/400 Distributed Communications Workshop	S6012
Implementing OS/2 Communications Manager	G3686

DATA STREAMS

3270 Operations And Design	I0031
Office Systems Information Architectures	33014

APPLICATION SERVICES

CNM Implementation Workshop With NetView	G3656
Intro. To NetView Facilities For Automation	G3690
Introduction To NetView Clist Coding	G3691
Automated Console Operations Using NetView	G3692

SAA Educational Courses (Continued)

Advanced NetView For Automated Console Ops. G3679

Office Systems Information Architectures 33014

SESSION SERVICES

SNA LU6.2 Data Flow G3664

AS/400 Communications Programming Workshop S6017

SNA LU Data Flow And Performance G3670

NETWORK

SNA LU 6.2 Data Flow G3664

ACF/VTAM, ACF/NCP New Release Enhancements G3688

DATA LINK CONTROLS

Token Ring Implementation And Management G3611

Token Ring Implementation Topics G3667

Planning For IBM X.25 Implementation Y1052

X.25 NPSI Implementation G3637-1

X.25 SNA Interconnection (XI) Implementation G3675

Data Link Protocols 32508

DISTRIBUTED DATA MANAGEMENT

AS/400 Networking S6021

D

Common User Access (CUA) 1989

The user interface is the means by which the computer system communicates with the user. Common User Access (CUA) is the IBM definition of those user interface components that are to be the same across applications. CUA is one of four fundamental components of SAA. The other three are Common Programming Interface, Common Communications Support, and Common Applications. The SAA systems include OS/2, OS/400, MVS, and VM. SAA is the IBM architecture for providing application portability across the broad range of IBM systems from OS/2 through MVS.

The fundamental objectives of CUA are usability within an application and consistency across applications. CUA is based on a set of generally accepted user interface design principles and is designed for ease of use and encourages learning by exploring. While it is certainly possible to design other usable interfaces, a key factor in usability is consistency across applications. Consistency allows users to transfer knowledge and reduces the amount of time it takes to learn new applications.

Computer users represent many diverse end user classes that can be supported by terminals attached as Workstations to hosts or by personal computers. The term used in this document to describe personal computers is *Programmable Workstation (PWS)*. The term used to describe terminals attached to a host is *Non-Programmable Terminal (NPT)*. The Personal System/2 with OS/2

EE is the Workstation of choice for the SAA enterprise system. Over time, users will migrate from the NPT because of user demand for the power and versatility of the PWS. To balance the value of consistency between NPT and PWS with the advanced capabilities of the PWS, CUA defines two user interface models: *Entry* and *Graphical*. Where practical, similar base components are used across the models to enhance user transfer of learning.

Entry is designed for the NPT environment and is appropriate for many applications developed for transaction processing systems such as CICS and IMS. It is intended for data entry intensive applications on the NPT and may also be appropriate for those same types of applications on the PWS. The OS/400 system demonstrates many aspects of the Entry model.

Graphical is designed for the PWS running with OS/2 and makes extensive use of the windowing capabilities of OS/2. The Graphical model includes action bars, pull-down windows and pop-up windows. User interaction techniques are supported for the keyboard and mouse. Additionally, the Graphical model defines the use of icons and standard graphical cues such as check boxes. It is intended for all PWS applications and for decision-intensive applications on NPT. The NPT subset of the Graphical model is called the *text subset*. It maintains close affinity to the Graphical model including action bars, pull-down windows and pop-up windows. The OS/2 system shell is an example of the Graphical model.

Workplace is an extension of the Graphical model that describes the integration of applications into an electronic version of a working environment. For example, a Workplace for the office might contain mail baskets, file cabinets, telephones, printers, etc., which all applications can share. The separate applications can be integrated as objects, which appear as icons in the Workplace environment. Workplace is designed for the use of the mouse for direct manipulation of objects on the screen. For example, to print a document the user drags an icon representing the document to an icon representing the printer. The OS/2 IBM office product is an example of the Workplace environment.

These models are described in two SAA documents: *SAA CUA Basic Interface Design Guide* (SC26-4573) and *SAA CUA Advanced Interface Design Guide* (SC26-4582). The *SAA CUA Basic Guide* is primarily for the NPT application designer and describes both the Entry and the Text subset of Graphical. The *SAA CUA Advanced Guide* is primarily for the OS/2 application designer and describes Graphical and Workplace. Together these two documents replace *Common User Access: Panel Design and User Interaction* (SC26-4351). The major difference between the previous document and the new design guides are the definition of the models and the increased consistency requirements. Specific differences include the following:

- Separation by interface model to enhance the clarity and usability of the document for the application designer.

- Selection of options based on a model. For each model, guidelines are provided describing how to use various interface components in order to enhance consistency.

- Inclusion of design principles and rationale for the user interface components that allows the application designer to extend the interface to meet the unique needs of the application while still preserving consistency across applications.

- Changes to some PWS user interface components to exploit the graphical capabilities of the PWS.

- Definition of additional user interface components to increase consistency.

Over time, CUA will be improved and refined and will include new technologies as implied in the directional statements in the "IBM Data Interpretation System" (289-215) and "Executive Decisions/ VM" (289-208) announcement letters. However, IBM changes will be incremental and applications developed to the current CUA definition will look and feel like applications developed to future versions of CUA.

Definition of the user interfaces is only one consideration in achieving consistency. The user interface must be supported by application development tools that enable the CUA definition with a high level of application developer productivity. There are two programming techniques supported by the IBM application development tools: *procedural* and *event driven*.

Procedural programming is the method of programming familiar to programmers who use languages such as COBOL. The current NPT user interface tools and the SAA Dialog Tag Language is a language for defining the definition of a user interface which is portable across NPT and PWS. The SAA Dialog Tag Language is used to support both the Entry and the Graphical models. Refer to Appendix C for the specific products supported in the SAA environment.

The OS/2 Presentation Manager and the supporting OS/2 Toolkit support *event driven* programming. When using the Presentation Manager, the recommended model is the Graphical model. Graphical applications are consistent with the user services provided by OS/2 such as file management, application selection, and user tailoring.

Similar services will be provided in a Workplace environment in future releases of OS/2. Applications developed using the Graphical model will continue to be viable.

The OS/2 IBM Office product has implemented a Workplace environment which includes OS/2 user services, as well as unique office applications. When similar OS/2 services become available in a Workplace environment, the IBM Office product will migrate to the OS/2 Workplace environment. Applications designers who want to provide a Workplace environment before the availability of OS/2 services may choose, such as IBM Office, to create their own workplace, or to integrate into IBM Office.

E
SAA Application Software Developers

SAA Application software benefits the user by providing consistent graphical appearance and simplified operation across IBM's product line. The following is a summary of the advanced cooperative processing applications developed by their respective companies.

AMERICAN MANAGEMENT SYSTEMS, INC. (AMS)

AMS will offer four SAA software applications: TieLine Telephone Bill Designer; Local Government Financial System; Government Financial System; and the College and University Financial System.

These products, used with OS/2 EE, exploit the power of cooperative processing and provide improved efficiency for day-to-day tasks. The TieLine Telephone Bill Designer, part of AMS's TieLine family, telecommunications industries advanced capabilities to respond to competitive demands. Functions for billing, administration and customer services are provided in an organized, comprehensive manner, with emphasis on flexibility and ease of use.

The financial system packages are designed to assist governments, colleges and universities in the performance of basic financial operations, human resource management, and tax administration.

AMERICAN SOFTWARE, INC.

American Software announced a new version of its Inventory Control & Accounting (IC&A) applications for Materials Management and Financial Control in the SAA computing environment. IC&A, running under OS/12 EE and DB2, offers users real-time integration with American Software's manufacturing, distribution, procurement, order processing, and financial control solutions. The application maintains information on finished goods, raw materials, and lot-controlled items. It also maintains the financial accounting for materials as well as their physical movement. As an SAA application, IC&A allows the user to choose how information is to be displayed and responded to on the Workstation screen. Simple screen formats and use of icons and dialog boxes present viable options in a consistent, uncluttered manner. These techniques make it easier for the user to learn the application and become productive in processing the information.

ARTHUR ANDERSEN & CO.

Arthur Andersen offers three new products for SAA platforms for use by management information systems and manufacturing professionals.

The new applications reflect the company's emphasis on software development tools and mission critical application software. They are: MAC-PAC (a fully integrated mainframe manufacturing planning and control system); MAC-PAC for the AS/400; and DCS/Logistics (a fully integrated mainframe system for managing distribution tasks).

COMSHARE, INC.

An international supplier of business management productivity software and services, Comshare announced new versions of its Commander Executive Information System (EIS) for use in SAA environments. The new releases are Commander EIS for the OS/2 EE, a Workstation application, and Commander EIS LAN version, which supports the IBM Token Ring LAN and OS/2 EE Communications Manager software. Commander EIS provides a graphic, colorful personal computer-based Workstation to help top executives increase their effectiveness.

INFORMATION BUILDERS, INC.

A new version of FOCUS, a fourth generation language/database manager for use in an SAA computing environment, was announced.

The new software, called PM/FOCUS, provides all the benefits of the FOCUS fourth generation language/database management system. FOCUS is the most widely used fourth generation language of businesses and government enterprises, including finance, transportation, utility and armed services customers.

INTEGRAL SYSTEMS, INC.

HR Vision is a family of human resource software for personnel functions such as decision support, time and attendance, payroll management, and benefits administration. The new product line, offered as an optional feature of Integral's mainframe-based Human Resource Management System (HRMS), is designed to integrate with OS/2 EE and OfficeVision.

MANAGEMENT SCIENCE AMERICA, INC. (MSA)

MSA announced that its BrightView series of cooperative processing solutions has been expanded for use on OS/2 EE. BrightView offers enhanced information management capability to users of MSA's financial, human resource, manufacturing, and materials management product lines. Previous releases of the software included elements of the SAA Common User Access framework, which stress a "common look and feel" to applications so they are easier to learn and use.

MCCORMACK & DODGE (M & D)

M & D, a supplier of financial and human resources application software systems, tools and services, announced the Millennium Workstation, a software enabling tool for use with SAA platforms.

A cooperative processing application, the Millennium Workstation provides greater flexibility, productivity and ease of use to customers using the PS/2 Workstation and the Millennium mainframe based product line of financial and human resource applications. Users benefit from a "common look and feel" across the product line, as well as relational access to information through SQL.

POLICY MANAGEMENT SYSTEMS CORP. (PMSC)

Six new products for the property and casualty insurance industry using SAA platforms were announced. The new applications are members of PMS/Series III family of integrated, cooperative processing solutions for automating insurance tasks. Three of the new systems are Workstation based and three are mainframe based.

SAS INSTITUTE, INC.

SAS, the nation's largest privately held software company, announced a new version of its popular SAS System for use in SAA computing environments. The SAS System, designed for data management, analysis and presentation tasks, is an integrated system of software that includes more than 125 applications, grouped into logical, modular components. Capabilities offered include data entry and retrieval, report writing and graphics, statistical and mathematical analysis, business planning, forecasting and decision support, operations research and project management, and applications development.

STERLING SOFTWARE ANSWER SYSTEMS DIVISION

Sterling's Answer Systems Division announced Presentation/ Answer, a new software program for moving data from IBM mainframes to desktop computers in the SAA environment.

Presentation/Answer, which runs under OS/2 EE, provides Personal System/2 users with direct and immediate access to large quantities of information stored in IBM mainframe databases. A cooperative processing application, the Presentation/Answer will extract and convert data from the host computer into formats compatible with popular PS/2 products—all transparent to the user.

TESSERACT CORP.

Tesseract expanded its Human Resources Management Systems product line with the announcement of HRMS Intuition, a software application developed for SAA platforms.

HRMS Intuition, offered as an option with Tesseract's fully integrated mainframe HRMS solutions, brings the benefits of cooperative processing to tasks such as personnel management, payroll and benefits administration. Using the full power of SAA interfaces (including OS/2 EE with Presentation Manager), the new product allows the user to take advantage of powerful mainframe applications through the graphical interface of the PS/2 desktop system.

ADDITIONAL SOFTWARE VENDOR ANNOUNCEMENTS

A number of leading software companies announced their intent to provide application development tools that will integrate with AD/Cycle. The companies are:

Adpac# Computing Languages Corporation

Aion# Corporation

American Management Systems, Inc.

Andersen Consulting

Applied Business Technology Corporation

ASYST Technologies, Inc.

Business Software Technology, Inc.

Cadre Technologies, Inc.

CADWARE, Inc.

CASEWORKS#, Inc.

Computer Command and Control Company

CGI-Informatique

D. Appleton Company, Incorporated

FB Technologies, Inc.

GAMMA INTERNATIONAL

Information Builders, Inc.

Learmonth & Burchett Management Systems PLC

Management Science America, Inc.

McCormack & Dodge Corporation

McDonnell Douglas Systems Integration Company

Micro Focus, Inc.

Nastec/Transform Logic Corporation

Netron, Inc.

Pansophic Systems, Inc.

Sage Software, Inc.

SAS Institute Inc.

Soflab GmbH

Softool Corporation

Sterling Software, Inc.

Synon, Inc.

Systematica, Ltd.

Texas Instruments Incorporated.

In addition, American Software, Integral Systems, Inc., and Policy Management Systems Corp. announced their support of the IBM AD/Cycle strategy.

Glossary

ADA A programming language frequently requested by government agencies.

API Abbreviation for *Application Program Interface*, which is a defined format and process of passing information from one part of a program to another.

APL A programming language.

Application Enabling A set of functions, such as languages like COBOL and services like database facilities, that are used in the creation of application programs.

Application A computer program that performs a series of tasks for an end user, which applies to his work task.

Batch Processing The submission of a series of computer applications to be executed with the results returned to the user at a later date.

C A popular programming language which allows user created functions.

COBOL Acronym for *Common Business-Oriented Language*, which is a programming language used for writing business applications.

Common Data Model The definition of the data as stored in the Repository.

Computer An electronic device that stores instructions and manipulates numerical, textual, voice, and image information.

Cooperative processing The relationship of application and system function on the intelligent workstation to the application and systems function on a host system.

CPU The central processing unit of a computer system.

Data Streams Govern the way in which data are handled and formatted when transmitted over a communications link.

4GL Abbreviation for *Fourth Generation Languages*, such as application generators like the IBM Cross Systems Product (CSP).

5GL Abbreviation for *Fifth Generation Languages*, such as those used for artificial intelligence application development.

Dialog The interchange or interaction between a user and a computer program. Usually a series of requests and responses to/for action or information.

Dictionary An application in which the Repository (CDM), repository manager and the function/tools are tightly integrated to make use of the meta data in the Repository.

Disk File An electronic media that magnetically records coded information that represents numerical or alphabetic values.

Enterprise System The totality of host systems, workstations, networks, systems, and applications software organized to serve the information needs of the enterprise.

IBM Strategy The IBM technical and business plan for a functional area, e.g. programming, generally specified over a 3 to 5-year horizon.

I/O Abbreviation for Input/Output.

Mouse A hand-held device that is electrically connected to a terminal and when moved around, positions the cursor on the display screen.

Operating Systems The collection of programming functions that are most often associated with interfacing to the hardware functions of a computer system on one side and the user functions, such as language on the other side.

Panel   An arrangement of information on a display screen.

PL/1   Abbreviation for Programming Language/One.

Protocols   Define the logic and rules for handling data formats occurring over a communications link.

Relational Database   Various pieces of information can be viewed in relationship to each other without predefining that relationship in the database structure.

Repository   1.(Webster) A place where anything is deposited, as for safekeeping. **2.** (Data Processing) An organized, shared, collection of information about business and data processing related objects.

Repository-Manager   An application program to support the collection, distribution and control of repository data.

Windowing   Displaying several panels at one time on the display screen.

References

1. Vincent E. Gierliano, "The Mechanization of Office Work", *Scientific American*, (September 1982): 154.

2. John Naisbitt, Megatrends (New York: Warner Books Inc., 1984) 6-33.

3. Frederick P. Brooks, Jr., *The Mythical Man Month* (Philippines: Addison-Wesley, 1975).

4. Robert Sobel, *I.B.M. Colossus in Transitions* (New York: Truman Talley, 1981), 228.

5. Jeremy Bernstein, *The Analytical Engine* (New York: Random House, 1963).

6. Thomas Wise, "IBM's $5,000,000,000 Gamble", *Fortune*, September 1966.

7. *IBM System Journal*, Volume 27, No. 3 (1988).

8. IBM Corporation, *Common Use Access*: *Paul Designs and Use Interaction*, SC26-4351.

9. IBM Corporation, *Writing Applications*: *A Design Guide*, SC26-4362.

10. IBM Corporation, *System Application Architecture*: *An Overview*, GC26-4341.

11. IBM Corporation, "IBM Customer/Confidential - SAA Joint Study Project Report," 10 August 1988.

12. Berry, R.E. "Common Use Access - A consistent and usable human - computer interface for the SAA Environments." *IBM Systems Journal*, Vol. 27, No.3 (1988): 264.

13. Ahuja, V. "Common Communications Support in Systems Application Architecture." *IBM Systems Journal*, Volume 27, No. 3, (1988): 264.

14. *The SAA Spectrum*, Volume 2, No. 3 (California: Killen and Associates, 1988).

15. McClellan, Stephen T., *The Coming Computer Industry Shakeout* (New York: John Wiley and Sons, 1984).

16. Lewis, Peter H. "The Executive Computer." *The New York Times*, 1 Jan. 1989, Sec. F : 10.

17. Bruell, Dietrich, "Customer Value of IBM Systems Software" (IBM Corporation, Task Force Report, 1988).

18. Scherr, A.L. "SAA Distributed Processing." *IBM Systems Journal*, Volume 27, No. 3, (1988): 370.

19. Aron, J.C. *The Program Development Process* (Massachusetts: Addison-Wesley, 1983): 275.

20. McGilton, H. *Introducing the UNIX System* (New York: McGraw-Hill Book Co., 1983).

21. *IBM 1988 Annual Report*, G505-1988 (1989).

22. *IBM Customer Briefs*, No. 1, (1989).

23. Killen, Michael, *IBM: The Making of the Common View* (Harcourt, Brace, Joranovich: 1988).

Index

Index